W9-BVT-417

LANGUAGE AND LITERACY SERIES

Dorothy S. Strickland, FOUNDING EDITOR

Celia Genishi and Donna E. Alvermann, SERIES EDITORS

ADVISORY BOARD: Richard Allington, Kathryn Au, Bernice Cullinan, Colette Daiute, Anne Haas Dyson, Carole Edelsky, Shirley Brice Heath, Connie Juel, Susan Lytle, Timothy Shanahan

(Continued)

For volumes in the NCRLL Collection (edited by JoBeth Allen and Donna E. Alvermann) and the Practitioners Bookshelf Series (edited by Celia Genishi and Donna E. Alvermann), please visit www.tcpress.com.

Literacy & Justice Through Photography

A Classroom Guide

Wendy Ewald • Katherine Hyde • Lisa Lord

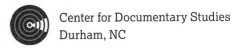

Teachers College, Columbia University
New York and London

Center for Documentary Studies
Durham, NC

KH

It is only as we collectively change the way we look at ourselves and the world that we can change how we are seen.
—bell hooks, *Black Looks: Race and Representation*

This book is dedicated to our students and fellow teachers.
—Wendy, Katie, and Lisa

Published by Teachers College Press, 1234 Amsterdam Avenue, New York, NY 10027, in association with the Center for Documentary Studies, Duke University, 1317 West Pettigrew, Durham, NC 27705-4854

Cover: Samuel's self-portrait from *The Best Part of Me* project, 2005

Library of Congress Cataloging-in-Publication Data

Ewald, Wendy.
    Literacy and justice through photography : a classroom guide / Wendy Ewald, Katherine Hyde, Lisa Lord.
       p. cm. — (Language and literacy series)
    Includes bibliographical references and index.
    ISBN 978-0-8077-5281-4 (pbk. : alk. paper)
    ISBN 978-0-8077-5282-1 (hardcover : alk. paper)
       1. Photography in education. 2. Documentary photography. 3. Literacy through Photography (Program) 4. Literacy—Social aspects. I. Hyde, Katherine (Katie) II. Lord, Lisa, 1951– III. Title.
    TR816.E93 2012
    371.33'52—dc23   2011034952

ISBN 978-0-8077-5281-4 (paper)
ISBN 978-0-8077-5282-1 (hardcover)

Printed on acid-free paper
Manufactured in the United States of America
Designed by Bonnie Campbell

19 18 17 16 15 14 13 12   8 7 6 5 4 3 2 1

9/19/12

Contents

Acknowledgments

WE FIRST WOULD LIKE TO THANK Club Boulevard Humanities Magnet School, where all the projects in this book took place. We thank the Club Boulevard students who took part in these Literacy Through Photography (LTP) projects for their creative, honest, and inspiring work. Many thanks also to Club's staff members (past and present) for helping LTP take root at the school. Thanks especially to Denise Friesen Baynham, who has worked with LTP in many capacities—for teaching these lessons so well to students and teachers, for writing about the connections between the lessons and good literacy instruction, for thoughtful feedback on all our work, and for helping to make this book a reality. Our appreciation goes to Jennifer Medley Harrison for her passionate teaching of *The Best Part of Me*, which always leads to students' artful self-portrait presentations. Thanks to Chrissy Slavinsky for suggesting the *Indian Boarding Schools* project and to Erin Pattishall for leading the *Girl Self/Boy Self* spinoff of *Black Self/White Self*. We greatly appreciate Principal Micah Copeland's commitment to keeping Literacy Through Photography as a core element in Club's curriculum. And finally, we thank Carolyn Ridout, retired principal, for accepting the invitation for Club Boulevard to participate in Literacy Through Photography.

We'd like to thank the Durham Public Schools, as well, for their partnership. We express heartfelt gratitude to Robert Hunter, a master teacher and LTP leader. We thank him for sharing LTP with countless students at Shepard Middle School and fellow teachers in the United States and abroad, and we're deeply grateful for his role in developing the *Black Self/White Self* project and curriculum. Thanks also to Cathy Fine and Emelia DeCroix for their collaboration on the *Black Self/White Self* and *American Alphabets* projects. We also thank all the members of the LTP advisory committee over the years. Thanks, especially, to Iris Tillman Hill and Alan Teasley for decades of wise guidance and generous advocacy. Along with inspirational educator Madeleine Grumet, Alan and Iris provided insightful feedback on early versions of this book's chapters.

Wendy would like to acknowledge the following people who courageously helped with the creation of the original projects during times when they were challenging the prevailing stereotypes: Megan Tingley at Little, Brown for recognizing the potential of *The Best Part of Me* as a children's book; DPS educators Marvin Pittman and Elsie Leak, who had the courage to promote the use of *Black Self/White Self* in the Durham schools; for *American Alphabets*, Maurice Berger and the Cleveland Center for Contemporary Art, which commissioned her to create the *African American Alphabet*; Adam Weinberg, Julie Bernson, and the Addison Gallery of American Art and Phillips Academy for their support in making the *White Girl's Alphabet*; Tom Finklepearl at the Queens Museum and Ellen Rudolph at Surdna for working with her to make the *Arabic Alphabet* a reality; and finally Marvin Heiferman, Marshall Weinberg, and the American Joint Jewish Distribution committee for giving her the opportunity to make the video *Memories from the Past Centuries*; and, most important, her co-teachers and artists Lisa Lord and Robert Hunter and their inspired students, without whom none of this would have been possible.

We also would like to thank the many Duke students and community members who've worked as volunteers or interns with LTP in Durham and in Tanzania. With their indispensable help, Literacy Through Photography has continued to evolve over the years and has reached thousands of children. Thanks in particular to Maya Robinson for her help with this book's technical pieces and for working with students on a *Memories from Past Centuries* project. Special thanks also to Kaitlin Rogers and Lindsay Kunkle for their work on the *Black Self/White Self* project with middle school students, and Emily Robertson for her insights on the *Girl Self/Boy Self* project she led with students in Kenya. Many thanks to Tia Maccari, as well, for her work on *The Best Part of Me* project.

This book would not have been possible without the support of the Center for Documentary Studies at Duke University, which has provided a home for the LTP program for over 20 years. We appreciate the support of our many colleagues at CDS, especially Iris Tillman Hill, Alexa Dilworth, Courtney Reid-Eaton, Bonnie Campbell, Lynn McKnight, Greg Britz, and Tom Rankin. Many sincere thanks to every former LTP staff member—especially those who worked with LTP during the time of this book. Thanks to Dwayne Dixon, Denise Friesen Baynham, Dave Devito, and Elena Rue for the brilliant ideas, ceaseless energy, and compassion that bolsters their work with art and youth. Elena Rue also provided important assistance in preparing the resource sections in this book.

Along with the generous support we've received from the Durham Public Schools and the Center for Documentary Studies, we're grateful for an Arts Education Grant from the National Endowment for the Arts, which funded this book's design and four teacher workshops about the themes within this book. Thank you to Demetria Martinez, Brett Cook, Daniel Wideman, Rebecca Walker, and Adam Weinberg for co-leading these workshops. Their provocative and inspiring ideas shaped the work presented in this book. We also give special thanks to Meg Lemke at Teachers College Press for her expertise and patience, to Danny Miller for his important editorial suggestions, and to the anonymous reviewers whose comments helped shape the direction of this book.

A sincere thank you to Bonnie Campbell for her intelligent and beautiful design. We appreciate the way the design creatively and artfully honors the students' work. Finally, we deeply appreciate Alexa Dilworth's insightful and inspired editorial leadership. In many ways she has held our work together—her patient guidance kept things moving as we continued traveling to different parts of the world, and her thoughtful editing threaded together the many voices in this book. We thank her for caring about this work—not only because her niece Eleanor Dilworth is one of Lisa's many talented students, but because of her respect for young people's expression and the complexity of words and images.

Thanks to the many other teachers, principals, and students who have kept LTP alive in Durham for over 20 years and the teachers with whom we've collaborated in Tanzania and Haiti—the many ways they've tried out the *American Alphabets, Best Part of Me, Black Self/White Self,* and *Memories from Past Centuries* projects have pushed our thinking for this book.

Introduction

OVER THE PAST COUPLE OF DECADES a growing number of artists have found ways of working more closely with their communities. They collaborate on artistic visions not ordinarily associated with museums or the usual art world sites. The results are artworks that express a variety of social and aesthetic positions and, very often, the work is intertwined with progressive educational philosophies and radical democratic theory.

As an artist who works with a camera, I take pictures that aim to show something of "reality." I am constantly aware that I'm collaborating with the world—with people and the environments they live and work in. I've thought a lot about how important it is to involve others in a meaningful way in my artistic process. When you get right down to it, the kind of photography I'm drawn to is a form of collaborative art. And as a teacher I respond instinctively to the idea of collaboration. Working in the classroom makes it clear that artistic practice can be a powerful avenue for self-expression and growth, not just for people who identify themselves as artists.

The open-ended process of making original photographs or videos—as opposed to the repetitive-work or corporate-think that society ordinarily requires—gives each of us a chance to offer our unique expertise. When non-artists work alongside trained artists, the results bring together many voices and tap into deep parts of ourselves that otherwise might remain mute. In educational terms, it's exciting to realize that this kind of exploration can lead young people to connect with what they care most passionately about.

In 1989, after years of working with children in various situations, I was invited by the Center for Documentary Studies at Duke University to start a program for the Durham Public Schools. Many of the students I met had trouble writing; typically, they would labor painfully over one or two sentences. Around this time, I began experimenting in elementary and middle school classrooms to see how photography and writing might cross-pollinate each other. The challenge of acknowledging the complexity of children's lives inspired me to imagine photographs that, with students' participation, would be truthful and penetrating. I also wanted to test my suspicion that an artist's ways of describing the world could help a student struggling with, say, a social studies paper. Could a lesson that begins with an image help students write with more detail, depth, and enthusiasm? In short, could an artist's way of thinking be the basis for certain lesson plans?

I found when the students worked from a photograph that had something to do with their own lives, especially a picture they had

Wendy Ewald
An Artist's Frame

taken themselves, they were able to write much more fluently. It was hard to escape the cause-and-effect conclusion that their writing began to flow when it was inspired by their immediate experiences. This was encouraging, but it soon became clear that many of my students didn't feel their lives were worth picturing or writing about in the first place. It was one thing to take snapshots memorializing family events like birthdays and weddings. But acknowledging the radiance of ordinary life in its unglamorized randomness—something that documentary photography has always been exceptionally good at—this was another matter, another world.

In order to expand the children's notions of photography, I gave them photo assignments that were relevant to their lives, starting with what they knew intimately: themselves and their families. Then we moved outward, into the neighborhood, and from there, to a more freewheeling concept—to their dreams. (In addition to making pictures, the students also wrote about these areas of interest.)

In creating the core concepts of what I began to call Literacy Through Photography, I identified certain formal elements of photography such as framing, point of view, timing, the use of symbols, and observation of details—all of which, of course, have parallels in writing. I asked students to think about and apply these concepts one at a time, or in combination. For example, when the kids were photographing themselves and their families, I asked them to concentrate on framing. If they were photographing their fantasies, I'd urge them to think about point of view. If we were talking about timing, we'd wonder aloud about the best narrative sequence for a series of images. As the students became more comfortable with the camera, I encouraged them to expand their ideas about picture making while staying close to subjects they felt deeply about. They discovered they could be the subject of their own photographs; they could transform themselves into "characters." The photographs that came out of these sessions broke new ground for the students. They began to see that it was possible to create any image and write any story they wanted.

My interest in the intersections of art and education has led me to more widely share the projects I've been doing for the past 20 years with teachers in the Durham Public Schools. My first book for educators, *I Wanna Take Me a Picture: Teaching Photography and Writing to Children* (Ewald & Lightfoot, 2001), laid out my process of working with children in schools and communities. Using photography and writing, the children described themselves, their families, their communities, and their dreams. The teachers I'd been collaborating with in Literacy Through Photography began to take an active part in shaping the projects for their own classrooms. This book presents four collaborative projects that many teachers successfully carried out in their classrooms. The lesson plans address issues of culture, identity, and language. The plans were developed by elementary teacher Lisa Lord with help from middle school art teacher Robert Hunter, 3rd- and 4th-grade teacher Denise Baynham, and Katie Hyde, an educator and sociologist. We hope these projects will be useful to teachers in many disciplines and many grade levels.

In order to explore how our projects could be used in a classroom setting and connected to a standard curriculum, we organized workshops for teachers based on each of the projects. For example, to lay the groundwork for the *Black Self/White Self* curriculum, 20 teachers attended a workshop that I led with Katie and writer Rebecca Walker, whose *Black White and Jewish: Autobiography of a Shifting Self* (2001) looks at her upbringing as a biracial woman. Lisa and Robert, whom I worked with on the original *Black Self/White Self* project, also taught in the workshop. The participants came from all over the United States as well as South Africa and Great Britain. We formulated goals for our new curriculum and had lively, sometimes difficult debates about how we see race in our schools. In the years that followed, Katie, Robert, and Lisa created and documented their own *Black Self/White Self* projects. Out of these pilot projects came the final lesson plans that were integrated into Lisa's elementary and Robert's middle school curricula.

Daniel Wideman, a writer, and Demetria Martinez, whose book *Mother Tongue* (1994) deals with the importance of one's native language and neighborhood patois, were visiting artists in the *Alphabet* project workshop. Artist Brett Cook led a workshop on portraiture for *The Best Part of Me* project. Adam Weinberg, now director of the Whitney Museum of American Art, led a workshop on curating, editing, and installing an exhibition, which stretched our thinking about presentation.

Some years ago, I was walking across the field in front of my home in the Hudson Valley, thinking about conversations I'd had about race with my students. Portraits of my students—as yet untaken—popped into my mind. The photographs showed—caricatured, rather, by means of scratches and drawings on the negative—each student as Black or White.

Could I bring those pictures into being through a process that would encourage honest self-reflection and respectful conversations about race? I was pretty certain that the resulting photographs, if I could make them happen at all, would be compelling.

In much the same way, each project in this book began with an image. Sitting on a Florida beach with my young son, who is Latino but was reluctant to keep speaking Spanish in *White America,* I was thinking about how to use photographs to teach language in its simplest forms. I envisioned a series of "alphabet photographs" with letters, words, and definitions written by students. Gradually, in the hope of transferring the energy of this concept to a workable project, I reverse-engineered the "alphabet" notion into a process to create those alphabet pictures with my English as a Second Language students.

I conceived of these projects as a way of making provocative photographs, but also as a way for teachers to bring political and social themes into their teaching. I hope these thoughtfully crafted lesson plans lead to learning and discussion that are as provocative as the images the students and I made.

Lisa Lord
A Teacher's Reflection

I AM AN ARTIST AND A TEACHER, and I was taught how to be an artist, just as I have been taught how to be a teacher. I remember the day my 7th-grade art teacher had us draw an orange using oil pastels. After watching us make orange circles on our papers for a while, he brought us up to his table to take turns actually holding an orange to examine it closely. He urged us to draw what we *saw*, not what we *thought* an orange looked like. Remembering another art teacher, I think of many Saturday mornings spent in the backyard studio of an artist in my hometown. She propped favorite paintings by Cezanne in front of us and helped us imitate his colors, lines, and strokes. One art teacher helped me be honest about what I saw, and the other taught me the techniques of the masters. I'm glad I learned both habits.

When I first met Wendy Ewald and participated in a Literacy Through Photography workshop for teachers, I immediately found myself immersed once again in habits of close, honest looking, and in learning techniques as an artist. Later, when I began collaborating with Katie Hyde in my classroom, I appreciated her questions and insights as a sociologist. She engaged in numerous in-depth, helpful conversations with students about their photography, writing, and planning—more interactions than are possible for a regular classroom teacher working as the only adult in a classroom. Katie not only was able to hear and record student conversations that I missed, but her questions and observations added immeasurably to my students' learning. On a practical level, for me and for other classroom teachers who will use this book, Katie teaches us useful questions to ask and gives us confidence that the conversations students have among themselves, as they work on these projects, are valuable, essential parts of the transformations that occur in our classrooms—even if we aren't able to participate in all of those discussions. Just as working with Wendy helped me refresh my skills as an artist and observer, working with Katie helped me improve the cornerstones of my teaching, particularly my questioning techniques and kid-watching strategies. We teachers constantly engage in action research in our classrooms, observing our students and evaluating the effects of our lessons; the better we are at kid watching, the better equipped we are for making instructional decisions.

Even in this time when states and districts and school administrators increasingly dictate components of the daily curriculum, I still make hundreds of independent decisions every day. Every year I make the choice to include at least one Literacy Through Photography unit in my lesson plans. That choice leads to two critical questions:

1. When can I do LTP? How can I find the time in our crowded days?
2. How can I present the LTP work as an integral part of the prescribed curriculum?

First, writing instruction includes work with brainstorming, details and elaboration, point of view, choosing titles—all key practices in Literacy Through Photography. We help children to read better by helping them to identify important details and main ideas, ask questions, make connections, describe characters, make predictions, and draw conclusions—all components of LTP projects. In social studies, we study particular periods of history, different cultures, and big themes such as the interaction between human beings and the environment and major movements of people and ideas. All of our science units include the goals of improving students' skills of observation, record keeping, and supporting conclusions with data. I work with an art teacher who expects students to learn techniques of all kinds of artists, from Mondrian to Monet, and how to view the work of others, whether their classmates or artists whose work is in galleries and museums. The guidance counselor and I strive to teach students empathy and respect for different points of view. Together, we seek to build students' self-concepts; times are designated especially for teaching writing, reading, social studies, science, and art.

Second, I fit one of the projects in as a major unit by adapting it to fit curricular objectives. I use the time set aside in the daily schedule for that subject matter. Social studies is a natural place to start with the *American Alphabets*, *Black Self/White Self*, and *Memories of Past Centuries* projects; *The Best Part of Me* most easily fits into language arts because of its connection to writing personal narratives. When I choose to *integrate* content areas, I think of the projects as both social studies and language arts, and use time from both of those parts of our day. This is my favorite approach—no matter where the project is rooted in the day's schedule, children can employ the skills they are being taught in other subjects.

I need my students to see enough relevance in all of the work we do that they will try hard and push themselves to think more deeply, write and read more fluidly, listen to others attentively, and look more closely for evidence to support their conclusions. Luckily, the LTP projects are so compelling that my students choose to participate wholeheartedly, and there is really no limit to what they can accomplish. These projects address their identity as learners, as people whose stories matter, as people whose attitudes and decisions make a difference. While LTP units are not part of the tested curriculum, they provide firm foundations in the areas that are tested.

These projects have been done with heterogeneous classes, with ESL resource classes, with gifted students, with students in resource classes, and in art classes. They have been done in public schools, private schools, elementary schools, middle schools, high schools, and colleges. They have been done in North Carolina, Tanzania, Haiti, Mexico, Saudi Arabia, Colombia, the Netherlands, and elsewhere. I appreciate the richness of different points of view when working with regular, diverse classes. I love seeing children's curiosity about their classmates' lives, the surprise when they learn new things about classmates they thought they knew well. Literacy Through Photography projects are structured so that every child is successful. Students are not turning to the gifted kids to learn what to do. Thus, students tend to be motivated and do their best work, which naturally leads to improvement in their reading, writing, and thinking skills. Their time is used in meaningful, productive ways. As a writing teacher I don't hear, "What do *they* want?" when students are trying to decide what to write (*they* being the publishers of textbooks and tests, and, sometimes, teachers when there is a "right" answer to an assignment). I hear, "What do I want to write?" Students automatically sense that they are the authorities, the *real* authors.

Teachers have led many LTP projects at my school over the years, and I have noticed results that I believe can be attributed directly to the projects: enormous school pride when there are exhibits, especially when we have had off-campus venues; an inclusive school culture in which students learn about one another's traditions; better behavior because students are feeling good about themselves; enthusiasm about school, which affects motivation in all academic areas; and students who have gone on to pursue hobbies, degrees, and careers related to photography and writing.

Ideally, students would expect to do a different LTP project every year as a regular part of school life, but realistically they may encounter only one teacher who offers this kind of experience. Yet a teacher who takes the initiative to implement an LTP project, especially if the students exhibit their work, may influence other teachers to try doing projects in their classrooms.

Remembering that we teachers are constantly making decisions, I've noticed that every time I participate in an LTP project, special circumstances arise. For example, in working on *The Best Part of Me*, I have had children with serious health challenges. While working with *American Alphabets*, I worried about the children who were English language learners. In *Memories from Past Centuries*, students have pointed out their reluctance to discuss issues of faith. In *Black Self/White Self*, students have been uncomfortable discussing race. In each chapter, Wendy, Katie, and I have described our own experiences with these "yeah, but what about . . ." moments in our teaching. In general, I believe that the "special" circumstances are a big part of the reason for inviting students to participate in these projects. These are the moments that allow for growth in everyone's appreciation of our diversity. One of the joys of leading an LTP project is experiencing a moment of surprise at an astute question or observation that emerges from a student.

Undertaking Literacy Through Photography projects might seem intimidating for a typical, stressed-out public school teacher (believe me, I know!), yet I have experienced again and again how these projects can reawaken the spirits of teacher/artists and rekindle wonder about the kids we're privileged to spend our days and lives with. Every time I include an LTP project in my class, I notice that I get the bigger picture all over again, and I think, Could this be a way to keep teachers in the profession? Could LTP be a way to increase teacher competence?

I urge anyone who picks up this book, no matter what subject or age group he or she teaches, to read all of it. The reader will find inspiration in the students' work and recognize connections to an array of curricular goals and successful classroom practices. All four projects can be adapted to meet different curricular purposes and situations. *The Best Part of Me*, the first and shortest chapter, is an excellent training ground for the other longer and more complex projects. Implementing *The Best Part of Me* takes less time than the other projects, yet it includes important components of the other three: emphasis on building a sense of community in the classroom, habits of brainstorming and pre-writing at the outset of a project, techniques for helping students improve their writing by starting with a picture, strategies for making pictures, and the importance of presenting pictures and writing to an audience.

I am encouraged to continue offering these projects to my students even without the presence and immediate help of a sociology professor and an internationally acclaimed photographer. I continue learning to teach more effectively by tapping my skills as an artist and fine-tuning my kid-watching abilities. I believe the photographs and stories in this book can equip other teacher/artists to offer students deeper, more personal experiences within the usual school curricula.

Katie Hyde
Through a Sociologist's Lens

BLACK FIGURES ON THE SAND and the sun rising over the ocean. This is what we see during the first few minutes of one of Abbas Kiarostami's visual meditations in his film *Five Dedicated to Ozu*. Only after one of the dark creatures lifts its head do we recognize them as sleeping dogs. As the horizon becomes brighter and brighter, we're invited to watch the dogs interact in the absence of people—we see them wag their tails as they rise, move around, greet one another, and again flop down in the sand, arranging themselves in new constellations. Kiarostami has commented that "'Watch Again' or 'Look Well' or simply, 'Look'" would be suitable alternative titles for this film. In showing us the dogs at sunrise sequence and four other poetic long takes—featuring, for instance, walkers coming and going along the shore or the moon's reflection on water—he asks us to pay attention to moments, details, textures, rhythms, gestures, cues, and contingencies. As viewers, as humans, we're asked to look well and see more.

The concepts of seeing and perception have always intrigued me. I became involved in Literacy Through Photography not through studying art, education, or photography, but through sociology. As a sociologist I am interested in the ways people see and understand their worlds and the paths that inspire or inhibit new ways of seeing and action. Sociology is, itself, about seeing. Like photography, it is a way of seeing. A sociological lens reminds us to look once again at the ordinary, and beneath its surface. It urges us to connect the large and small scale, the local and worldly, the bewildering and mundane. A camera lens likewise helps us look more closely at our world. As we frame pictures and time our shots, we slow down our looking, giving subjects due attention, seeing them anew. We isolate our subjects, deciding how to strip away or give context. We decide how others will see our subjects with framing that adds mystery or enhances meaning. Looking at and carefully reading photographs of all kinds—images on billboards or Facebook pages, within historical archives, family albums, or school yearbooks—require and reinforce sociological mindfulness. Both sociology and photography invite us to gaze at the familiar or personal with fresh eyes and to identify the personal significance and substance of the foreign.

I first learned of Wendy's work as I was finishing my graduate work in sociology. Reading about her *Black Self/White Self* project, I was compelled by the idea of using different tools (documentary photography, for example) to study the same topics that interest sociologists, but with different, or at least broader, goals and audiences in mind. I began exploring the field of visual sociology, taking courses with Wendy and other professors at the Center for Documentary Studies, and when the opportunity arose I grabbed the chance to work with LTP full time.

My work involves training teachers, teaching undergraduate students, and facilitating and overseeing LTP collaborations locally and internationally. Every time I have the opportunity to work with teachers and students on classroom LTP projects, I remember why LTP first appealed to me as a pedagogy that allows students to see deliberately and more expansively. LTP assignments help students create thoughtful self-representations; they cultivate critical thinking that encourages students to pay careful attention to what's in front of and around them, regardless of whether they have a camera in hand.

Each project in this book appeals to me as an educator interested in critical and creative connections among the personal, social, and historical. I have come to appreciate their potential and complexity as a co-facilitator of Wendy's workshops, as Lisa's collaborator within the classroom, and as a keeper and "curator" of students' LTP work. As a co-author of this book, I have spent countless hours reading and re-reading students' images and words. The more I look, the more I see.

Looking closely, the seemingly ordinary objects and scenes in students' pictures become remarkable. The examples in this book abound with discoveries, comprehension, compassion, and vision. A favorite example is Nytrepa's *Best Part of Me* portrait of her hands (see Chapter 1). In other portraits featured in this book, we notice Nytrepa's hands holding onto the branches of the tree she's perched in, or tipping a watering can just enough to let water trickle onto the school's garden. Here Nytrepa's hands are isolated, taking up three-quarters of the frame. The tips of one hand's fingers touch the other's tips and point toward the camera.

By showing us less, Nytrepa invites us to see more. Alongside their portraits, other students wrote titles, descriptions, explanations, and poems. Nytrepa poses questions, ones that directly engage the viewer: "Do you know your hands can make people feel sad?" "Do you know your hands can help you do everything?" "Do you know your hands can make people feel really good?" Seeing Nytrepa's hands, reading her questions, I see four hands fluttering in sign language, a dancer's graceful pose, a protestor's fist, punches thrown by frustrated siblings, a father patting a shoulder, a mother wiping away tears; I see hands writing letters, hurting or healing bodies, waving good-bye. I see Nytrepa looking at her own hands through her family's eyes. "My mom, dad and sister always say I have big black hands," her portrait's title tells us. I'm reminded of the set of words Nytrepa listed in planning home pictures for the *American Alphabets* project—aunt, brother, dad, friend, mom, sister, loving, hug, understanding. I see hands holding, caring, tending.

Every student's photographs and writings radiate with layers of both personal and broader meaning. Nytrepa's questions are explicit, yet all students' self-, imagined, and historical portraits elicit questions. They evoke stories, memories, emotions, and histories from within and outside the frame.

In creating a visual alphabet about "school" for another assignment, students designated "A for art," "L for learning," and "Q for questions." Like sociology, like photography, these Literacy Through Photography lessons promote and require seeing—active, curious, inquisitive seeing. In reading representations and making them, students gain the tools to question themselves, appearances, stereotypes, and injustices, and to express their thoughts, feelings, and discoveries.

About This Book

ALL OF THE PROJECTS described in this book begin with an introduction by Wendy in which she tells the story of how she conceived of the project. She shares how she collaborated with students and teachers to create original, meaningful works of art. Wendy's introductions provide a guiding voice as she describes the inspiration behind each project's conceptual framework.

The heart of each chapter is an in-depth, step-by-step look at the project as later put into practice in various classrooms. Here the chapter's narration moves from Wendy's voice to a collective story that reflects the book's three authors. In every chapter we draw from our range of experiences to offer straightforward guidelines in undertaking project activities.

In our explanation of each project, we feature students' images and writings. With only two exceptions, all the work presented in the four chapters was made at Club Boulevard Humanities Magnet School in Durham, North Carolina. There are a few cases where we use a pseudonym for a student, otherwise we credit our students using their real names. Club Boulevard is an urban school with an economically and racially diverse student body. Some students live in wealthy areas near the local universities where one of their parents might work, other students come from impoverished neighborhoods and more than half participate in the school's free and reduced lunch program. Club Boulevard's student body has a fairly balanced mix of African American, White, and Latino/a students, and a small percentage (around 5%) are multi-racial. In Chapter 1, *The Best Part of Me,* we include examples of Club Boulevard students' photographs and writings over the course of 10 years, but in each of the book's three subsequent chapters we narrow the focus to one implementation of the project—explaining the process in general terms while sharing the story of how a particular class worked together to explore themselves, their home lives, and American and world history.

The book has an easy-to-follow structure. Each chapter opens with an overview of the project's theme and process, followed by specific, self-contained photography and/or writing activities. We recommend following the sequence of activities as presented in each chapter. Individual activities typically require 1 hour of class time (class periods of 45 to 90 minutes are ideal). The length of time needed for an entire project will vary depending on how many activities are completed in a given day or week. We typically lead two activities a week (often during writing, reading, or social studies instruction), which means the projects are spread out over the course of 2 or more months. The length of each project also will depend on the amount of equipment available—when students share a set of cameras and/or computers, more time will be needed.

In each chapter, we also include a "Talking About" section specific to a project's subject matter and larger themes—for instance, "Talking About Race" in Chapter 2, *Black Self/White Self*. In student-centered classrooms, teachers are accustomed to differentiating instruction and recognizing individual strengths and needs. When leading the projects in this book, teachers can choose where and when a scaffold will help their students deal with the risky subject matter and provocative themes. Each chapter's "Talking About" section cautions teachers about potentially charged moments, and suggests a mix of academic readings, children's literature, and classroom activities that can preface, complement, or conclude the LTP projects. We believe that a primary reason for doing these projects is that they provide students the chance to explore—with honesty, creativity, and critical thinking—important social, personal, and political topics that otherwise are easily avoided in the classroom. We hope that with these suggestions (some of which are appropriate across projects)—and the recommended readings at the back of the book—teachers will feel prepared to dive in. Some chapters also present suggested variations of the project. At the conclusion of each chapter, we share closing thoughts in the form of "A Teacher's Reflection" by Lisa Lord and "Through a Sociologist's Lens" by Katie Hyde.

The chapters are in order of the breadth of the project focus. This structure is reminiscent of Wendy's book, *I Wanna Take Me a Picture* (Ewald & Lightfoot, 2001), which explains the progression of LTP themes from the self to the family, then to the community, and finally to the symbolic and imaginative world of dreams. Here, again, we suggest that students begin with an in-depth exploration of themselves. In Chapter 1, *The Best Part of Me*, the chapter that introduces the LTP methodology, students keep the focus on their own bodies. The *Black Self/White Self* project, described in Chapter 2, involves self-portraiture but entails a more complex look at identity and how identity can be tied up with ethnicity, race, and culture, as students consider how they would portray themselves as "other." While all LTP projects marry and blend words and images, Chapter 3, *American Alphabets*, looks at language itself. In creating a visual portrayal of words that constitute their home language, students reveal their different ways of naming and representing their world. As students investigate home, community, culture, and language, the *American Alphabets* project also moves them through increasingly complex layers of writing, making photographs, and making decisions about representation.

Whether looking at the body, identity, race, culture, and/or language, the projects in Chapters 1 to 3 begin and end with the students' own experiences. The book's final chapter, *Memories from Past Centuries*, is a point of departure. Here students begin by looking at archival portraits and histories of children in another place and time. Like *Black Self/White Self, Memories from Past Centuries* pushes students to imagine themselves as an "other," in this case, by building on factual accounts of children who were rescued during the Holocaust. (In this chapter, all the children's names for the archival Joint Distribution Committee photographs and case histories have been changed to pseudonyms.) Students create multimedia portraits that combine still images, writing, and video recorded performances. They bring their own personalities and biographies into their historical fiction, full of powerful messages about individual choices and actions.

Literacy Through Photography, as a philosophy and practice, is about students learning to read and write by *doing*, by creating their own works of art (rather than studying someone else's) that combine words and images to express an idea and to tell a story. Throughout LTP projects we purposely use the term "art" in talking about the students' work because we suspect that in their eyes, art projects are more fun, more impressive, and on a larger scale compared with "just writing." Art means creativity and imagination, and implies an audience. Students make connections across different genres, blending fact and fiction, and conceptualize, as individuals and as a group, how the many pieces will fit together and be understood by an audience. Not all students think of themselves as artists, but as a final activity in each one of these projects everyone produces a piece of art.

ONE | The Best Part of Me

Questioning Appearances, Exploring Identity

IN ADDITION TO BEING A POWERFUL PROJECT IN ITSELF, *The Best Part of Me* introduces the core processes we used in creating all the projects presented in this book. This chapter explains how photography and writing projects depend on and help to establish a respectful classroom atmosphere, and describes how the projects are woven into readers' and writers' workshops. The detailed descriptions of reading, making, and presenting photographs are relevant to every chapter in the book.

In *The Best Part of Me*, each student creates a self-portrait that features a favorite body part. The project begins with students collecting ideas for a self-portrait by mapping memories and observations about different parts of their bodies. Students brainstorm their self-portraits by "reading" family photographs and interviewing one another about the stories contained within those pictures. After narrowing down their ideas and creating a photograph of one specific body part, students write about their photographs. Finally, they transform their work into banners and make a large installation for an audience.

The Best Part of Me pushes students to observe details, call up stories and sayings, and choose what they wish to show an audience about themselves. Besides boosting students' sense of the value of their uniqueness, the self-portraits invite conversations with others about the way they are seen and how they are understood through the portraits they present. While working on a photography assignment or a piece of writing, students step back to consider the part with the whole. Throughout the project, we see students develop the flexibility, agility, and habit of looking more closely, of considering the "big picture." They recognize new thoughts, look again, adjust their message, become open to new insights, and experience *surprise*. *The Best Part of Me* teaches students to enjoy the view and rewards their willingness to keep looking.

Wendy Ewald
An Artist's Frame

WHEN I BEGAN making photographs, I decided that portraiture was what I was most excited about. The fascinating thing, it seemed to me, was that however one went about making portraits, there was always an intense relationship between subject and artist, a deep courtesy that called, if only briefly, for the recognition of mutual humanity.

The ongoing, half-mute dialogue between the photographer and the subject (and inevitably the viewer) became for me the essential point of a photograph. I gravitated toward the work of master portraitists like Nadar, August Sander, and Judith Joy Ross, who seem as a matter of course to deliver uncanny glimpses into the personalities of their subjects and the times they inhabit.

My Hands

I like my hands because they turn the pages of a book slowly and magically. Reading makes me happy. They wipe my eyes when I am sad. They threaten the things that make me mad. They pull the covers over my head when I am scared. They feel my forehead when I am sick. They write what I am writing now. They touch the precious earth and ground. They dance. They act. They're slender and unige. They're mine— thats all, slender and unique.

Colette Cosner

Colette's self-portrait, 2000.

The fact is that many people feel uneasy or unbeautiful or downright frightened in the presence of a camera. So how do they choose to stand or pose? How do the clothes they wear signal things about their personality, their desires? How do they show or hide themselves? And how, finally, does an artist render someone's "life" in an image; how does the subject influence that image?

Recently, photography has gotten more and more interested in the human body and in issues that arise in the portrayal of children. The specter of impropriety hovers over photographers who make pictures of their own children. Still, no one has given much thought to what the subjects might have to say about all this. I began to wonder whether, if given the chance to express themselves on the subject, children's views of their own bodies might change—and perhaps improve—the way adults read images of children.

As an artist and a teacher, I often ask people to create self-portraits in words or photographs. Many times I've heard children describe themselves, and their family ties, by focusing on parts of their bodies: "I have Mom's eyes," one of my Kentucky students told me. "They're real little." Observations of this sort, on the part of children, have the power and resonance of secrets revealed. Self-awareness can be scary.

Of course, children grow and change, and their attitudes toward their changing bodies shift. At Shepard Middle School, I started by asking 8th-grade students to select a part of their body that I might photograph. But I was disappointed by the images we made. One girl's photograph was of her hands holding a briefcase; a boy chose to focus on his foot perched on a soccer ball. These pictures were more

My Hands
By: Tramika Davis

Ohhh. My hands. My old wrinkled hands. Can't you see the triangles in both of them? In the picture I have on 2 real rings, 1 plastic ring, and 1 fake tweety bird ring. I have no ring on my thumb. My hands are big, I say strong. I lift some -things that are heavy. Maybe thats why they're big and ugly. The reason why my nails are'nt long is, because I bite them off.

I write with my right hand but if write with my left it looks sloppy. See the reason why I choose my hands is becau--se I like them even if they're big and ugly.

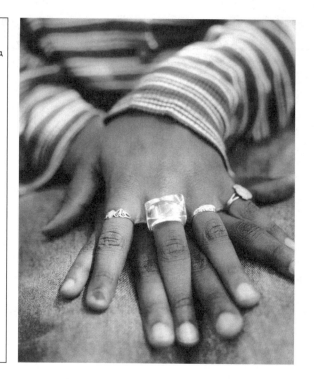

Tramika's self-portrait, 2000

about the objects than about parts of the body. One of my educator friends suggested that I'd been asking the wrong question of the middle schoolers; I should have asked them to pick their *worst* body part.

I moved on to 2nd- through 5th-grade students at Club Boulevard Elementary School and asked them to choose the parts of their bodies they liked best or that explained the most about them. Since they hadn't reached the more self-conscious middle school years, their choices turned out to be much more about themselves and less about how they wanted to be seen.

I set my camera up in the schoolyard and worked one-on-one with each student. I used a view camera to take a Polaroid of each child in order to maximize texture and details. The student and I looked at the photograph together and discussed changes in composition or background that might better reflect the child's vision of him- or herself. Once we were satisfied with the image, the child took it back to the classroom and worked with teacher Lisa Lord in her classroom.

The students' words drew out the meanings of the camera's scrutiny of each part of the body. Alejandro fixed on his spike-like teeth, which he compared with a shark's—and with his cousin Lara's. Beverly had me photograph her back and her hair. In her writing she likened herself to a Barbie doll. Tim asked me to photograph his chest because he counted on it, he said, to protect himself. To this strikingly sensual image he added layers of pride and irony with a poem that began: "Chest, chest, you're the best." When I looked at the pictures and text altogether, I was startled by how revealing they were. I was struck, too, by the different ways in which different cultural groups might conceive of their bodies. Tramika, who is African American, and Colette, who is a White girl from a more affluent family, both chose their hands, but they described them very differently. Tramika's description alluded to the manual work they'd done; Colette's to the graceful, magical protection they gave her.

I was asked to put together some of the work for a children's book. I asked Lisa's students to help me design it. Tiffany came up with the title, and the other students worked on a dummy book and title pages. We wanted to be sure the book reflected the diversity of students in the Durham public school system, so a few more photographs were made, a few more poems written. The last photograph I took was of Nada's hands in prayer. She titled her poem "All Mine."

I hoped the book would give children a chance to talk about their bodies and share their candid sense of themselves with adults, for whom intimacy and what is plainly, innocently visible are often at odds.

OUR STAGE IS A CLASSROOM in which children develop habits of working together that allow them to excel in writing and photography and to gain greater understanding of themselves and others. Creating a safe classroom environment, brainstorming ideas, and teaching students to read photographs, three essential components of all the LTP projects, as well as information about the readers' and writers' workshops, are described below. Brainstorming, as the first activity, is described in the first section. By the time students engage with the activities of mapping memories of their bodies and reading one another's family photographs, they are already becoming more comfortable on "stage."

Setting the Stage

Creating a Safe Classroom Environment

During the first few weeks of school we teach students about the classroom community we envision. We help them articulate the expectations for how we treat one another and how we work together. A great deal of class time is devoted to community-building games and to teaching specific procedures for how we use our time and materials. From then on the students work all year to build and protect a safe learning community.

The students' experiences with photography described in this book strengthen community spirit and help create a respectful environment. At the beginning of the year, no students could be expected to produce personal, honest, and meaningful writing required of *The Best Part of Me* project, or any of the others, if they didn't first feel like

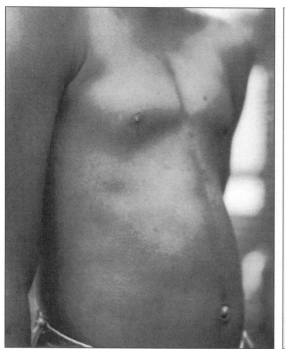

Tim McKoy

Chest, Chest you're the best.
I like to rest on you, oh yes.
I wake up. I depend on you
to protect my body too.
Chest, Chest, you're the best
you're a big Success you might
be the best in the west.
Chest, Chest, you're the best.

Tim's self-portrait, 2000

members of a safe community. In our classes students gain a sense of safety because of a series of decisions we make as their teachers.

First, we value students' choices—of books to read, stories to write, partners with whom to study, specific topics to explore, and images to photograph.

Second, we recognize that we teachers don't know everything that our students know. We are in a position of calling upon their authority —especially about their experiences, opinions, and preferences. We structure our classes in a way that encourages our students to be themselves and to contribute their knowledge to the community.

Third, we display student work and equip our classroom with the necessary materials and tools: an extensive class library, walls adorned with student art, and bins of supplies accessible to students. These basic elements of the classroom build students' pride in their work and their responsibility for caring for equipment and using supplies appropriately. We also arrange the classroom furniture in a way that encourages the students to work as teams and to get help and feedback from classmates. There are quiet times in our class, but there are many times when the students are talking to others about their projects.

Finally, we plan field trips and projects that invite the students to learn through experience.

Initiating and maintaining a safe classroom environment may, in fact, come from shared photography and writing experiences early in

My back

I picked my back because if
I did'nt have my back then I
couldn't move because every thing
counts on my back.
And I put Hair in the picture
because I like my hair.
I can put barrets in my hair
and I can braid it. My mom
braids my hair a lot. she
Says I am her little Barbie.
My hair is longer than my Short
Sleeve shirt.

By: Beverly Benton

Beverly's self-portrait, 2000

the school year, like creating books or displays called "The Best Part of Our Class" or "The ABCs of Our Class." Consequently, when students begin deeper thinking about themselves and risk honesty about some of their most precious ideas later in the year, they are already accustomed to making independent choices and expressing individual opinions.

Brainstorming:
Mapping the Body and Discovering Uniqueness

We have carried out *The Best Part of Me* project with groups of all ages—elementary, middle school, and high school level students, as well as teachers—and in many places, including North Carolina, New York, Ohio, and Colorado, in addition to Tanzania and Haiti. We think it is an excellent introduction to the Literacy Through Photography philosophy and structure. As we describe *The Best Part of Me* project in this chapter, we draw on insights from many iterations of the project. Most of the student work we present and discuss was made in 4th- and 5th-grade classrooms at Club Boulevard Elementary School during the years 2003–2010. We also draw on examples from Wendy's original pilot in 2000, as well as a project Lisa led in Haiti in 2010.

The Best Part of Me project begins with brainstorming, a routine part of the LTP creative process. In this book's projects, brainstorming takes form in a variety of ways, such as diary entries, drawing, alphabetical lists, or note taking in a word processing program. For *The Best Part of Me*, students brainstorm by making a "map" of their bodies. We ask students to draw themselves from head to toes on a large sheet of paper, or glue a pre-cut paper silhouette of the human shape onto a piece of construction paper. Because students quickly become engaged with and engrossed in their drawing, teachers may prefer to use silhouettes to maximize time for storytelling and note taking. We ask students to label their drawings or silhouettes with notes about any memories or stories they associate with their eyes, hands, feet, hair, elbows, knees, and so on.

The purpose of this brainstorming exercise is to generate a wealth of details—memories and observations—that will help students generate better, more complex, and interesting ideas for self-portraits. Rather than simply identifying feet on their body maps, students include details like, "My feet used to fall asleep and I used to walk on my tippy toes. But now I don't do it"; "My feet are so flexible it's like they have no bones sometimes"; and, "I love to build up the soles of my feet by walking barefoot on rocks." Letting students know that their brainstormed work will not be "published" lets them relax about mechanics and get excited about writing. They consider the physical sensations of their emotions with notes such as, "My face burns when I'm going to cry, but I fight it," and, "When I did something wrong or bad my heart pounds and I think everyones accusing me of something."

Frequently the mapping process leads students to remember experiences that have long been forgotten. In addition to notes about features such as a "unabrow," long hair, and dry lips, they share unforgettable moments: "This only happened once but once I woke up at around 12:00 and could not breathe." Nearly everyone maps his or her injuries, scars, or signs from past operations. Regardless of their age, we find students maturely and respectfully annotate memory maps of their bodies as preparation for their self-portraiture. Teachers may want to advise or remind students that certain body parts are off limits for this project, although we haven't found this to be necessary.

We start out by looking at identical "bodies," but this quickly and easily evolves into a sharing of particular memories and associations from each student's life: Elijah's injuries include a busted chin on the Champs-Élysées, while Clarice reports a hickey on her arm from licking it, and Shaniqua remembers her cousin stepping on her earring while it was still in her ear. We soon realize that talking about the body maps is an excellent way to get to know our students. Kierra draws a line to her knees and writes that everybody will laugh at her ashy knees. She also writes, "When I was little I had six fingers and had one cut off."

The stories flow. Labeling his nose, Elijah remembers "the first time I smelt Paris." Bragging begins. Next to his ear, Javontre writes, "I have a good sense of hearing. I can hear a dollar drop a mile away." He must have heard that said before. Pointing to his skin, Isaac writes that he is a blood-sucking insect magnet, just like his mom. Elijah labels his foot with a note that he first used a piano pedal when he was 3. Cole writes about his ability to cross his eyes and show his ribs by sucking in his breath. Students' notes reveal facts of their family history as well as things other people say about them—for instance, Breonna writes that her skin shows that she is half Indian, or at least that's what her mother told her.

The fact that students fill large sheets of paper with notes about specific events, talents, and characteristics shows us that they are involved in an important assignment. We see students become comfortable writing and talking about their bodies. As pages fill up with notes, it is evident that paying close attention to parts of their bodies leads to a fuller understanding of themselves as whole individuals.

Since students are the resident experts on the stories and memories linked to their hands, heads, bellies, and so on, and because they choose what to include and what to omit from their maps, *The Best Part of Me* can be powerful rather than problematic for children dealing with issues of difference or with health concerns. Establishing a safe, child-focused classroom environment allows children the security to express themselves regardless of family or physical distinctness. When many students report things like, "I fiddle with my ears when I'm thinking, just like my dad," or "Everybody say I look like my mama," we worry that students like Samuel, who was adopted when he was old enough to remember escaping "from war" in Liberia, might feel alienated. But Samuel's body map (and eventually his self-portrait) allows him to emphasize his physical strength and his sophistication—the notes on his body map are about coolness and pride in his maturity. Although we rarely see notes about body size, students who are overweight or underweight may be uncomfortable writing about their bodies. The child in the class who we worry might be the most sensitive about his body is Larry, who is overweight. On his body map he writes about his mother's hospitalization for diabetes and his grandfather's death from cancer, and the time he had to go to the hospital when he fell playing basketball because it was too hot. Larry writes that he wished "no one would be sick any more." Along with his concerns, Larry also recalls accomplishments: "1 time I played for the YMCA and I won the championship and we all got trophies and took a team picture." We realize that students are less sensitive or embarrassed about their families or their bodies when we provide a safe way to deal with their concerns. When embarrassing or awkward things come up in discussions, teachers have important conversations with individuals and may decide to rearrange which students work individually, with partners, or in small groups.

TALKING ABOUT THE BODY

THE BEST PART OF ME *is both valuable and challenging because it calls explicit attention to how students are unique and different. In asking students to consider their own and classmates' distinctive physical, mental, and expressive qualities, teachers should prioritize three overlapping guidelines: establish parameters about an appropriate and respectful use of language; anticipate the body-related topics with the most emotional charge; and help students see how the social world influences perceptions of the body and of beauty.*

Address students' use of language and name-calling. *The body is familiar terrain in health and science classes dealing with internal systems, nutrition, body types and shapes, and reproduction. Setting parameters about the appropriate vocabulary for* The Best Part of

Me *activities will help keep students focused—students' body maps are meant to be a springboard to memories and in turn richly detailed self-portraits. Since some students may interpret the task of mapping bodies as an invitation to talk about anatomy, we are also careful about the language we use to introduce the project. Especially when working with teenagers, we frame this as a self-portrait project—rather than a project about favorite body parts; we begin by asking students to use an entire piece of 8.5 x 11 paper to draw themselves (rather than their* bodies) *from head to toes as a first step in making self-portraits.*

Teachers can promote a respectful use of language by linking The Best Part of Me *to "No Name-Calling Week," a national event organized by GLSEN (Gay, Lesbian and Straight Education Network). The excellent lesson plans provided on GLSEN's website (nonamecalling. org) integrate writing, media literacy, and literature, and directly relate to many elements of* The Best Part of Me *project. Since it deals with body-related name-calling, we especially recommend GLSEN's "Using Literature as a Tool to End Name-Calling" middle school lesson plan, which is framed around an excerpt from the classic story* Blubber *by Judy Blume (1974). Teachers can segue from* Blubber *or another piece of literature—such as* Loser *by Jerry Spinelli (2002) or Gordon Korman's (1998)* The 6th Grade Nickname Game—*into a conversation about students' own exposure to and/or experience with name-calling and bullying. Teachers can guide dialogue or journal writing with essential questions like: What names are used to single out students in this school? What do these names mean? Within what spaces and under what circumstances does name-calling occur? Other GLSEN lesson plans will help students recognize how to respond as a victim or bystander of name-calling and establish guidelines for respectful classroom dialogue.*

Anticipate emotionally charged issues. *Like all LTP projects, this one delves into the unpredictable territory of students' interior lives and subjective realities. Teachers should anticipate the vulnerability students feel in recognizing distinctions (real or perceived) tied to bodies, families, and special talents. The sensitive topic of body size should be addressed in terms of both the highly visible issue of obesity as well as the often hidden struggles involved with anorexia and bulimia. Like* Blubber, *other stories about weight struggles—such as* Full Mouse, Empty Mouse: A Tale of Food and Feelings *by Dina Zeckhausen (2007) for grades 2–4;* Fat Chance *by Leslea Newman (1994) and* The Cat Ate My Gymsuit *by Paula Danziger (1974) for middle school students, and the memoir* Thin *by Grace Bowman (2007) for high school students— generate empathy and invite consideration of the social pressures that contribute to eating disorders and self-esteem issues concerning body image. Students can speculate on the cultural habits that influence obesity,* as well as the kinds of limitations and problems obese children face. Another useful resource is the downloadable Educators' Toolkit *on the National Eating Disorders Association website (www.nationaleatingdisorders.org). We also recommend addressing ideas about athleticism, which also encompass gender and body issues.*

Furthermore, students also may differentiate their bodies along the lines of intellectual capacity and academic success, especially in inclusion classrooms. We suggest using Patricia Polacco's picture book The Junkyard Wonders *(2010) to discuss the social ostracism that may accompany students' learning or developmental disabilities and to reinforce the value in uncovering and honoring all kinds of genius. For middle school students, we recommend* Rules *by Cynthia Lord (2006), about a female protagonist's struggle with her younger brother's autism, and June Rae Wood's* The Man Who Loved Clowns *(1992), about the relationship between the 13-year-old protagonist and her uncle who has Down Syndrome.*

Finally, as students reflect on family connections in this project's activities, be aware that students who are adopted, living in foster care, or living with parents in a same-sex relationship may be unable to list and write about family traits that have to do with physical resemblances. When asking students to create their body maps and reflect on family photos, remind them to consider not only physical appearance, but also the unique ways family members have taught or inspired them to use their hands, eyes, legs, brains, and so on.

Consider the body in a social context. *When leading* The Best Part of Me *project, teachers should keep in mind that social identities (gender, sexual orientation, age, race/ethnicity) and family/cultural traditions condition the ways students experience their bodies. It's important to help students understand how society influences the way we see and feel about our bodies. Conversations about stereotypes will help students examine the assumptions—often false—we make about difference. Teachers will find a wealth of useful essays and lesson plans about stereotypes (and many social justice issues in education) in the journal* Teaching Tolerance, *as well as its companion website (www.tolerance. org), which is published by the Southern Poverty Law Center. Among many useful lesson plans that address stereotyping (relevant to all four projects in this book), is an activity called "We and Thee" that utilizes Shakespeare's* Romeo and Juliet *to examine the dynamics and destructiveness of the "us versus them" mentality.*

Teachers should help students see that stereotypes often rest on inaccurate or distorted assumptions about bodies—physical and mental capabilities, personalities, and so forth. For teachers wishing to consult research about school practices and curricula that perpetuate gender and race stereotypes and inequalities, we recommend Still Failing at Fairness: How Gender Bias Cheats Boys and Girls in Schools and What We Can Do About It *(Sadker, Sadker, & Zittleman, 2009) and* Bad Boys: Public Schools in the Making of Black Masculinity *(Ferguson, 2000). Students can investigate gender and racial stereotypes by looking at classic fairy tales or Disney movies, as well as contemporary advertisements and children's toys. Lessons on stereotyping should involve three main goals: identifying stereotypes, understanding their impact, and learning how to address and change behaviors and language that reinforce stereotypes. It's also important to help students see that difference, itself, is not bad, but that the manner in which we relate to difference is often problematic. Books that portray characters who defy cultural expectations about gender, for example,* Jose! Born to Dance: The Story of Jose Limon *by Susanna Reich (2005), are also useful in this regard. Another recommendation for older students is Mark Hardy's* Nothing Pink *(2008) about 15-year-old Vincent, the son of preacher, who comes to accept the fact that he's gay.*

bell hook's picture books Happy to Be Nappy *(1999) and* Skin Again *(2004) and* I Love My Hair *by Natasha Anastasia Tarpley (1998) challenge myths that narrowly define beauty in terms of only certain skin and eye colors, hair textures, and body shapes. The documentary photography in Lauren Greenfield's* Girl Culture *(2002) and* Thin *(2006) provides a critical look at beauty standards and practices and is appropriate for older students. Similarly, a suitable novel for middle school students is Sharon Flake's* The Skin I'm In *(1998), which deals with appearance-based identity issues that are tied to race and gender. Finally, media literacy lessons will sharpen students' awareness that beauty standards are often distorted and unattainable as well as racist and sexist. We recommend the educator resources provided by Center for Media Literacy, such as their "MediaLit Kit" that can be downloaded from www.medialit.org.*

Reading Photographs

READING PHOTOGRAPHS is a core activity that directly links photography to literacy by establishing the idea that photography is a language. This practice, used in every project in this book, equips students with the tools necessary to communicate stories and concepts visually and in writing. Students begin by reading and discussing an array of historical and contemporary photographic portraits, which prepares them to create their own pictures more intentionally as they foresee the outcomes entailed in making certain choices, such as background and point of view. As they begin to experiment with their own portraiture, students can draw on these examples of

Tanya's family photograph and drawing (opposite), 2010

how photographers build a story with gesture, expression, clothing, and props. What's more, students use the process of reading images to think about and discuss their own photographs, which only strengthens their literacy and communication skills.

We have three goals when we read photographs with students. The first goal is to develop a student's habit of looking carefully at the details of photographs. Students discuss what a photograph's subjects are doing, what emotions are evident in their gestures and facial expressions. They notice hairlines, body types, the style and season of clothing. They pick up on clues regarding relationships— how closely two children are sitting next to each other —and whether people are grouped in a public or private space—a kitchen or a crowded school bus. In reading photographs, a student also notices the background, the architecture of a house or a building's doors and windows, trees and their shadows on walls and sidewalks.

Reading images also enables students to decipher or infer a photograph's story based on concrete details. To reinforce this, students are asked to support their verbal or written arguments with facts; they are expected to articulate their reasoning by pointing to details in the photograph.

A final goal of reading photographs is to help students identify and understand the choices photographers make with framing, timing, and point of view in order to communicate a particular story and/or feeling with an image.

There are several key exercises that we ask students to do. We start by spending 30 minutes or so noting as many details as we can while we look at an interesting photograph projected on our classroom screen. The photographs we use might be the work of professional photographers, images drawn from the LTP archive of students' work, pictures students have brought from home, and/or the photos students are making as part of *The Best Part of Me*. We have contests to see who can find the most details in one photo. We then ask the students to write a narrative based on the photograph. We may prompt students to form hypotheses about the photograph: What happened just before the picture was taken? What happened afterward? Who is the photographer?

When looking at a portrait, in particular, we ask: What does the background tell you about the subject? What about his or her expression, body position, clothes? Where is the camera? How does the position of the camera affect your reading of the picture? For example, if you're looking up at the subject, she might seem imposing. What do you think the photographer is trying to tell you about the subject?

Reading Family Photographs

During the body-mapping activity, students think about parts of their bodies, tell stories, brag, and remember events from their past. The next part of *The Best Part of Me* involves reading family photographs to allow students to consider how they are each part of a bigger group. Our families influence our understanding of ourselves—family members give us nicknames, compare our characteristics with those of other members of the family, and help determine the way we see ourselves. Some students understand the word "family" as extended and multigenerational, while others think of the people with whom they live—biological, adoptive, or perhaps transient or temporary. Some think of positive, supportive families, while others worry about volatile or traumatic situations.

Building on the students' body map comments about what people in their families say about them, we hope that bringing a favorite photo of their family to class will reveal yet more dimensions of how students perceive themselves. Body maps elicit a network of relationships, the history of events. To model the reading photographs activity, Lisa shows students a snapshot of her and her brother standing in front of a downtown appliance store when they were in 2nd grade and kindergarten, respectively. Students point out as many details and observations as possible: Lisa's brother's cowboy suit, his glasses, painted images on the store window, people not centered in the photograph, the prediction that the painting on the window was important. We record what the students have to say without comment. When they run out of ideas, Lisa reveals a little more information: The picture was taken because she had painted the window as part of a citywide Halloween contest and she had won honorable mention. The questions the students ask Lisa invite her to tell them more about her brother and her childhood.

We then ask students to choose partners to "read" each other's family photos for about 5 minutes, listing on paper as many details as possible without asking questions or having discussions. When it is time to talk, partners point out what they notice, ask questions, and listen to lengthy elaborations. When the conversations subside, we ask students to write about their families.

Jackie is prompted to include more information about her photo because of her partner's list about her photograph: "Pretty. It was your birthday. Your family. They take a picture. Dress. Crayons, People. Presents." After talking with her partner and re-examining her photograph, Jackie writes: "I'm at my 8th birthday party. I'm having a cousin picture. My cousins Alex, Kevin, Johnny, Maycon, Luis, Kimberly, and Lesly. I have a balloon at the top. I have presents beside Kimberly. There is a bag on the table. Kevin is by the happy birthday sign. I have on a purple long dress. All the girls are wearing a skirt but not me. It was fall during my birthday. My cousin in the yellow has a picture beside him for me."

Tanya brings a family portrait from 2007 and draws a picture of her family in 2010. Her partner notices changes and differences in Tanya's pictures when she writes this list: "Dad dressed in western wear. They are all smiling. It's a colorful background. Tanya is in a dress. She didn't have braces. Her brother's wearing jeans and striped shirt. Her other brother dressed in shorts." Tanya writes, "Me being part of this family makes me feel weird, happy, sad. We are not a normal, typical family. Some of us now look different. Well . . . most of us, my older brother has a Mohawk, is 13, and 5 ft. 2 inches. My little brother is now 3 years old but still a clumsy naughty little boy, and me—now I have braces, shorter hair and am a lot taller than before, and my parents, well, they haven't really changed much except my dad. Now he only has 1 cell phone, and I'm more of a drama queen now."

As a last activity before moving on to making photographs, we direct students back to their body maps to think again about what their family members say about them. Looking back at specific notes related to the photographs, we notice students beginning to generalize. Luis writes, "My mom says I am a good son." Sam writes, "I'm a big brother who tries to help my brother and sister. Responsible, most of the time. Spoiled rotten." "I feel proud to be an only child. I am proud to have a wonderful family," Johanna writes.

About Readers' and Writers' Workshops

One of the reasons students in LTP classrooms can handle sensitive, personal subjects is that they are accustomed to the habits and attitudes of readers' and writers' workshops. Teachers everywhere have adopted the spirit and practices of readers' and writers' workshops. In these classrooms, the teacher is very active in equipping and supporting photographers and writers, assisting students in interviewing and questioning one another, and helping display students' art. Students and teachers routinely participate in workshop-style literacy instruction, including individual conferences; likewise, in LTP projects, teachers and students communicate constantly during the planning and making of photographs and pieces of writing as well as at exhibits and presentations. By way of introducing the ground rules for working and communicating in our classes, we offer a summary of the important elements. Teachers can find detailed information about implementing these practices in many excellent books by Nancie Atwell, Lucy Calkins, Donald Graves, Paula Denton, and Roxann Kriete.

Readers' Workshop. Reading photographs well takes time, as explained above. Appreciating the wealth of understanding we gain from the investment of time and attention to a single photograph, we can apply the same appreciation and care to developing skills in reading books and other texts. Conversely, the more accomplished students become as readers, the more associations they bring to a photograph. Readers' workshop is a routine part of the school day and the backbone of reading instruction. The components are described below.

Classroom shelves are loaded with a variety of children's books: paperback and hardcover novels arranged in baskets according to authors' last names; nonfiction books organized in tubs labeled with different topics; special shelves designated for poetry books; big bins of miscellaneous picture books, ranging from *"More, More, More," Said the Baby* (Williams, 1990) to *The Librarian Who Measured the Earth* (Lasky, 1994). The former book could easily be enjoyed with a toddler, while the other teaches about Eratosthenes and ancient Greece. If a classroom doesn't have its own library, bins of books should be borrowed from the media center. A great variety of reading levels, topics, and genres should be available. The books we mention as resources for the LTP projects are available for students during independent reading time, as well as when we may choose to read aloud an excerpt.

We set aside 45 to 60 minutes a day for readers' workshop. Budgeting time this way teaches students what our priorities are. Students know the routines and expectations for their work during readers' workshop. They choose the books they want to read. They choose a place in the classroom where they can focus on their reading. They keep required records of their reading—lists of books, brief comments, some journal entries. They participate in individual and small-group conferences with the teacher about their reading. Some students read better with a partner as they work toward the goal of reading independently.

We teach whole-class and small-group lessons about reading strategies. These lessons usually are led with excerpts from a variety of types of literature, usually passages that are relevant to topics being studied or types of writing being encouraged in writers' workshop. Often the passages enhance the subject matter of LTP projects. We read aloud to the students every day.

Students discuss their reading regularly with friends. We lead conversations about books and passages that are highlighted in reading lessons. Because of these daily lessons and routines, students are accustomed to being read aloud to. They are accustomed to questions like, "What did you notice about this book?" and "How does this book compare with that one?" They are accustomed to expressing their opinions about books, to relating books to life experiences or to other books they know, and to supporting their comments with examples from their reading.

Writers' Workshop. Writers' workshop is a routine part of the school day, the chief opportunity for instruction in every aspect of writing, from spelling, handwriting, and grammar to strategies for composing various genres. Writers' workshop is often the setting for organizing and presenting knowledge and ideas gained from reading and participation in all other parts of the curriculum. As with readers' workshop, our work with photography enhances writing instruction, and our writing instruction enhances students' image making. Here are the components of writers' workshop, which also takes 45 to 60 minutes a day.

Students know the routines and expectations for their work and they choose the majority of their writing assignments. Working quietly and independently, students produce a required quantity of drafts each week. They keep records of their work. In individual and small-group conferences, students share and discuss their writing, give and receive compliments, ask questions, and provide suggestions about one another's writing.

We lead brief lessons about writing, emphasizing a variety of objectives. At times particular assignments are made and a sequence of lessons guides the students' work on those assignments.

We decide how much to emphasize editing and proofreading with each student. We choose to help students build skills and confidence as writers with unique voices as a priority over perfecting the mechanics of writing. When student compositions are going to be read by an audience beyond the classroom (such as being included in a class book or exhibit), we find an excellent opportunity for lessons and conferences about producing the best final copy possible.

Because of the daily habits of writers' workshop, students enjoy their individuality as writers. They rarely say, "I don't know what to write," or ask, "Is this long enough?" They learn to identify a new writing task for themselves when they believe they have completed another job. Because of the variety of literature being shared in reading and writing lessons, they have the habit of seeking good writing models everywhere they go.

WITH THE RICHNESS and honesty of their recent thinking, and their multitude of ideas, the next step for students is to choose one part of themselves as the focus of the rest of this project. We ask students to consider the one part that represents them best. What is most important? What is their favorite? What is the "best"? What defines them as a person more than any other part?

Now we are ready to teach children how to be photographers and how this instruction can help them become better readers and writers. During readers' and writers' workshops, students enjoy the work of authors who have written about their bodies, and each student works with a partner to photograph one part of his or her body. After reading their own photographs, they work on writing about their "best" body part. With the workshop approach to teaching writing, the substance of *The Best Part of Me* is personal. The teacher doesn't have a list of correct approaches or responses. And as with the workshop approach to teaching reading, *The Best Part of Me* depends on interviews and conferences; conversations between artists and writers/readers lead to discoveries.

Making Photographs

We ask that students learn how to master the use of a camera—digital or analog—so they are able to use it in an intentional and powerful way. Some of the core concepts of photography—framing, the use of symbols, timing, and point of view—have strong parallels in writing and are used in each project in this book.

Framing. Framing is the most important element of photography, and students learn to make conscious decisions about what to include and what to leave out of their photographs. One way to help

Planning and Making Photographs and Writing About Them

Ja'Vai's self-portrait, 2003

students become aware of the edges of their frame is to ask them to cut a rectangle in a piece of paper, close one eye, and hold the paper up to their other eye. Wherever they turn their head, they are seeing their surroundings through a frame. Before starting to shoot photographs, ask students to look through the camera they'll be using while moving it from side to side, up and down. Then ask them to choose an object to look at through the camera and write a description of what they see, including the edges of the frame.

Using Symbols. Understanding the use of symbols in photography gives students much more control of their picture making. For example, if students are asked to photograph their community, they might think to photograph the outside of buildings, not realizing this wouldn't show the activities or conflict of the neighborhood and its inhabitants. To help students generate more specific ideas for photographs, we ask them to list adjectives and activities that name the things that they like about their communities. We then ask them to list words associated with things they don't like. From there, we talk about how photographers use symbols to represent the emotional quality of places—for example, a hug outside a church at the end of a service—and how photographers use symbols to stand in for things that are unsafe to photograph—for example, a pair of shoes hanging from a telephone wire to represent gangs or drugs.

Timing. Photography is unique in its ability to divide an action into segments of time that otherwise we would not see or stop to contemplate. Students must become conscious of when to click the shutter to express a feeling or action. It's helpful to ask students to choose a situation that is changing over time, such as an activity on the playground, and have them each shoot a picture from the same spot. When we look at a selection of the photographs, we discuss how a fraction of a second can change a picture. We also arrange and rearrange photographs in a sequence, regardless of whether they were intentionally taken in a certain order. We ask the students to describe the passage of time and create a narrative from the various sequences.

Point of View. The camera also can be moved to emphasize different aspects of the subject and change the photographer's and viewer's point of view. For example, if you photograph something from above, it will appear smaller; conversely, if you photograph it from below, it will look larger. Also, what is close to the camera will appear larger than what is farther away. We ask students to choose a subject to photograph, like a person or a computer, with a plain background. First we ask them make a list of all the angles from which they could take their picture. Then we ask them to look through the camera and describe how the subject changes as they change their point of view, and finally to make the photographs from each angle on their list.

Lillie's self-portrait, 2003

Isaac's self-portrait, 2005

Isaac

Choosing and Picturing One Part of the Body

Whether it is because they have been told their eyes, hands, or feet are just like those of someone they admire or because they notice the connection between some part of their body and something they love to do, it usually isn't difficult for students to choose one part of their body to photograph. For example, what Tanya saw as distinguishing her from her family members—braces and short hair—inspired the choices she considered for her project. Most students don't seem at all self-conscious about photographing themselves; the brainstorming and storytelling activities that lead up this part of the project put them at ease, with the task and with one another. If teachers notice students who are struggling with this part of the work, they may assign partners who are especially encouraging.

Choosing what to photograph is the beginning of an artistic collaboration. Each student now needs someone to take his or her photo. The collaborator needs to follow instructions well and be able to discuss the choice of background, pose and point of view, framing and timing, and the use of props. Partners help negotiate what looks good or how the image may be perceived by viewers. Both directing and taking the photographs empowers each student.

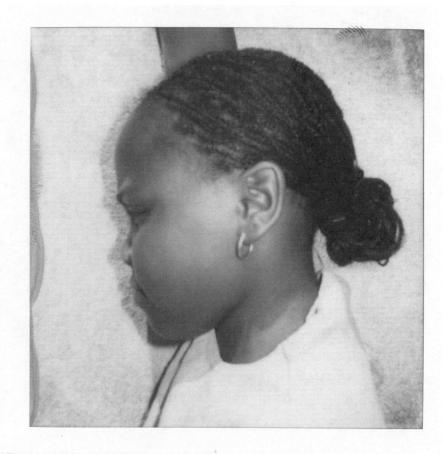

Shaniqua

Shaniqua's self-portrait, 2005

The ability to choose various locations around the campus gives collaborators an additional sense of freedom and power. (Digital cameras provide so much freedom that it may be helpful to limit the number of shots and the amount of time each team has.) Noticing choices of different textures for a background and interesting props increases students' recognition of the range of possibilities for how they present their featured body part. Chain link fences, brick walls, metal banisters, and wooden tables provide sleek, solid, permanent backgrounds. Trees, flowers, lawns, and fabric may look softer and more flexible. Collaborators help each other notice their options and feel comfortable with checking how well the photograph would represent the ideas and stories they have discussed about their bodies.

(When Lisa originally did this project in 2003, students made their first photograph with a Polaroid instant camera. They made full body portraits and then used permanent markers to draw a frame around the desired close-up part of the image. More recently, students have used digital cameras to make a "rough draft" image. Partners examine the image on the camera, adjust the zoom, and take a new photograph. When the new version is approved, students

Elijah

print the photo on a portable printer. Watching the completed print emerge from the printer causes excitement and anticipation.)

We are amazed not only by the variety of body parts the students choose, but also by the different ways each part is featured. When Wendy first did this project, she used a large-format camera that required students to sit very still. This limited students' choices in presenting their hands. In later projects, when students became the photographers and used a variety of cameras, the positions of hands became much more varied: Nytrepa's hands are clapping, fingertips toward the camera; Mario's are gripping a railing, knuckles inscribed with the letters of his name; Elijah's are poised as though they were over a keyboard; Jayleen's are barely in view as he drums with pencil "drumsticks"; Destiny's are stretched along a fence in the sunlight.

Jessica and Cherica showed their hair from the back, while Amber had her photographer focus on the top of her head, to show her hair as well as part of her face. Jessica seemed to be celebrating her distinction as the kid with the longest hair, while Cherica seemed especially proud of her intricate braids and interesting beads. Samuel flexed the muscles of one arm with his head bent over, face still visible, and Alex demonstrated his strength by framing his shoulder while doing a push-up.

The partners and artistic collaborators are friends. Friends tend to notice both small and large differences about one another and still choose to be friends. Samuel was not only different from his classmates because he was adopted, he was also different from them physically. He was older and more developed than a typical 4th- or 5th-grader. His formal schooling began when he arrived in the United States from Liberia. Rather than covering up this difference, he chose to photograph and celebrate his impressive biceps. He wrote about being a "man." Jonathan also chose his arm muscles as his best part. In his photograph he posed as a diminutive weightlifter in front of a huge brick wall. In the notes on his body map, Jonathan revealed the miracles of his survival as a baby born prematurely, writing, "Now I'm OK." He enumerated many of his distinctive qualities. Showing concern for his appearance, he wrote that he had worried about looking ugly when he got glasses at age 3. As a 4th-grader he was growing much more comfortable with himself: He was known to have worn a diaper over his clothes on Halloween to represent his favorite book character, Captain Underpants.

As teachers of *The Best Part of Me*, we have learned to not shy away from assignments that invite children to reflect on their uniqueness. For instance, at a home for students with physical and mental disabilities in Haiti, teachers asked students which part of their body they thought was the "best." Teachers made the photographs the way students directed. Some of the students chose their hair, their heads, their smiles—just as students in most classes do. One girl had the teacher retake her photo of her hair after she had put colorful barrettes on her braids; she was particular about the details, just as all children are. Many photos don't reveal unusual differences. In contrast, another girl chose her foot to photograph and wrote about how she wished it would help her move around as easily as others moved.

Physical differences are one aspect of all students' identities; encouraging them to recognize and appreciate their uniqueness in the safety of a learning community may strengthen their self-concepts at a critical time in their development. In making photographs of one part of their bodies, students also think about how their photos will be understood by an audience.

Because they are making photographs for others to see, students not only make choices about what will be in the photos, but they also *look* much more closely than before. The best part is no longer a matter of memories, reputations, and hearsay stories from their families, but an objective record. Other people, even strangers, will see this photograph. Will they get the message the student had in mind?

Destiny's self-portrait, 2003

Reading and Writing About Bodies

The Best Part of Me project starts with brainstorming prompted by a generic "body," and progresses to a written collection of memories and sayings about parts of students' bodies, some of which come from reading family photographs. Next kids produce close-up photos of one part of their bodies, so it is logical that the process moves to an examination of the details of that photo and to a written piece.

Anticipating students' first reactions to the writing assignment, we put ourselves in their shoes—"My body? You want me to write about my body?" A sensitive topic and task, to say the least. Note taking, storytelling, writing about families, and photography have become comfortable and natural things to do. When it comes to writing specifically about our bodies, one source of courage for embarking on this project comes from knowing that other authors have written about theirs.

Two of our favorite poets, Nikki Grimes and Naomi Shihab Nye, have written many pieces about children appreciating their bodies, their heritage, their strengths, and their abilities to overcome hardships. We read selections from the poets aloud and discuss what students notice about the techniques the authors have used. This prods the students' thinking about their bodies and suggests ways they can shape their thoughts in writing. For example, in "Running Shoes," Nikki Grimes (2000) helps children realize that their feet matter much more than the best running shoes. In "When You Come to a Corner," Naomi Shihab Nye (2000) leads them to explore a new neighborhood when they are faced with a move: "You still have your feet." Grimes (1999), in "His Hands," examines an older person's hands to help young people inquire about the stories their loved ones have to tell. Whether skinny or overweight, students can identify with the voices and feelings of the narrators in "Sideways Beauty" or "Wallet Size" by Grimes (1997). Nye's "My Body Is a Mystery" (2005) is an excellent choice because she mentions so many specific parts, uses them metaphorically, and looks at the body as a whole— something awesome, mysterious, and worthy of consideration.

Every time we read someone else's work in class, we ask the students what they notice. They may point out rhymes, repetitions, alliteration, interesting vocabulary, or figures of speech. Later, when they are writing their poems, without being assigned a particular format or structure, the students naturally imitate what other writers do, while including the messages of their own work.

After reading poems by Nye or Grimes, we ask students to choose a partner and to silently "read" each other's photograph, listing as

Caity's self-portrait, 2003

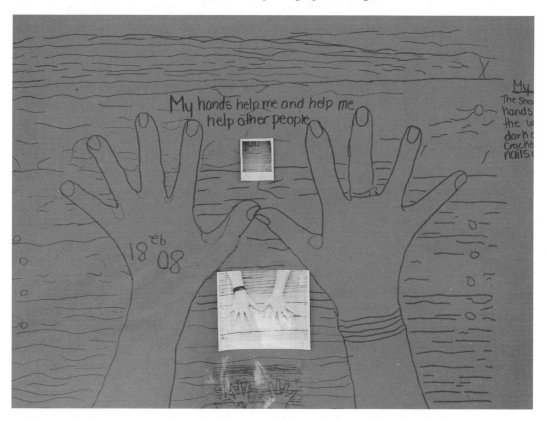

Jessica's self-portrait, 2005

many details they see as possible. Then partners discuss the lists of details they notice in the photographs. The reading, listing, discussing, questioning, and answering gives students more material and experience and prepares them for writing about their own photo. By working with partners, they have another reminder that they are writing for an audience.

In their writings, some simply list the reasons they chose their part, while others write about how much they appreciate a particular part of their body, even ones impossible to photograph, such as the heart or the brain. One way they show appreciation is to imagine life without their best part. For example, Alex, who chose his arm as his best part, wrote:

Amber's self-portrait, 2003

Cherica's self-portrait, 2003

Look at my arms and tell me what you see. You see strength and power. But if you had no arms, what would you see? Nothing. Nothing at all. If you had no arms you couldn't do cartwheels. You couldn't sharpen a pencil if you had no point. If you had long, silky hair you couldn't rub through it with your hands or grab it. If you didn't have arms you couldn't fluff up your pillow to make it softer when you're going to sleep. You couldn't shoot rubber bands and make them say ouch. And you couldn't play video games. Especially video games! I'm just making a point here to say if you didn't have arms anymore you would wish you were dead a long time ago. So if you want to have a good life you better wish you're keeping those arms for the rest of your life. Look at those arms go!

Samuel's self-portrait,
2005

Samuel

Others describe their features or write about what their best part can do. Jayleen wrote, "I use my hands to play the drums." Still others write about their connection to families and culture. Lillie addressed her eyes as though she were writing a love poem to them. "I love you, eyes, because of all those little lines. You are so detailed and beautiful. You show my culture. I am Jewish and most Jews have brown eyes." Nytrepa framed her poem as a series of "do you know" questions about the connection between hands and emotions. "Do you know that hands make people scared when they throw things?" "Do you know that hands make people cry?" Her photo shows happy, clapping hands. Mario seemed to be making promises as he wrote "siempre mis manos": promising to use his hands only for defending himself, not for creating violence; and to use them for doing his homework, and never for smoking. During the time we were working on this project, Domineck's father was on crutches because of a leg injury. It wasn't surprising that Domineck wrote about things he can do because of his healthy knees and about his concern for people who have "cramps or broken knees." Domineck closed his writing

with, "I love my knees. It would be good if someone asked why."
This project encourages students to ask themselves and one another
about their bodies. What do they appreciate and admire and why?

Creating Work for an Audience

WHETHER IT IS A PHOTOGRAPH mounted on a piece of construction
paper and clipped to a clothesline, a photocopied book, or an iMovie
viewed on a large screen, students present their work in all Literacy
Through Photography projects. In *The Best Part of Me*, students learn
some of the techniques of contemporary artists as they make beautiful banners that will hang on the walls of their school. Instead
of making banners, some students will "publish" their photography
and writing in a book that will be read many times.

The overarching concept of considering parts and wholes in *The
Best Part of Me* relates to the importance of "publishing," curating,
or exhibiting student work at the conclusion of each project. In all
the projects, individuals call on their personal interpretations and
choices when they photograph and write; yet in all four projects, the
impact of viewing an entire class's work provides viewers and artists

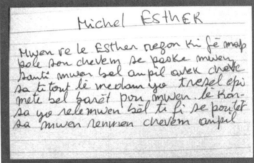

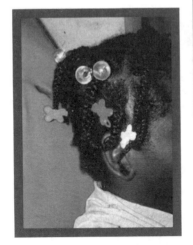

Esther's self-portrait, Haiti, 2010

I am Esther.
The reason I am talking about my hair is because I feel that I am very beautiful with my hair, especially when the women fix it and put beautiful barrettes on me. That's when they call me beautiful girl and that's why I like my hair.

with new understandings. Combining unique, individual parts creates complex, interesting wholes.

Presenting a Collective Vision

We always inform students that we will "publish" their Literacy Through Photography work. Knowing others will be viewing their pieces motivates them to do their best. How could typical textbook assignments inspire such dedication and care? Throughout the LTP projects students take a lot of notes. They creatively list, label, compose, and share their writing. It is mostly during the exhibiting/publishing phase of the project, however, that we effectively emphasize conventions of spelling, punctuation, handwriting, and capitalization without worrying about inhibiting anyone's creativity. Now, they realize, other people will read exactly what they have written.

We hope *The Best Part of Me* enhances students' self-concepts. We show students respect as artists and writers when we provide special supplies for creating an exhibit and when they see viewers examining their work or when viewers ask them questions to learn more. If we choose a special venue, host an "opening," and serve

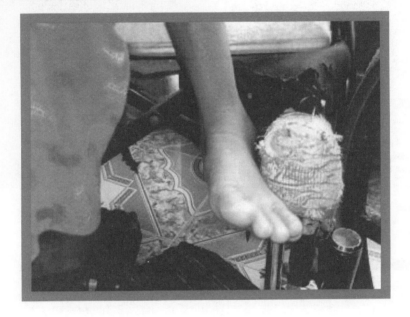

I would like to walk in all the houses and see all my friends that live near me, but because of my foot I'm not able to walk.

LaZar Michiel
Mwen ta Renmen mache nan
lout Kay la, epi mwen soti al wè
tout Zanmi ka viv bene, mwen
men akòz pye m' fem pa ka
mache.

11

Michiel's self-portrait, Haiti, 2010

refreshments, we contribute even more memories to the students' experience of being an artist.

In addition, working on exhibits helps students better appreciate what they see in galleries and museums. Just as they improve their own reading by creating pieces for others to read, they learn exhibition viewing from exhibition making. In Literacy Through Photography, creating an effective, appealing exhibit is another valuable process to master. Combining students' work in an exhibit pushes the meaning in their work to a higher level.

Whether it's during the work of "hanging the show" or while witnessing viewers admiring their work, students and adults find themselves reflecting on the choices made by the photographer/writers/artists. Early in *The Best Part of Me* each child considers parts of his or her own body. At the end, each student sees himself or herself as a part of a larger whole—a community of artists.

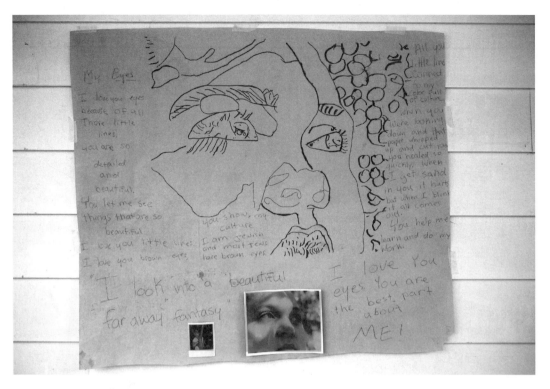

Making an Installation

Inspired by California artist Brett Cook, who makes giant colorful portraits from photographs that often are made collaboratively with a community and placed outside as murals and billboards, we next work on making an installation for the school hallways. Our first step is to make the students' self-portraits much bigger, so, still focusing on one "best part," we set out to make 4 x 6-foot paper banners. When Cherica was asked what she thought about making such a large picture of her hair and hanging it in the foyer, she said, "I'd feel like the most popular kid in the school." We would love for every student to experience that feeling.

In a conversation with Wendy, Brett describes the importance of creating installations in this way:

> Like curriculum development for students with a variety of learning styles, installations are engaging by appealing to a variety of intelligences. A well-made installation considers the technical and conceptual implications of the space it is in. Harmonious examples use tangible elements like scale, color, and materials in combination with non-physical considerations like the social environment and history of a place. The disparate elements can each serve as vehicles to bring separate parts and people of a locale together to talk about an array of issues or ideas.

Lillie's banner, 2003

Lillie's banner, details, 2003

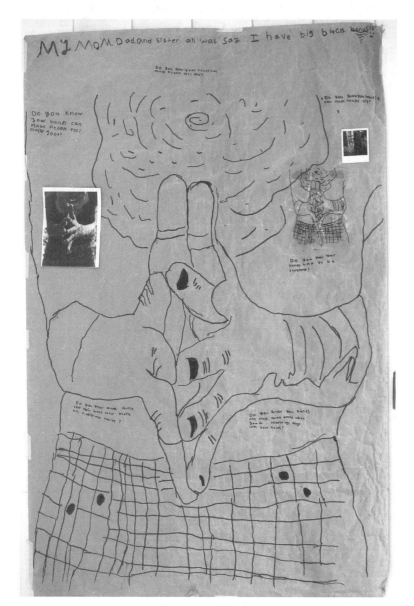

Nytrepa's banner, 2003

Nytrepa's banner, details, 2003

By having participants share the experience of collaborating on an installation—which may include developing questions, participating in an interview, having a photographic portrait made, drawing their portrait, and then coming together to draw projections of themselves from their acetate drawings—the participants become connected to each other with a collective intention.

Following Brett's techniques, students tape a blank transparency sheet over their photograph. They draw lines on the transparency, tracing the edges of their body and details in the background, and

Anthony's banner, 2003

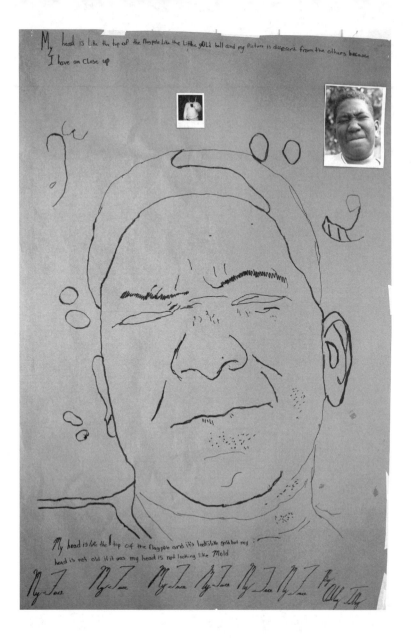

making lines that indicate shadows and textures. Brett prepares his students for this with an exercise he calls "Looking to See."

"Looking to See" is a drawing exercise used to practice awareness of the visual world and ourselves that challenges us to draw only what we truly see—not a memory of what we have experienced before, and not what we think we want the future audience to see. It starts by inviting participants to help define what a line is. Typically the conversation will produce a geometric definition for a line, and on rare occasions the painterly response that a line is a place where a dark value and a light value meet. Sometimes the borders between dark and light are obvious in portraits, like the edge of a shirt collar, or the curve of a cheekbone; other times the gradation from dark to light is subtle, even invisible. Having participants trace lines over

Hands help me defend myself
And not create Vidence
Never To smoke
Do my homework
Siempre mis manos

My Hands ~ My Hands

My Hands Are for Peace
Not War ~

Mario Guzmán

their photo portraits requires deep looking. The details that each person documents in his or her drawing are subjective, but the act of looking deeply is universal.

This is hard work, demanding great attention and care. Students focus so intently on their drawings that they seem to forget that they are reproducing an image of themselves. These drawings become independent objects. Next, students take turns placing their transparencies on an overhead projector and projecting the line drawing onto a 4 x 6-foot piece of paper taped to the wall. Students move the projector closer or farther away as they decide how large they want the drawing to appear on the banner. Once the projector is fixed in place, the students begin to trace the projected lines onto the banner with markers. As Anthony finished tracing the lines, he stepped back and exclaimed, "It looks just like me!"

Surprise is appropriate. This self-portrait project lasts several weeks. Students work together to read photos and make body map notes at the beginning. After these initial stages, a few weeks pass as pairs of students take turns using the cameras and developing and printing photographs. Then, back together as a class, students make their transparencies on the same day. Another few days pass as they take turns with the overhead projector, transferring the drawings onto the banners. There is a lot of methodical effort, a focus on lines and shapes that become almost impersonal—these images of bodies become abstract objects. As the banners near completion, the images once more represent real people. If there originally was any timidity about photographing and writing about one's body, pride quickly takes over. The banners are big, beautiful, and about to be seen by a wide audience.

To complete the banners, students copy their written compositions about their photographs onto the banners. Many students also attach the pieces involved in producing the large drawing: the original photograph and the transparency. Finally, they compose a title, a short message to write in large letters on the banner—a statement they would like to make to the world. Indigo wrote, "My ears hear things." Alex's banner about his arm includes the message, "Don't judge a book by its cover."

Mario's banner reflects the kinds of choices students, as artists, consider when putting together their banners. He chose emerald green paper. He chose to back the projector as far away from the banner as possible in order to make a huge image of his hands. He traced the projected lines carefully, accentuating some areas in order to make the hands stand out. Mario also labored over writing his poem in the top corner. He decided to tape his Polaroid photograph, black-and-white close-up, and transparency to the banner, making it possible for viewers to see all the steps of his work. Or maybe he wanted us to see his hands over and over to underscore his message. Finally, he decided on the motto that would serve as the statement to represent his work: "These hands are for peace not war."

An additional step Brett has included in his installation pieces is to place a collection of important personal artifacts in front of the banner. When a group of teachers did this project with Brett and Wendy, one teacher incorporated the fire extinguisher on the wall into his exhibit by cutting a hole in the banner. Memories of his fireman father had figured into his "best part." Our students benefit from knowing they are using the techniques of artists, including their teacher, and noticing that well-known artists and teacher/artists too get their ideas from family stories and family heroes. Fi-

Emmon's self-portrait in
The Best Part of Me class
book, 2006

I'm glad I have my arms. Because what would I do without them? I couldn't tie my shoe or I couldn't play video games. I would have lots of trouble riding a bike, and it would be a disaster if I tried to go rock climbing. That's why I'm glad I have ARMS! By: Emmon Roth

nally, students notice that their art is treated like *Art* when we choose special paper for making the banners, get permission to display the work in prominent places at school, and invite the community to view our work.

Making a Book

Instead of making banners, some classes make books that resemble Wendy's resource, *The Best Part of Me* (2002), which included the self-portraits and writings of all class members. Some make exhibits of the photographs and the writings without creating larger banner drawings. Books are more convenient than banners in terms of being kept and reread, and students enjoy seeing their work in a class book. Multiple copies of the book, PowerPoint slideshows, or web pages can be valued keepsakes.

The Karate Legs

I like my Legs because they help me in my sport karate. They me to do my side kicks, and my roundhouse kick, and my front kick. They help me run faster than my dad and The Same speed as my brother. My Legs help me to stop right away! My Legs can help me jog and jump! my Legs can help me run away from Danger! I really love my Legs so so much! They can help me ride my Bike and my skooter and to skate. I love my Legs so so much!

By: Deon Leach

Teachers can create class books in several ways. Jennifer Harrison at Club Boulevard Elementary School imitated the layout of *The Best Part of Me* by mounting each child's photo on a full page and placing the child's handwritten composition on the opposite page. Photos and writing from all the members of a class can be compiled in one volume in this way, a treasured part of the classroom library. Teachers can hand-stitch the pages or have them spiral-bound with laminated, student-decorated covers. Some teachers purchase blank, hardback books or spiral-bound journals and manually affix the photos and student compositions to the pages. In these cases, teachers produce multiple copies of the class collection of photos and student compositions by making photocopies and stapling the pages. Many find it simpler to showcase student work electronically, a method that may convey the quality of the students' photographs better than a photocopied version.

As teachers, we are privileged to stay in touch with many of our student artists. Mario, who as a 5th-grader emblazoned his knuckles with the letters of his name and wrote on his banner the words, "These hands are for peace, not war," in 11th grade had a Facebook profile photo that looked remarkably like his *Best Part of Me* portrait. No matter where students go, how many years go by, how many friends change, schools change, families change, they still have their bodies. Their bodies change too, of course, but what do they remember about creating images and writing about their bodies? They remember the care they took in making pieces of art. What do they remember about the attention and questions of a partner and other classmates, a teacher, a member of the audience, their parents? They may remember their surprise that the banner looked "just like me" or the feeling of being "the most popular kid in school" when a banner was displayed, but, more important, this self-portrait assignment expands students' inner view of themselves while also broadening the understanding of the people around them. Through this project we all look more closely and appreciate the wealth of differences in our bodies. As teachers, we hope students form *lasting* impressions about their value as unique individuals.

Lisa Lord
A Teacher's Reflection

The Best Part of Me—the title says it all. My students wear shirts with phrases like, "It's all about me," and "Me, Me, Me." Someone purchased those shirts for the children. Even if children don't wear proclamations of their self-centeredness, everyone who spends time with children or remembers being a child knows the natural, irresistible pull of attention to one's self. If something is important to teach, especially a process or habit, can I find a way to teach via personal attention to the student? Why not start with what's irresistible?

Beyond taking advantage of students' expertise and interest in themselves to promote literacy skills, the magic of the project from the students' point of view is the emphasis on themselves. Their comfort level in choosing subject matter for photographs lies in the idea of *best,* which, for many, calls on their ever-ready spirit of competition. I believe strongly that this project has the power to strengthen students' self-concepts. *How could it not?* Every step of the process lets the student be the authority.

Self-portraiture leads students to recognize their own personal history and bank of memories—treasure troves of writing possibilities. The interviews about what people say about the child, how he or she is like other members of family, build connectedness and history.

Donald Graves (2001) challenges teachers to be able to name all our students from memory and to be able to name specific experiences and interests of each person. Even better, our assignment gives kids the job of presenting who they think they are . . . and teachers the opportunity to show how much they care about who the kids are. The invitation and the presentation lay the foundation for an accepting, inclusive classroom community that tells each child that he or she is "the best."

As a teacher of writing and reading, I am especially thrilled with the workout students get in moving back and forth between parts and wholes. All kinds of artists and learners practice the process of moving back and forth between close-up looks at parts and far-off considerations of wholes.

I might have an idea and sketch it with charcoal. Then I paint lines with neutral thin paint and as quickly as possible with thin layers of colors. Then I begin the work on a focal point, something that has grabbed my attention. I mix colors and use thick paint and make deliberate strokes. After a while, I stop and back up. I look at the whole canvas, compare what I see with the still life, model, landscape, or photo that was the source of the idea. I back up some more and squint. I see what's good and what needs to be changed. Sometimes I see a pleasant surprise, a different idea from the original plan. I go back to the canvas, make changes, know where the next effort goes, develop the new idea. Soon I'll be backing up to look at the whole picture again.

Katie Hyde
Through a Sociologist's Lens

THE STUDY OF THE BODY, the physical self, often is reserved for science classes. In this project students observe the parts, details, and intricacies of their bodies with the care of scientists and as creative, critical thinkers and writers examining the broader meanings. As the project that most centers on the individual self, *The Best Part of Me* also encompasses the range of social themes contained within this book—identity, culture, history, place, family, memory, language, and home. Through mapping, photographing, and drawing the physical body, students tap into distinctive and nuanced memories and stories with social relevance.

For example, in capturing their favorite parts, students think of their relationship to others. At times this reveals loving connections to families—"I love my face because every time I go somewhere people say I look like my parents"—and other times it brings to light students' awareness of the troubled dynamics between peers—"[I use my feet] to run away from a bully." One student wrote, "I like my hands . . . my hands are best because I can . . . help my mom take the clothes to the laundry. Sometimes I help my dad fix or clean his car, or go to the store and select food. I use my hands to push the cart around the store and I use my hands to point to the food I want."

Students' pictures and writings evoke other places and times as well as other people. On his body map, Elijah wrote, "The first time I heard my grandma play piano." In reflecting on why she chose her brain as her best part, Carima wrote, "This brain of mine is like no other, it takes me to places I've never been." Several students reflected on where their feet or legs could take them in real life or their imagination—"I want to be running at the speed of light."

Through their self-portraits students embrace the challenge and opportunity to distinguish themselves from others by using clever frames for their pictures and writing. Deon featured his Karate legs: "They help me do my side kicks, and my roundhouse kick and my front kick." Also writing about her legs, Oesa announced, "I have more than 22 birth marks on my left leg." In a photograph about his arms, Emmon dangles from a metal bar; since we can't see his feet, we can't tell how high he is above the ground. His writing adds, "I'm glad I have my arms. Because what would I do without them? . . . It would be a disaster if I tried to go rock climbing."

Students' thinking about bodies also called forth emotions. Nailah wrote, "My face burns when I'm going to cry but I fight it." Nytrepa asked, "Do you know your hands can make people feel scared?" Another wrote, "When I am mad, I punch things with my hands," and contrasted this feeling of aggression with the peaceful gesture conveyed in his picture. We see only his hands isolated in the corner of a generic concrete space. They are cupped as though catching water or making an offering.

Although the conversations presented in this chapter do not directly address gender, *The Best Part of Me* provides a space for students to feature traits and interests that challenge gender stereotypes—a boy's ballet feet, or a girl's wild eyebrows. Likewise, the many pictures of boys' flexed arms provide an opportunity to talk about how our culture uncritically links gender identity to physical characteristics (like muscles and strength), and often intellectual and emotional capacity as well.

It is interesting to notice that while this project emphasizes individuality, the portraits also make a broader statement—we are all, in many ways, alike, regardless of gender, race, and economic diversity. Looking at the collection of portraits and recognizing boys' and girls' parallel pride in their hands, faces, arms, and legs can be especially powerful. It is virtually impossible for young people to escape messages about the multitude and meaning of differences among boys and girls, given the gendering of children's toys and clothing, and the ever-present gender stereotypes in popular culture and even within some educational curricula. Any opportunity for boys and girls to see themselves as more similar than different, and even more significant, to recognize physical similarities, can be groundbreaking.

The Best Part of Me also can make a statement simply through the presentation of large banners on school walls; these portraits require viewers (students, teachers, school visitors) to spend the time to look and *to see* the complexity and depth of children's identities. One Latino student titled a beautiful portrait of his upturned, sunlit, smiling face, "Without my face, I wouldn't be somebody." Students can look upon their own images again and again, with pride. Like all the projects in this book, this one promotes self-awareness and reflection.

The project encompasses the core Literacy Through Photography themes of self, family, community, and dreams presented in *I Wanna Take Me a Picture* (Ewald & Lightfoot, 2001). As a starting point for the other projects in this book, *The Best Part of Me* underscores the relevance and power of starting with children's lives, of starting with concrete images, and of integrating the arts into the curricula.

Lesson Plans | *The Best Part of Me*

Brainstorming *Mapping the Body & Discovering Uniqueness*

TIME NEEDED: 1 HOUR

1. Distribute a piece of 18 x 12-inch paper to each student.
2. For teachers who want their students to create drawings, ask students to spend 10 minutes drawing themselves from head to toes, using the entire sheet of paper. Another option is to provide each student with a generic silhouette of a human body and ask students to glue the silhouette to their piece of paper.
3. Ask students to label their drawings or silhouettes with notes about any memories or stories they associate with their eyes, hands, feet, hair, elbows, knees, and so on. Follow up by suggesting that students include notes about their favorite features, the way they enjoy putting their hands and feet, and so on, to use, and the parts of themselves that remind them of their parents or other family members.
4. Allow students to share their body "maps" with fellow students and tell one another more details related to the notes.

Reading Family Photographs

TIME NEEDED: 1 HOUR

1. Prior to this lesson ask students to bring a photo of themselves and their family to school.
2. Have students exchange photographs with a partner. Allow students who didn't bring a photograph to make a drawing that represents their family.
3. Have partners "read" each other's photographs and list as many observations and details as they can.
4. Ask partners to talk with each other about what they "read" and ask questions to learn more.
5. Give students time to write about themselves as *part* of a family.

Choosing and Picturing One Part of the Body

TIME NEEDED: HALF AN HOUR FOR EACH PAIR OF STUDENTS; TOTAL TIME DEPENDS ON THE NUMBER OF AVAILABLE CAMERAS.

1. Ask each student to choose the best part of himself or herself to feature in a close-up portrait. Ask such questions as: What is your favorite part? What part shows your best feature? What distinguishes you most from others?
2. Allow partners to photograph each other's "best part." Remind them to make careful choices as photographers. What is the background? What point of view is best?

Reading and Writing About Bodies

TIME NEEDED: 1 HOUR

1. Ask partners to "read" each other's photographs: to examine, make notes, and discuss observations, ask questions, and elaborate more on notes.

2. Read selections from *The Best Part of Me* (Ewald, 2002) or other selections aloud to students (for recommended readings, see References and Additional Classroom Resources for Teachers and Students).
3. Discuss the features of the authors' work: What did the author do that you might do in your writing? Which ideas from your previous writing about your body do you want to include?
4. Follow writers' workshop procedures for completing a poem, story, or essay to accompany the photograph (brainstorm and make notes, write drafts, share with partners, revise, proofread, and publish).

Making an Installation

TIME NEEDED: 1 HOUR, DEPENDING ON AVAILABILITY OF OVERHEAD PROJECTORS AND WALL SPACE

1. Show students how to transfer a drawing made from a photograph onto a banner. Follow these steps: Tape a transparency over the photograph. Use a marker to outline objects in the photograph and indicate shadows and shading. Tape a large paper banner to a wall. Use an overhead projector to project the drawing on the transparency onto the banner. Trace the projected lines onto the banner with markers.
2. Ask students to write the poem, story, or essay on the banner with markers.
3. Allow students to add other items to the banner such as the photograph, the transparency, and so on.
4. Ask students to write a "motto" or saying in large letters. What would you like this banner to say to the world?
5. After obtaining permission, display the banners in the hallway of the school.

Making a Book

(You can make either a digital book on the school's website or a paper book.)
1. Arrange students' photographs with their writing on the opposite page.
2. Lead a class discussion to choose a title for the book.
3. Include a title page, an introduction to the project, and a list of students' names.
4. Give students an opportunity to read the book to other classes or audiences.

TWO | Black Self/White Self

Playing with the Ideas and Imagery of Race

FOR PEOPLE OF COLOR who have experienced racism and/or racial stereotyping, talking about race can be painful, frustrating, and exhausting. Whites may feel uncomfortable talking about race for fear of sounding ignorant, offensive, or insensitive. The *Black Self/White Self* project offers students a way to talk openly about race, a topic many teachers avoid.

The project begins with students creating a self-portrait. Although kids are accustomed to having their photos taken for school pictures and family snapshots, they often have little control over the technology. Here students choose their point of view and make pictures that reveal what they want people to see. In making their self-portraits, students decipher, discover, and highlight their unique identities. In the second part of the project, students work with what have become familiar tools to explore the unfamiliar terrain of representing this imagined, other self. In making portraits of other, imagined selves, students work together as critical thinkers and decision makers, asking questions and offering one another advice as they talk about racial identity and ways of expressing their ideas creatively. Beyond emphasizing that race matters, this project also encourages students to ask questions about both differences and similarities among their diverse group of classmates. In their writing, students make historical connections as they try to understand race relations in the past, and articulate visions for change in the future. Grappling with the challenge of representing someone else cultivates in students a deeper appreciation for the complexity of all people—themselves included.

Wendy Ewald
An Artist's Frame

I STARTED EXPLORING the question of race in Durham public elementary schools in 1992 when a merger of the city and county school systems, which would effectively integrate the schools, was still being hotly debated. From the early 1980s, more and more of Durham's White population moved to the suburbs, and the schools became segregated along city–county lines. Proposals to merge the systems were stymied by objections from both sides. By the mid-1990s, the inner-city schools were almost entirely African American, and the county schools predominantly White. Many of the African American students that I worked with in the city had never attended school with Whites, and many said they preferred it that way.

Local newspapers began publishing articles about Durham's failing communities and troubled schools. School administrators and teachers wanted to counter these disheartening messages by encouraging their African American students to portray their communities in a positive light. As usual, the kids did not take this directive as literally as their teachers. Tiffany, a 5th-grader, took a picture of her

Damien's Black/White self-portraits, 1995

aunt sitting on her boyfriend's lap and titled it "My aunt and her boyfriend." The principal, citing this as a poor representation of the African American community (an intimate portrayal of an unmarried couple!), asked that the picture be removed from an exhibition hanging in the school. The more I worked in Durham classrooms, the more it became clear that race, although a crucial issue for students and teachers, was an all but taboo subject.

I offered workshops after school and during the summer with the idea of training Durham teachers who wanted to use photography and writing in their curricula. Our workshops took place in a conference room with a long table in the center. The White teachers took seats at the table while the African American teachers invariably sat in chairs at the edge of the room. When I asked about the racial climate in the classrooms, the White teachers were quick to reply that in elementary school the students were a "happy family" but by middle school, every once in a while, a student would mention race. The African American teachers kept quiet. I realized I would have to create a different atmosphere before all the teachers could take part in this conversation.

It occurred to me that looking at race in a faraway context might make it easier to talk about. I showed the teachers *The Transported of Kwandebele: A South African Odyssey* (Goldblatt, 1989), a book of photographs with visual documentation of the daily round trips made by Black workers into White neighborhoods in South Africa, and the

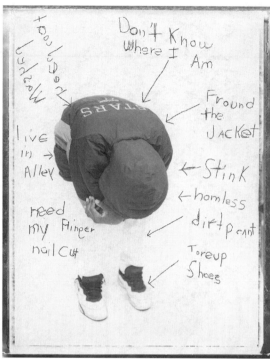

Antonio's White and Black self-portraits, 1995

violence that often erupted. I asked the teachers to write about what they thought was going on in these pictures.

Meanwhile, in my Literacy Through Photography classes in the city schools, I had several frank conversations with my African American students about incidents they'd experienced in local malls and other public places. These conversations, the upcoming school system merger, and the African American students' apprehension about attending classes with White students, led me to wonder whether I could create a process of making pictures that dealt directly with racial identity. I imagined a series of black-and-white portraits of my students posing as themselves and as their "other" selves. To these images would be added their words, drawn over the images.

Cathy Fine, a White 5th-grade teacher, and Robert Hunter, an African American middle school art teacher, agreed to work with me on the project, which the students came to call "Black Self/White Self." Cathy's classroom was two-to-one White/African American; Robert's was completely African American.

In keeping with my usual practice, we asked the students to write a self-portrait, then follow up with a second self-portrait, this time imaging themselves as a member of another race. Many of them squirmed in their seats at this suggestion. I'd asked them to do something shocking. Then they began asking questions: Could they change their names? Could they live in a different neighborhood? Could they have different friends, a different family?

In Cathy's elementary school classroom, the students worked in racially mixed pairs, interviewing each other. In the African American middle school art class, they had to rely partially on their stereotypes of Whites. Soon they were writing freely.

We looked at portrait photographs to see how professionals use background, clothing, lighting, and gesture to describe a person. We started with the work of Nadar, a 19th-century Parisian whose images remain influential to this day. Because of the rudimentary technology of Nadar's time, he had only a single light source and a bolt of drapery to work with. Even so, the Durham students were able to draw sophisticated conclusions about the sitters as fresh human presences.

We also looked at photographs by James Van Der Zee, who worked in Harlem during the 1920s and 1930s using elaborately painted backdrops and luxurious furniture as props. We studied the work of Hans Namuth, who photographed people against a white wall in a Guatemalan village. Typically, Namuth's subjects dressed in their finest clothes and displayed some object dear to them—a doll, a radio, a soccer ball. We went on to examine the work of many other portrait photographers. The idea was to get students acquainted with the variety of elements they could use in creating their self-portraits.

We used large-format Polaroid positive/negative film, which simultaneously produces a positive print and a film negative. This enabled us to look at the positive and decide on tweaks we could make. I asked the students to choose partners and help each other pose for their pictures. I operated the camera.

My teaching assistant and I were the only White people in Robert Hunter's entirely African American middle school art class. One of the students, Najma, decided to partner with me to make her portraits. She suggested we go to the mall and pick out an outfit for my Black self-portrait. After shopping in several stores, Najma selected for my outfit black biker shorts with white polka dots, a white tee shirt, and large silver hoop earrings. The students were pleased when I showed up in my new ensemble. In making a portrait of me as my Black self, Najma directed me to pose with my right hand on my hip.

It was difficult for some of the students to visualize themselves as the "other." Since White children rarely dealt with the Black world's perception of the White world, they had almost no idea of how to pose. The African American children, on the other hand, didn't need coaching. They had a clearly defined sense of how they were seen by White people, and of how White people viewed themselves. Sometimes they internalized these ideas; they might talk about their White selves as being "nicer" or "smarter." Rachel, an African American 6th-grader, told me that she put all her dreams for the future

Chris's Black self-portrait, 1995

into her White self. In contrast, Antonio posed for his White self as a homeless person and, for his Black self, as a doctor. A White boy of his age, Antonio explained, would not have a close-knit family and community, as he did. As for the White children, they seemed more hopeful, optimistic; Chris made a portrait of himself as the first African American president (this was 1992).

The next step was to use ideas from the written portraits to alter the Polaroid negatives. The notion of transforming their own physical features excited and challenged the students to think conceptually about the technical process of black-and-white, negative-positive photography. They had to scratch away the emulsion of the negative in order to produce a black line on the positive print. To make a white line in the print, they had to add a black mark on top of the emulsion. They had to think very carefully and methodically about black and white. Black and white, negative and positive, took on meanings both conceptual and physical. Jeffrey, an African American student, had been photographed with a football for his White self. The negative was so underexposed that only his outline was clearly visible. Jeffrey highlighted his outline with a black Sharpie, making it white in the print. Then he drew wings on his back, transforming himself into a white angel.

It came time to decide how to display the photographs. How would the viewers know which picture was which, or who made it? Once the students had scratched or written on their negatives, their racial identity was obscured. We talked about titles for the pictures. As a start, the students began writing "Black self" on one image and "White self" on the other.

With trepidation we decided to show some of the photographs to school administrators. It was a risky move; although the school systems had just been merged, the photographs and writings were a vivid reminder of the ongoing racial divide in Durham.

Marvin Pittman, the new head of the middle schools, reacted enthusiastically. With the merger, teachers were mixing as they never had before; they needed ways to talk with one another. Mr. Pittman asked if we could conduct *Black Self/White Self* workshops with all the teachers in the district. He hoped that by making their own self- and other-self portraits, the teachers would become sensitive to one another's personal struggles with racial identity.

The Durham school merger, of course, was a complex and messy process. Over time, as the merger zigged and zagged, I could see the students' portraits changing, too. Early on, the only portraits that showed students reading books were "White selves"; then there were African American readers. Also, more and more immigrants—

especially Latinos and Asians—were moving into Durham; the area's racial mix was changing. An African American 5th-grader named Courtney, in what looked like a play on the blackface pantomimes, redefined contemporary ethnic divides by creating a self-portrait in which she painted one side of her face White.

In the first part of the *Black Self/White Self* project, students study photographic portraiture and then create their own self-portraits. Where *The Best Part of Me* project asks students to narrow in on a particular, physical part of themselves, the self-portraits created for this project allude to more abstract ideas about students' entire beings—their personalities, special qualities, and unique interests. Their portraiture again requires careful thought, as students first sketch and plan pictures with writing and drawing and then work with partners to shoot their photographs. Next, students read their own and each other's photographs; this dialogue encourages students to re-examine their pictures and themselves. Making, and then reading, self-portraits sharpens students' visual communication skills and helps students gain a better appreciation for the process of representation.

Reading and Understanding Photographic Portraits

Before looking at any photographs, we begin by posing the question, "What is a portrait?" The 4th- and 5th-grade students respond with a variety of answers: a picture of someone or maybe a family; a picture of a face; an image showing a person's entire body; a photograph; a painting in a museum; a spray-painting on a wall.

We spend an entire class period looking at a selection of photographic portraits. We deliberately sequence these images to move from very simple compositions and backgrounds to more complicated ones in order to highlight the different components of how portraits supply viewers with information. We start with a 19th-century daguerreotype of a wrinkled hand against a plain black backdrop taken by Nadar, one of the first portrait photographers, and finish with a portrait of a young boy in a classroom by contemporary photographer Nicholas Nixon. For each image we ask students to begin by reading the concrete details available to viewers. Building on these details, students invent a story or stories that go along with the image. Like detectives, students refine their ability to see. Not knowing any information about the photograph makes this exercise more fun and suspenseful. Students are obligated to defend their storylines by pointing to details in the photos. Later, this refined way of seeing will influence their picture making. Narrowing in on the details,

Setting the Stage

on the background and composition, students notice the decisions available to photographers and the way these decisions about framing, background, and timing affect what viewers see in a picture.

Neil looks at the image of the wrinkled hand and suspects that the simple backdrop was chosen so that "our eyes don't give attention to the background; the focus is on the hand." Noticing and deciphering the details, students deduce that the hand, with all its lines, belongs to an old person. One student thinks the black background gives the image a scary feeling because it looks as though the person's arm has disappeared.

The next photograph we use in this exercise also has a simple background but provides more information about the subject. This time we can see a woman's face, shoulders, and chest. We suggest that one way to read the story of a portrait is to look at the subject's facial expression. Some of our students read her expression as sad, others as serious. We reiterate that in asking them to read the photographs, we aren't looking for a right or wrong response but rather for concrete details that we can later interpret. One student comments, "She won't stop looking at me." "Like Mona Lisa's face," another chimes in. We talk about the woman's eyes as an important part of this portrait. "They make the whole expression," as one student puts it. "She's focused on the camera, like she's going to jump out." Another student responds, "But the photograph would be blurry if she were really moving." Taking time to notice the details, the students understand the photograph more thoroughly.

Another slide features a young Guatemalan boy in front of a plain backdrop—a photograph by Hans Namuth, who asked his subjects to bring an object with which to be photographed. Right away the students notice a difference between this photograph and the previous two photographs. In this image the subject is holding something in his hands, a soccer ball. We discuss how the inclusion of objects is another way to build a story within a photograph.

Students notice the subject's balled-up fist. We ask, "When do you have your hand in a fist?" Students answer, "When you're going to fight." "When you're flexing your muscles." "When you have energy." We also want to know what the students see in the boy's face. One student thinks it looks like the wind is blowing, because of the boy's tousled, possibly wind-blown hair. Another says, "He's sad, serious, unique." Someone offers a different interpretation and suggests that "he wants to laugh." Several people think he looks determined or proud because of the way he has his hand on his hip.

When we ask about the boy's clothes, they comment that it looks like his shirt has a different kind of waist. The clothing seems un-

familiar to them, and they guess that he is from a different culture. They say they think he is "more Hispanic—from Mexico, Cuba, or some other Latin American country." Although the photograph is black and white, the students guess that there are bright colors in his patterned shirt.

Whereas the subject of this photograph poses for the camera, the students notice that the subject of the next image—an image made by the African American photographer James Van Der Zee—is "right in the middle of something." She looks like she is studying, writing notes . . . doing something. Perhaps she is a teacher grading papers at her desk. Or maybe she is an author. Students comment that we can see her whole body, and that there is light on her face and that she is looking outside instead of at the camera. "Maybe she doesn't even know that someone was taking her picture." As we gather clues about her life from her facial expression and her environment, which seems to be a classroom or an office, students feel as though the photograph is telling them her story.

Planning Self-Portraits

The next day's activity focuses on planning portraits. In order to get students thinking about how they'll make their own portrait, we show them a few examples of photographic portraits from books around the classroom, and we look at photographs of authors and sports figures, for instance, and talk about how they've chosen to portray themselves. As a further example, we ask students to think about what they would or wouldn't do in order to make their self-portrait. When Lisa said she won't be wearing fancy jewelry, high heels, and a jacket, students laugh because they know their teacher never dresses that way. She won't pose as if she's about to throw a football or choose a silly facial expression like sticking her tongue out at the camera. That wouldn't represent who she is, either. Certain props, like a football, would be out of place. "So would a pigeon pose," Imani says, explaining that this is a yoga position. Lisa said she won't have the picture made in a doctor's office, because the background would be misleading. Someone playfully responds, "But, you are a doctor!" referring to her doctorate in education.

We discuss the choices we have in making self-portraits—the things we can control in representing ourselves with pictures. We came up with the following list, which we copied on the blackboard:

- Facial expression
- Background
- Where will the image be made? (Inside—in the classroom, in the hallway, in the gym? Outside—in the courtyard, on the playground, by the basketball court, in the woods?)
- What to include in the photograph
- Will you hold something? What props? What to bring from home?
- What to wear
- Clothing, jewelry, hats
- Posture/pose
- Acting, sitting, standing
- Action
- Doing a cartwheel, swinging a bat
- Angle
- Where is the camera?
- Light
- Where is the light coming from?

Looking at the list of photographers' decisions, students make notes for their portraits. Jayleen carefully follows the list of choices on the blackboard and makes a specific plan for his self-portrait photograph. Caity's plan includes a drawing showing where she'll stand in the rectangular frame of her picture.

Other students' written plans also include careful, detailed choices. Amber commented, "I want my picture lying down outside and the sun shining in my face. My purple yellow and white outfit. Or my lion outfit. And a regular expression. The camera looking down at me." And Domineck's description also shows creativity and intentionality: "1) I want it to look like I'm flying. 2) I'll look bigger because the camera will be below me."

Students' plans suggest an understanding of the camera as a tool they can strategically maneuver. They simultaneously reveal their creativity in choosing how to express their individuality through clothes, colors, team loyalty, and intellectual and athletic activities.

Making Portraits Together

In the next stage of our project, we work individually with pairs of students as they make their first portraits. We begin by looking at each student's written sketch to think about location. Most of our students choose the school courtyard or playground as the setting for their photographs. After explaining how to use the camera, Katie asks students to experiment by looking through the viewfinder and trying out different distances and angles. Students take their time setting up their shots and double-checking to make sure that they aren't accidentally including anything in the background that might distract attention away from the subject of the photograph.

The students work well as two-person teams. Rather than using a self-timer, each student entrusts his or her partner to make the picture. Using digital cameras allows students to review their work immediately. After giving each other immediate feedback, students can reframe their pictures as desired. Each person can take two or three shots if he or she wants to.

As planned and directed, in Cherica's self-portrait the camera is looking up at her, and our attention is drawn to her outstretched arm that reaches gracefully and effortlessly above her head. By contrast, the camera looks down at Amber, who is sprawled out, soaking up the sun.

Each pair of students needs about 30 minutes to make its pictures. Sometimes the process takes longer, for instance, when there is an action shot. Anthony has his heart set on a portrait in which he is leaping into the air, shooting a basket. It takes several tries before he and Jayleen perfectly time the action and capture a picture with Anthony's feet off the ground.

Some students come well prepared with costumes and props. Lillie holds photographs of herself in her hand and wears blue ribbons

Above: Tray's self-portrait, 2004

Right: Jayleen's self-portrait plans, 2004

Jayleen   My Portrait   Feb 13
                      Basketball

Clothes: My Iverson jersey and my wrist band,
my head band, and my Nic Force ones, and my black
pants off chester.
pose: I am doing a lay up.

facial expression: excidulated

props: My Carolina Basketball

where: outside on the basketball court on the
playground.

camera angle: straight

light: in the shade.

pinned to her waist to symbolize her love for horses and her accomplishments in riding competitions. Before making his photograph, Tray disappears into the bathroom to change into his baseball uniform. He brought his shirt and pants, hat, socks, and cleats with him from home. In his portrait planning, Tray considers two options "1. I might Be in my Baseball Jersey holding a Bat in my position. 2. Or I might have a glove on in the air catching a ball." On this particular day, Tray chooses to kneel down on one knee, hands and chin resting on his bat, looking directly at the camera.

Sometimes students have to make do without props. Because Neil doesn't have a basketball with him, he decides to use the angle of the camera (facing and looking up at Neil) to communicate more dramatically the action of shooting a basketball. His photograph captures the moment right after the ball leaves a player's hands for a shot.

By and large, the students take their picture making seriously. They concentrate on perfecting their photo's composition and consult with and advise one another. After looking at her first shot, Takeira asks her collaborator to reposition the camera to show her face and hands.

Amber's and Neil's self-portraits, 2004

Several students climb one of the trees in the school's courtyard, and despite the repetitive background, each portrait is unique. While we see a serious, somewhat aloof expression in Alex's profile, Nytrepa chooses to face the camera with a smile, arms outstretched as she holds onto two branches. With the shadows of branches across her face, shirt, and arms, Nytrepa seems to be part of the tree, while Alex is merely perched in it. Chris is sitting in a tree, immersed in his book. Looking at the different photographs, it's interesting to see how students naturally use a variety of angles and distances without knowing what their classmates have done with the camera.

Chris's and Nytrepa's self-portraits, 2004

These collaboratively made pictures tell us about each student's individuality. In the next phase of the project, the students' writing—with its impressive and creative attention to detail—underscores this individuality even more.

Delving Deeper—
Reading and Writing About Portraits

To prepare for writing about the self-portraits, students first select their favorite self-portrait among the two or three images they've taken. Next they sit with a partner and "read" their photographs. We ask them to list everything they can see in the photograph, encouraging them to focus on concrete details, making very specific descriptions of the photos. We also suggest that they might want to imagine being in an art gallery and pretend that they don't know anything about the person in the photograph except what they can find in the image.

Students have the option of reading their own photograph or reading their partner's. Working with a partner helps students get started and allows the two to get to know each other. In some cases, it also produces better writing. We have noticed in this and other photography projects that some students are more interested in the less familiar and potentially puzzling details of someone else's picture. They are able to elaborate on the details and invent a story for a photograph more freely, fully, and imaginatively if the photograph is not their own.

We give students about 10 minutes to list as many things as they can see in the photo. Jessica meets the challenge by listing 30 items about her own photograph. In addition to details that stand out in the background of her photograph, such as the school's trailer classrooms, their windows, and supporting cinder blocks, Jessica includes the kind of details that ordinarily might escape a viewer's notice when looking at a photograph for only a moment. She lists such details as shadows, blurs, reflections, telephone wires, window shades, street lights, leaves, wind, mulch, flying hair, and bending knees.

Students sit down on the floor with their partner to work with their photographs and lists of details. Using the lists as a starting point, their next assignment is to write about the person in the photograph. The goal is to develop a piece of writing that introduces the person, and, again, they can choose whether to write about their own or their partner's photo. Instead of using the first person, we ask students to write in the third person, using their name or third-person pronouns. This helps them detach from the photograph, to see it as a stranger might. Jessica writes:

> Jessica thinks jumping is fun and exciting. She also loves the sun! She is looking to the side with her hair flying wildly behind her. She is jumping off of the deck on to the dirt in front of the hose.
>
> Jessica is bending her knees and raising her arms. The hood of Jessica's sweat shirt is flying up as she jumps. The branches of the trees are shading her to keep her cool in the hot hot sun.
>
> She is making a shadow as she jumps. There are lots of things behind Jessica. The things behind her are big things like cars, trailers, and trees.

The following day, the students take their writing a step further. Still thinking of their photographs as a starting point, students now bring more imagination into their writing. They elaborate beyond what they can see in the picture, or what they already know about the person in the photo. As our students begin writing, someone asks for clarification: "Does it have to be in the photo?" We explain that what they have written so far has to do with what they know because of what they can *see*. In this next stage, they are to consider what else they could add. We suggest they imagine interviewing themselves or their partner. What else do we want to know about the person? What other sides are there to this individual?

Quizzing students, we ask, "What's the main difference between today's work and yesterday's?" Someone responds that "today we can't necessarily see or prove what we're saying." Another student offers a helpful analogy: "This is like the behind-the-scenes information." We ask students to continue using the third person, and write

Jessica's list of details
about her self-portrait,
2004

Jessica

1 Shadows
2 Hair
3 blur
4 Cars
5 Trailers
6 reflections
7 Dirt
8 Trees
9 cinder blocks
10 Telephone wire
11 hose
12 Decks
13 window shades
14 Windows
15 street light
16 Pants
17 Stomach
18 Wind
19 Sweat shirt
20 Tires
21 eyes
22 light dirt
23 leaves
24 mulch
25 Branches
26 Flying hair
27 Bending knees
28 Part of a House
29 ramps
30 Screens

notes on some students' papers reminding them what this looks like
("he/his/him"). Some students make notes to themselves to remind
themselves to write about "what you can't see in the picture."

After students spend time writing, the next step (on the same day)
is to share with their partner. Jessica elaborates on her first writing,
adding details (especially about intentions) that can't be seen directly
in the photograph:

> Jessica loves nature that's why she took her pictures outside,
> near lots of trees and flowers. She doesn't know why she
> chose to be in the shade because she absolutely loves the sun.
> Especily the sun in the park or even in her own back yard. Or
> sometimes when she's on vacation she likes to sit on the beach
> and draw or read all afternoon in the hot sun.
>
> Man oh man did Jessica love the way the wind flew in her
> face as she jumped off of that deck, it felt cool and refreshing

and like a new day had begun. Her hair was flying all over the place it was wonderful.

In following a sequence of steps in making pictures (reading photographs, planning photographs, and finally shooting pictures) and then writing (reading photographs and then writing in two stages, often with lots of input from classmates), students produce rich and layered portraits. For example, Jessica expands the final version of her writing to include six paragraphs with more vivid details, such as:

her hair flying wildly behind her . . . the branches of the trees are shading her. . . . She is making a shadow as she jumps. . . . She doesn't know why she chose to be in the shade because she absolutely loves the sun. Especially the sun in the park or even her own backyard. OR sometimes when she's on vacation she likes to sit on the beach and draw or read all afternoon in the hot sun.

Heeding advice, students don't limit themselves to writing about what anyone can see when looking at the picture. For instance, Tray's action-packed writing complements his quiet picture; we feel as though we're in the stands, listening as the announcer dramatizes the game moment by moment. We feel the suspense, the player's nerves, the excitement in the air:

He's acting like he's about to do a speeding pitch. He's standing in the huge Club Blvd. School field. He is so nervous he thinks the batter is going to hit a home run. The ball is on fire in his eyes. The last guy had got scared of him because on the boy's first strike. There was not strike two. He ran back to the dugout. There is no telling what he's going to do now. Tray is a nice guy and a good pitcher. He likes to pitch and to strike people out. When he's on the field he feels like a super star.

Having classmates read their photographs encourages students to look at themselves with deliberate attention—this time through someone else's viewpoint. They learn that different viewers see different things in pictures—sometimes more and sometimes less. This feedback then shapes students' writing by providing them with new ideas and/or helping them focus or connect their abundant ideas. Likewise, it helps strengthen a student's point of view and writing voice. Furthermore, this dialogue among students allows them to see which details are crucial to capture interest and which ones are important to communicate something clearly. Students push their classmates to write more sophisticated pieces about the familiar subject matter of themselves.

THE TIME AND CARE that go into making self-portraits provide an essential foundation for making other-self portraits. The process of portraying someone with a different racial/ethnic identity involves several steps: conceptualizing images, creating images, altering images, writing about images, and preparing a class book. Each stage includes plenty of input from others—mostly classmates. Inevitably, students encounter, refer to, and even rely on stereotypes in their open-ended conversations and, at turns, serious and playful enactments of their "other" selves. The *Black Self/White Self* project's multiple stages are designed to help students develop the tools needed to create thoughtful and complicated portraits, while making discoveries about and confronting stereotypes.

Allowing students room for uncensored dialogue and exploration, while also strategically framing conversations and writing exercises, helps students plan and execute their ideas and delve into their own perceptions and language. As a whole, the process of making portraits (in images and writing) invites critical thinking and insight about the stereotypes that emerge in the students' work and conversations, and those that they hear/see all around them, whether on TV, at the kitchen table, or in video games, newspapers, movies, or even school materials.

Imagining Another Self

Students now have more experience in making portraits, and as a result of their writing exercises they've also gained an appreciation for all the information available in a photo. They have read their own photographs, responded to their partner's image, and listened to others' responses to their pictures. Even though they've become skillful at looking at the familiar through someone else's eyes, not all 4th- and 5th-grade students have the tools to articulate the important ways race shapes their life experiences, interests, opportunities, and everyday reality. Since our photography project requires this kind of critical reflection, we need an appropriate way to transition to the next part of the *Black Self/White Self* project. Talking about U.S. history provides a foundation for addressing race in contemporary culture. One idea is to begin with a single issue—for example, school segregation in the American South—to consider how lives were blatantly divided along the lines of race and how racist ideas resulted in racial disparities and inequalities. We then can focus even more specifically by studying the life of one person—Ruby Bridges.

At Club Boulevard Elementary School, students have a rare opportunity to hear Ruby Bridges speak. The timing of her guest visit at their school offers a perfect segue into our *Black Self/White Self* project. In front of hundreds of children who sit on the carpet in

Portraying Imagined Selves and Understanding Others

the school's media center, Bridges vividly recounts her challenging, heartrending, and courageous experiences as the sole Black student attending a newly integrated New Orleans school in 1960. Sharing her photographs and stories, she invites students to consider what it felt like to walk past angry protestors who shouted with fists in the air. She helps the young students imagine being a 6-year-old walking to school with the court-mandated protection of federal marshals. Her words help them envision the threats, doubts, conflicts, and suffering that she and her family endured.

Foreshadowing what would be our next photography and writing activity, Bridges carries out a thought-provoking, role-play activity. (Teachers can build a similar role-play activity around Bridges's 1999 autobiography, *Through My Eyes*. In addition, they can invite to the classroom a local leader to share his/her experiences in advocating for racial equality.) Bridges asks for a young volunteer to step back in time and take her place in a debate with Louisiana's White governor. In front of an audience of his peers, Ethan, a White 4th-grader, nervously makes his case for why he deserved to attend the almost all-White school. Bridges, acting as the governor, badgers him with arguments for racial segregation. Classmates empathize with Ethan as they watch him fumble in his role as Ruby Bridges. And they enthusiastically join in, offering Ethan a variety of arguments and defenses, confident that right is on their side.

Planning Other-Self Portraits

The following day our students are still excited about Ruby Bridges's visit when we explain the next assignment is to make a second portrait—this time with students pretending to be someone other than who they are. Lisa goes on, "This assignment could involve pretending to look very different. What if I looked like Ruby Bridges? Would my life be the same?" We explain that we want students to pretend to be someone of a different race. Neil asks if it is like "living in a different neighborhood." Someone says, "Or maybe [it's someone] at this school, but a person of a different race." Lisa breaks the ensuing silence, saying, "Start to see yourself as someone else and to think about what people might notice about you."

In order to plan their other-self portraits, we instruct students to concentrate on two questions: *What will the portrait show? What symbols will I include to communicate my idea?* We remind students of the first portrait discussed weeks before so they can recall how the wrinkles on the hand symbolized the person's old age. They remember, too, that a hand alone can tell us different things depending on its position: for instance, whether it's pointing, or resting on a leg. We ask students to spend 5 minutes writing plans for a portrait of an

_____Alex_____'s Pretend Portrait

Idea: I would like to put myself in Martin Luther King's shoes. When I do, I would do everything in my power to put black and whites. I would have to be speaking infront of millions an millions of people each day to make them their difference.

The Symbol: will be a poem hard thought to spread peace around the nation.

Alex's and Lillie's other-self portrait plans, 2004

_____Lillie_____'s Pretend Portrait

Idea: My hand will be in a fist. I will be holding and pulling on a rope. I will have a bit of red on me. I am a slave.

Symbol: A Fist, blood, labor, to be a hard working slave.

imagined self. By writing first, students each pursue their own ideas. We don't want one person's comments to dominate everyone else's thoughts.

Eager for a glimpse of students' ideas for their other-self portraits, we discover that a few have misunderstood the assignment. Jayleen, who is African American, writes that he wants to be Michael Jordan. Alex, also African American, writes, "I would like to put myself in Martin Luther King's shoes. . . . I would have to be speaking in front of millions and millions of people each day." We clarify two things. We remind students that the intention is to portray themselves as a person of another race. And furthermore, we explain that the person doesn't have to be another living or famous person; we encourage them to create a fictional persona.

To help students understand the inventive thinking we are look-ing for in this assignment, we draw a parallel with reading literature, explaining, "When we read books, it's like we're meeting people.

We imagine putting ourselves in someone else's shoes." Likewise, we remind our students that Ruby Bridges asked a student to imagine himself as someone else, while she pretended to be Louisiana's White governor.

We encourage students to use their imaginations, asking, for instance, what Jayleen's portrait might emphasize if he were White? Would his life be different? In what ways? We want students to reflect on how their own lives might be the same or different if they had another racial or ethnic identity. To explore this new concept, Chris writes bulleted notes on his paper:

- live somewhere else. (Maybe)
- look different/wear different clothes
- be different from what I am

Lillie brainstormed about how switching races (from White to Black) would make significant changes in her life: "I would have a whole different history and background. I could have ancestors who were slaves. I could have been someone helping Martin Luther King, Jr. I wouldn't probably have the same religion. I would have different friends. Many different features. My hair, my eyes." In Lillie's written plan for her other-self portrait, she imagines her life as a Black person from another time in history.

Also pointing to the past, Caity's "pretend portrait" concept was especially clear and powerful:

Idea: To be in Ruby Bridges shoes to be a young African American girl having to go to a white school and having to face the people and there threats. To be the only one in her class.
Symbol: me and people around me like the body gaurds or me with segragators in the back. Me walking up stairs with signs about don't immagrat.

Some students focus on the physical characteristics they believe will indicate their race in the new portrait. For instance, several White and Black students refer to eye color and hair (length, texture, and color). Mark, a White student, writes the following:

Idea: Being Chinees
Black hair
A bit darker skin
Shorter
Eyes more slanted
Different clothes
Symbol: Piece of paper with Chinees symbols.

Indigo also emphasizes physical features while imagining herself as a White girl:

> *Idea:* A 14 year old girl that has long cirly hair all the way down to her waist. She has light skin and golden brown. She is very fit but not too skinny. She has very bright blue eyes and is very nice. Her name is Iris.
> *Symbol:* Big blue eyes with long eye lashes.

Like Indigo, a few other students name their imagined selves. Cherica's Chinese self is called Taki. Rather than highlighting physical characteristics in his writing, Mario relies on a cultural stereotype in his short description. In noting how he might portray a Native American self, he writes, "Home: the wild." Two other students choose to represent a Native American identity for their other-self portrait, also relying on conventional stereotypes about place and lifestyle (riding horses, shooting with bow and arrows) in their preparatory writing. In addition, Lydia draws a teepee on the back of her paper.

Talking About and Making Other-Self Portraits

When it is time for students to shoot their second set of portraits, they again work in pairs outside the classroom with a co-teacher, volunteer, or teaching assistant. We actively facilitate the students' photography but hold back as their dialogue unfolds. Since students are still getting used to the idea of imagining another identity, they need time and space to talk through their ideas. As students set up their pictures on the school playground or in the courtyard, their spontaneous conversations help them elaborate and examine their first thoughts about portraying an imagined self. While the pre-writing activity jump-starts their thinking, talking with a partner pushes the students further. They ask each other's advice, test out ideas on each other, and offer provocative suggestions and questions. They challenge each other, too.

When collaborating with someone with a different racial identity, students recognize the utility of soliciting an opinion, getting a different perspective, or simply gathering information from their classmate. Sometimes students joke with or tease each other playfully. Indigo, an African American student, reminds us that she wants to have long (and straight) hair in her White-self portrait. She explains that she'd have "weird stuff tied in my hair."

> Katie: Weird stuff tied in your hair?
> Indigo: Well, not weird.
> Indigo (after tying a scarf in her hair): Do I look Spanish?
> Her partner: No, you look like a clown.

Our students express themselves candidly, at times encountering their own and others' stereotypes. Knowing they will have the chance to reflect again on these stereotypes, we try not to intervene at this stage even though we may be missing good opportunities to talk about race.

The following examples suggest the kinds of comments and questions that are likely to emerge in any implementation of the *Black Self/White Self* project. We offer questions or comments that can be explored in greater depth either on the spot as small groups collaborate, or as part of a large-group discussion after students complete their other-self portraits.

"I think everybody's the same." Several students hesitate when it is time to make their pictures, in spite of the planning they've done. Clearly, the idea of imagining one's self with a different racial identity is an unfamiliar challenge. When a White student announces that she wanted to portray a "Hispanic" self, she adds that she doesn't know how to make her portrait. Mario, the only Latino student in the class, comes to her mind. She continues, "They talk a lot. Maybe I'll be someone from Honduras." Wanting to help her explore how to translate her ideas into a picture, we ask, "How will you show that?" She says, "I think everyone's pretty much the same."

Do students believe that everyone is the same, or is this something they've learned to say? Most likely she believes groups are both similar and different, but feels uncomfortable drawing attention to difference. Intentionally, this project asks students to consciously think about and discuss their own and classmates' racial and cultural identities. This is something that, ironically, multicultural rhetoric about equality and sameness can discourage. We hold the assumption that avoiding the topic of race can perpetuate general misunderstandings, including the notion that difference, in itself, is bad.

Considering this tendency to downplay or avoid race, putting structure on this part of the *Black Self/White Self* assignment is essential. When teachers define the terms of this project more loosely by asking students to create two portraits—a self-portrait and an other-self portrait—without mentioning race, students tend to avoid any explicit reference to race. Instead they portray two sides of themselves, such as their serious and playful selves. Such portraits can be compelling, but they don't help students delve into the ways that identity is conditioned by history and culture. Establishing strict parameters (in other words, explicitly telling students to address race) actually can give students freedom to explore and express their thoughts and experiences related to race instead of avoiding the topic—whether because they feel it is rude or uncomfortable, or because they lack an awareness to see aspects of race in their own lives.

Another way to provide structure for students is to talk about vocabulary—such as the term "Hispanic" used by several students. A starting point could be to identify when and where the term is used—for example, in North Carolina, schools districts, television news stations, and social service organizations use "Hispanic" in reference to immigrants from Mexico and Central America. Such a discussion would consider how the label, like all racial/ethnic labels, has limitations. Students also can talk about who is included and excluded from the "White" label. By taking a historical look at the label "Indian," which appears in the next example, students learn about label's origin and the reasons why some people prefer the term "Native American."

Finally, while encouraging students to explore the possible ways our lives differ along the lines of race, it's also important to delve into students' ideas and claims about sameness. When students suggest "everyone's the same," encourage more dialogue with open-ended, follow-up questions such as, "How so?" or "In what ways are we the same?" or "What do you mean?" Another question could be, "What's the value in people being similar as well as different?"

"You should be Black, because you act like you're Black."
Mario, a Latino student, hesitates when it is his turn to make his second portrait, saying, "Can't I be Hispanic?" We clarify that for this exercise he should portray himself as someone of another racial or ethnic identity and suggest, "You could be African American, Asian, White, or multiracial." Mario responds, "I actually never thought about it." His African American partner, Larry, then chimes in, "You should be Black, because you act like you're Black." Mario responds, "I want to be an Indian, but I don't know how to act." Mario concludes the discussion by saying, "I don't know what I want to be."

Mario drags his feet, but seems perplexed by and interested in the comments and questions. Mario is the only Latino student in his class. An appropriate follow-up question to Mario's plea might be, "What would your Latino portrait look like?" We also could tie the conversation to his original self-portrait, asking him to remind us of its content. Did he see his self-portrait as representing a Latino self? In his self-portrait, Mario looms large as he stands atop a school railing looking down and directly at the camera. In Mario's other-self portrait, he's seated on the same railing, with his chin resting on his hand, looking down, as though dejected. A possible variation on this project could include three portraits: a self-portrait, a race-conscious self-portrait, and an other-self portrait.

Unlike the other students in the class, Mario moves back and forth between his Spanish-speaking home and his English-speaking classrooms. Larry's comment suggests that Mario identifies with the Black community. To follow up on this exchange about enacting racial identities, one might ask: "Can anyone act Black (White)? What would this look like?" or "If an African American kid tells a Latino or White kid that they 'act Black,' what does that mean? What's an example?"

"What does that have to do with being Chinese?" While Mark prepares to shoot his Chinese-self portrait, he proposes various ideas blending mostly made-up notions about Chinese people with some knowledge of Chinese writing and athletics. He comments, "They're more active, they start touching what they want to buy." His partner challenges, "What does that have to do with being Chinese?" Mark does not answer, but abandons the idea. Later he tells us he imagined holographs (meaning, characters) everywhere in his portrait, but then thought twice about including the symbols as "no one will know what it is." He also remembers doing "those things" in the gym, referring to Chinese push-ups. We suggest that his portrait show that, but he declines, insisting the push-ups were "ugly, no one liked doing them at all, even though they're a whole lot better technically than other push-ups." Finally, Mark designs a portrait in which he is hanging from a tree.

Asking students to share the story of their photograph encourages reflection on the reasoning and assumptions that went into making it. Students might reveal the kind of back and forth thinking that went into Mark's photograph or the assumptions students are making regarding what viewers would/wouldn't understand. The follow-up question Mark's partner posed is fine as it is: "What does X have to do with being Chinese (or White, Black, and so on)?" This question is not meant as a critique, but as an invitation to share a story, akin to the way students are asked to describe the pictures in their mind as they read.

Like Mark, Cherica also envisions a Chinese-self portrait; she plans to show that her hair is straight and black. Her response to the question, "What does that have to do with being Chinese?" would likely differ from Mark's; she might have answered, "Every (almost every) Chinese person I've seen has straight black hair." These conversations can help students develop a more intricate understanding of stereotyping. Such discussions would help them distinguish between two kinds of generalizations—those based on observed patterns (a statement that many Chinese people have straight black hair) and those based on something seen or heard only once (in person or on TV) and/or simply made up (for instance, the suggestion that Chinese customers touch everything in stores). Discussions that build on students' own comments also will help students distinguish between benign versus harmful and offensive generalizations.

Mark's, Chris's, and Mario's other-self portraits, 2004

"Some African American kids do make bad choices in school."
Although Chris's written plan is to portray himself as a Black basketball
player, on shooting day he ventures into more dangerous and complicated terrain, electing to represent an African American student "making bad choices in school." Whether consciously or not, Chris's words
allude to the disproportionate amount of disciplinary action that, in
some schools, is heaped upon Black students, boys in particular. Chris's
choice of words is telling. In saying "*Some* African American kids *do*
make bad choices in school," Chris suggests that he knows this doesn't
apply to all African Americans and that he might have to account for
this statement—possibly to his African American partner, Alex. Rather
than guessing about Chris's intentions, we could use comments like
these to remind students that it's inaccurate and dangerous to suggest
that only a certain group of kids makes bad choices.

It's also impossible to know, but still interesting to consider, what
went through Alex's mind when he added another layer, linking bad
choices to coolness. As Chris poses for his picture (standing next to a
"tobacco free" sign on a school wall), Alex offers this advice: "Don't
be smiling. That looks cool, a whole lot better." Perhaps Alex is simply reminding Chris of the importance of expression to successful
portraits. (In fact, their advice giving is reciprocal. Later, when Alex
is stumped as to how to distinguish his other self as White, he says
to Chris, "What would a White person look like? You're White."
Alex signs his writing in the final booklet "by Chris and Alex," again
pointing to their collaboration, something no other student thought
to do.) But beyond giving photographic advice, is Alex distancing
himself from Chris in pointing out something that escapes Chris?
Is Alex offended by Chris's portrait idea but uncomfortable saying
so? Is he, himself, critiquing the idea that being bad is cool? A useful
follow-up question might be: "What does looking cool have to do
with making bad choices?"

**TALKING ABOUT
RACE**

THE BLACK SELF/WHITE SELF PROJECT *works best within a school/
classroom that is already committed to an anti-bias curriculum, in other
words, one that fosters the development of "personal strength, critical
thinking ability, and activist skills to work with others to build caring, just, diverse communities and societies for all" (Derman-Sparks &
Ramsey, 2011, p. 5). Each teacher will decide how best to incorporate
the project into his or her writing, reading, and social studies classroom.
We suggest that teachers read about race and connect this project to children's literature dealing with such topics as exclusion, racism, interracial
friendships, multiracial identity, and so on. See the list of recommended*

resources at the end of this book. Here are four other general suggestions to scaffold the *Black Self/White Self* project.

Agree on ground rules. *When introducing* Black Self/White Self, *teachers may want to remind students about the ground rules, established at the beginning of the year, for cooperative behavior and respectful speaking and listening. On top of this, it's useful to establish ground rules specific to conversations and explorations of race. In* Courageous Conversations About Race: A Field Guide for Achieving Equity in Schools, *Glenn Singleton and Curtis Linton (2006) propose four agreements essential to courageous conversation: stay engaged, expect to experience discomfort, speak your truth, and expect and accept a lack of closure. These are presented as necessary conditions for adults talking about racial inequities within schools, but can be proposed as guidelines for conversations with and among students. As an alternative to these four agreements, teachers may ask students to generate their own short list of guidelines for dialogue about race.*

Examine prejudice. *As implied in the above agreements, it's important for teachers to accept that lessons dealing with the complicated dimensions and implications of racial identity and racism have no clearly defined end point, but rather are a starting point for an ongoing discussion of race in the classroom. In the* Black Self/White Self *project, conceptualizing, making, and discussing other-self portraits draw out students' otherwise unspoken notions—the process puts ideas on the table, which then can be explored further through children's literature addressing the topics of ethnic/racial exclusion, civil rights activism, and interracial friendships. Examples include Millie Lee's* Landed *(2006) about the prejudice experienced by Chinese immigrants in the early 20th century,* Harvesting Hope: The Story of Cesar Chavez *by Kathleen Krull (2003), and Patricia Polacco's* Pink and Say *(1994) about the emergence of a friendship between one Black and one White teenaged soldier during the Civil War. In addition to the suggested activities dealing with prejudice mentioned in "Talking About the Body," we recommend Paul Fleming's "Small Steps: A Tolerance Program" posted on www.tolerance.org. This essay describes useful activities that constitute "small steps" in examining prejudice: identifying stereotypes, examining the process of labeling, and understanding the consequences of intolerance. Another important resource is the lesson plan "Who Are the Arab Americans?" which also can be found on www.tolerance.org.*

Listen to students and follow their lead. Everyday Anti-Racism: Getting Real About Race in School, *edited by Mica Pollock (2008), presents more than 60 concise essays that are both theoretical and practical. One such essay, "Following Children's Leads in Conversations About Race"* *by Kimberly Change and Rachel Conrad, provides a nuanced discussion of two short conversations about race, illustrating effective and less effective ways of engaging with students' spontaneous questions and comments about race and racism. The authors suggest that teachers avoid playing the role of the all-knowing adult and instead "'be willing to use children's terminology, build on children's ideas, and try to understand their racial statements in the context of children's experiences" (p. 38). Facilitating dialogue requires that adults ask open-ended questions and chime in with their own ideas without dominating or stifling the conversation. Under "Talking About and Making Other-Self Portraits" we provide examples of open-ended questions that could be useful in generating in-depth dialogue about race in response to students' uncensored comments.*

Address Whiteness. *Teachers should be prepared to address Whiteness. When White students think about race, they may not be accustomed to thinking about its impact on their own lives. It is essential that White students recognize their racial identity and the possible ways their Whiteness shapes their lives in terms of their opportunities, friendship choices, school success, and so on. In* What If All the Kids Are White: Anti-Bias Multicultural Education with Young Children and Families, *Louise Derman-Sparks and Patricia Ramsey (2011) propose important strategies for teachers committed to talking about race in all-White settings. These strategies are likewise useful in mixed-race classrooms. In addition to offering suggestions that are central to any anti-bias curriculum, their work also provides White teachers with tools to understand their own racial identities, and the ways that children learn racism and anti-racism. In addition to the book's focus on racism and Whiteness (and White superiority), it also looks at White resistance to racism and includes practical teaching strategies, such as the chapter on "Fostering Children's Caring and Activism."*

For teachers, we also recommend Eye of the Storm *(1970), a film that documents the controversial blue eyed–brown eyed exercise devised by educator Jane Elliot to teach her White southern 3rd-graders about racism and prejudice after the assassination of Martin Luther King, Jr.* Blue Eyed *(1996) documents how a group of adults struggle with the powerful lessons of Elliot's "experiment" as they endure her hands-on, anti-prejudice training.*

Reconsidering Other-Self Portraits— Altering, Writing, and Reflecting

Students make fascinating and imaginative other-self pictures. But their work doesn't stop with the photographs. This last activity illustrates how students refine their work—altering other-self images by drawing and writing *on* the pictures; contextualizing the pictures with students' own and classmates' writing *about* the pictures; and assem-

Ja'Vai's before and after other-self portraits, 2004

I choose to be a teacher because when I grow up I want to be a teacher. a teacher.

bling final work (portraits and writings) in a classroom book. These stages are meant to help students refine their portraits so that they produce final pieces that reveal careful thought and deliberate complexity.

We encourage students to study their other-self portraits to determine what finishing touches are necessary. We explain that they can alter the appearance of their photographs with drawing and writing if this will help them more clearly portray themselves as another person. We suggest, for example, that they might change the look of their hair, clothes, or skin. In addition, we suggest that students might want to add words to their picture or draw something in the background to help establish context. In her other-self portrait, Ja'Vai intended "to be in Miss Medley's [another Club Boulevard

teacher] shoes to be a teacher." She embellished her photograph, in which she's standing at a chalkboard, by drawing math equations and writing the word *Teacher* across the top.

In our project, students can alter the negative itself. When using digital cameras, students can draw and write directly on the print. It's helpful to allow students time for practice by having them place their image in a plastic bag or underneath acetate paper and use permanent markers to re-imagine their picture. Another option for altering digital images is the use of photo manipulation software.

After altering or decorating their images, students write and edit pieces inspired by the other-self portraits. Finally, they revisit their original portraits and make choices on how best to edit and assemble both portraits. They choose whether to stick to their own writing, or to include their classmates' contributions as well. Each student is responsible for contributing one page to a class book, which can be called something like *Portraits in Black and White*.

Indigo's page illustrates the kind of critical thinking we hope for in the final stage of the project. The process of shooting, altering, and then writing about her other-self portrait has made it more than a picture of curly-haired Iris with blue eyes and long lashes. The other-self portrait has evolved into a story about how things used to be. Her writing begins, "A long time ago . . ." There is a knowing look on Indigo's face in her White-self portrait, which is taken at a close distance and at eye level. She truly looks like a different person compared with the carefree Indigo perched in a tree, smiling down at the camera and "waiting and waiting for something to happen for a change."

When we look at the juxtaposition of portraits on one page and among booklet pages, students' approaches to exploring identity reveal themselves. Only one of these approaches involves directly building upon stereotypes, as seen in Chris's two portraits. Another strategy is to highlight history, as seen in Lillie's careful portrait of a Black self resisting slavery. She knows precisely what her portrait should look like and works hard to accomplish her vision. She intends to show more than her shackled hands; she also wants to show struggle. Putting all her energy into her extended arms and leaning back, she carefully frames the image to exclude her face and instead features her arms and hands. (By contrast, because Lillie's self-portrait includes more of the school's courtyard in the background, viewers must look carefully to notice her horseback riding ribbons, which symbolize her pride and success.) Lillie drew a rope within her image to make the story more explicit. By choosing to write in the first person, Lillie made her piece intimate and direct. She calls attention to the details of everyday life; she imagines being awakened early, living in segregated housing, having her hands tied and her movement restricted. In essence, she imagines and shows herself being at the mercy of a ruthless master. In their class book, Lillie's and Indigo's pages face each other, as if deliberate counterparts—Lillie's highlighting the suffering of slaves and Indigo's piece emphasizing the privileges traditionally enjoyed by Whites.

Caity's work, inspired by her admiration for Ruby Bridges, presents a deliberately favorable and uplifting historical portrait. In fact, she includes the theme of strength in both of her portraits. In Caity's self-portrait, she faces the camera with the determined look of a serious, strong player. One arm rests on the soccer post, and one foot is holding the ball in place. In Caity's Black-self portrait, her upright

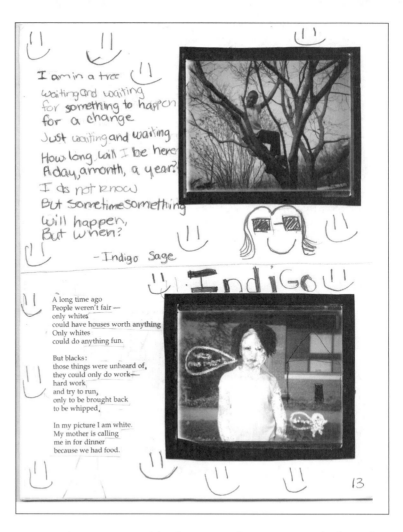

Indigo's self- and other-self portraits from class book, 2004

I am in a tree
waiting and waiting
for something to happen
for a change
Just waiting and waiting
How long will I be here
A day, a month, a year?
I do not know
But Sometimes something
will happen,
But when?

—Indigo Sage

Indigo

A long time ago
People weren't fair —
only whites
could have houses worth anything
Only whites
could do anything fun.

But blacks:
those things were unheard of,
they could only do work—
hard work
and try to run,
only to be brought back
to be whipped.

In my picture I am white.
My mother is calling
me in for dinner
because we had food.

posture also suggests pride. In a second portrait, we don't see her face; we see where she is going. Caity's Black-self writing is full of emotion and vivid details from Bridges's story.

Another approach to exploring racial identity is to present two portraits that together convey the message that race doesn't or *shouldn't* matter. Ja'Vai's two pictured selves, seen earlier, both reveal a studious, academic identity. In one, she's learning; in the other, she's teaching. About her White-self portrait she writes, "I choose to be a teacher because when I grow up I want to be a teacher. I don't have to become white to be a teacher." Her words consciously address race, although in an ambiguous, open-ended way. Does Ja'Vai mean that race will not limit her aspirations and that she can be anything she wants to be? Or does she intend to say that teaching is a profession accessible to Black females? Whatever the case may be, in both portraits Ja'Vai advocates the pursuit of knowledge.

Talisha's writing also alludes to race and how things "should" be. In her portraits she reveals her own passion—dance. Sitting comfortably in the "splits" position, Talisha smiles at the camera

Lillie's self- and other-self portraits from class book, 2004

Lillie
By Talisha Herring

Lillie is standing in the courtyard.
She has ribbons on the side of her pants.
She is standing between
a big rock and a little rock.
The courtyard is in the middle of the school.
Her hair is behind her.
She has wrinkles in her pants,
they make her pants look cool!
Lillie loves horses,
you can tell they make her happy!
She love's to take care of her dog
and horse!
She looks like she just won
the best horse rider award,
but there is no such thing!

Slave
By Lillie Hart

My master wakes me up early in the morning. He told me he is going to sell me. He walks me past my friends, and family. He walks me past my home, and many others.

For my picture I drew in two slave houses, to show where I lived. And a rope tied to my wrist showing how he walks me around. My cuts show how I have been hit and beaten.

He tied me up with his rope. He pulls me, not gently as he promised. You see my cuts and burns where my master whips me and the sun burns me.

in her self-portrait. In her other-self portrait she poses with equal confidence in another yoga position—"dancers' pose." Next to this White-self portrait, she writes, "I like the applause by every color in the auditorium it makes me feel like no matter what skin color we are all the same we should be treated equally."

Other students convey more implicitly a connection between the two selves they've presented. In Cherica's preparatory notes she wrote, "If I were to put myself in someone else's shoes I would have to act like that person and at the same time be myself." True to her words, the differences between Cherica's two portraits are subtle. Her self-portrait and her Chinese-self portrait both feature gracefully choreographed gestures. Nytrepa's description of Cherica's self-portrait is spot on: "Her body and face looks like she is saying I love it." In her Chinese-self portrait, Cherica's profile reveals a calm expression. She's squatting in a yoga position with one hand placed over the other. To distinguish one self from the other, Cherica removed her hair tie and leaned upside down to shake out her hair. Later she drew on her image to exaggerate her long, straight, black hair.

Nytrepa's self-portrait and her White-self portrait are both themed around nature. In the first, Nytrepa climbs high into a tree. Her classmate writes about Nytrepa's portrait: "She also likes to feel the fresh air. She really likes to be up real high. Nytrepa thinks climbing is fun and exciting." In her other-self portrait, where she's posing as a White person, Nytrepa's appreciation for nature becomes a professional identity. As we go outside to make her portrait, Nytrepa is thinking that she will hug a tree in her White-self portrait. We talk about what she wants to show with this gesture and discuss how some people's work involves taking care of nature and the outdoors. Looking around the school's courtyard for a way to show this, Nytrepa finds the watering can we see in her portrait. As in her self-portrait, her expression here is convincing. She lovingly attends to the flowers. Nytrepa carefully arranges the picture to show the flowing water. Later she frames the top of her portrait with the long word *environmentalist*.

Finally, Neil uses his other-self portrait as an opportunity to comment on the very process of representation. His portrait and writing imply an awareness of offensive, racist portrayals of Black culture, as well as an awareness of the way pictures can be distorted. Facing the challenge of creating a portrait of his other-self likely deepened Neil's awareness. Wary that his portrait might be misinterpreted, he very consciously constructs what he sees as a positive image. He composes his image carefully and has his partner take several pictures to get it right. He then draws on the image and, as a result, his white shoes are almost glowing. In the class booklet Neil also adds a quotation from Martin Luther King, Jr.'s "I Have a Dream" speech.

PROJECT VARIATION

A Middle School Approach to Self

Black Self/White Self

WHEREAS ELEMENTARY-LEVEL CLASSROOMS may open conversations about race through the use of read-aloud literature, such as *Pink and Say* (Polacco, 1994), *The Other Side* (Woodson, 2001), *Remember the Bridge* (Weatherford, 2002), or *The Watsons Go to Birmingham* (Curtis, 1995), middle school teachers may choose to begin by talking about the students' own experiences. For example, in middle school art classes, Robert Hunter, who is African American, begins by asking students to write about their first experience of race. In the following examples, 7th-graders elaborate on both lived experiences as well as stereotypes—about how race influences the clothes and hairstyles people wear, the places they live, the way they speak, and the way they are respected and/or mistreated. One White female student confesses that she "truly didn't know," while a White male classmate remembers, "In kindergarten or 1st grade I heard crying and I went over to see what was going on and both Black and White

Cherica's self- and other-self portraits from class book, 2004

children were taunting another child using the 'n' word." A Black male student writes, "In 1st grade I started noticing it. I had similar interests with Black people, not Whites. On the phone they think my mom is White." An African American female writes about stereotypes and expectations about how to enact race: "A lot of people judge me because I'm not the most 'ghetto.' I'm not ashamed; I went to a White school. They say, 'Oh she talks proper, she's White.' But White people talk slang and have cornrows." A biracial female student wrote, "My dad is White, my mom is Black; I never saw my dad. I'm mixed. My mom talks 'White.' People try to treat me right because I have White in me, but they treat my mom differently because she's Black." The details in students' memories provide ample material for in-depth discussions about how race affects people's lives in

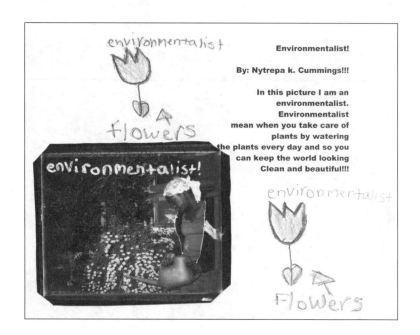

the realm of school, work, friendships, language, and so on. Students'
writings also provide useful material to tie into their visual portraits.

As stereotypes inevitably arise, this activity can segue into a productive conversation about the dangerous and commonplace nature
of stereotypes. As another opening activity, Hunter has shown students the work of photographer Nikki Lee, which, like *Black Self/
White Self*, deals with imaginary or manipulated realities and constructed identities. Lee creates series of self-portraits in which she
poses as members of different communities, from White punk rock-
ers to Korean schoolgirls, from young Latina mothers in L.A. to
yuppies in New York. She creatively uses setting, clothing, props,
expression, and so on. Her photographs raise questions about how
we make assumptions about other people, what we base these assumptions on, and what positive and negative stereotypes are associated with different groups of people.

Hunter also asks his middle school students to define race, ethnicity, nationality, and culture. Clarifying such terms and identifying examples helps students avoid misconceptions and mistakes
such as conflating race and religion. Discussions are meant to equip
students with a more nuanced vocabulary for investigating the differences and similarities among groups, and eventually for portraying other selves. Hunter also asks students to list five questions
they'd like to ask a person of a different racial identity, and to think
of several people of different racial identities and to list five positive qualities and/or accomplishments of each person. Throughout
his projects, Hunter expects students to keep a journal that they
may or may not share with others. All of these activities—which can

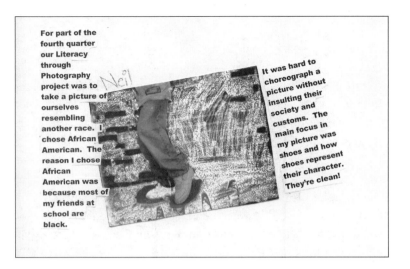

For part of the fourth quarter our Literacy through Photography project was to take a picture of ourselves resembling another race. I chose African American. The reason I chose African American was because most of my friends at school are black.

Neil

It was hard to choreograph a picture without insulting their society and customs. The main focus in my picture was shoes and how shoes represent their character. They're clean!

Neil's other-self portrait from class book, 2004

be integrated into the framework of *Black Self/White Self* described above—encourage students to remain open and inquisitive.

Girl Self/Boy Self

Yet another approach to other-self portraiture involves an exploration of gender. Erin Pattishall asked her 4th- and 5th-grade students at Club Boulevard Elementary School to make photographic and written portraits revealing their "girl" and "boy" selves. (She followed the same general process, where students planned, shot, and wrote about each self-portrait independently.) Along with their self-portrait pictures and writings, Pattishall's students engaged in weekly debates on gender issues, read fairy tales in order to identify gender stereotypes, wrote letters to various companies and organizations to raise awareness of gender issues, and conducted research reports about individuals who have resisted gender conventions.

Two male students wrote the preface to their class book, which is titled "Breaking the Barrier." Their preface reads: "Did you ever wonder how it would be like to be the opposite gender? In this magazine we used that as a stem of writing. We saw a lot of different sides to people, while breaking barriers along the way. This was a great experience because lots of boys thought they would never think about being a girl. But in the end, they came through. Many boys seemed to be terrified of being a girl. It was the same with the girls. We hope you like our portraits!"

As their preface reveals, people are often terrified by difference. These projects allow kids the opportunity to play with, explore, name, manipulate, challenge, and even disregard difference. They help build students' self-awareness and confidence, along with their empathy. The process of representing themselves and their imagined selves sharpens students' skills in written and visual expression as well as their critical thinking.

Lisa Lord
A Teacher's Reflection

I THINK EVERY ADULT should consider how he or she would do this assignment. My White self would feature me wearing my usual "teacher" attire: comfy shoes, machine-washable clothes, reading glasses, simple jewelry. I'd be smiling in front of a tall, messy bookshelf loaded with children's books. My fingers would have marker marks on them, my gray hair would probably be sticking out, and my lipstick would be faded. If I were completely honest, I'd include my small desk with its spilled coffee and avalanching piles of paperwork. I don't have any trouble brainstorming the details I'd include in my self-portrait.

My Black self would have to be a Black teacher, wouldn't she? How would that teacher be different from my White self? Am I stereotyping when I think that I've never known an African American teacher who didn't dress more formally than I do? What about when I conclude that my Black self would have a neater classroom? Brainstorming the details for the portrait of my Black self pushes me to think of individuals I've known over the years. Are the differences I'm remembering because of the difference in our races? If I happened to be part of a diverse group of teachers doing the *Black Self/White Self* project, would my planned photograph offend my African American colleagues? What would they think? Would they help me get it right?

I think this portrait-planning is difficult. It pushes me to remember the segregated Mississippi public schools I attended in the 1950s and my experiences as a rare White teacher in a historically Black school in the '70s. I've witnessed adult participants in teacher workshops struggling with the difficulty of this assignment. They were very creative in finding ways to avoid making an other-self portrait about race, and they sometimes voiced their discomfort and resistance. Even though students seem to struggle less than adults, many students in our class avoid making other-self portraits featuring the most prevalent races in our class. There were no Asian or Native American children in the group, so those seemed to be safer choices than Black, White, or Latino.

Participants have a range of choices, some more challenging than others. Choosing to represent a famous person of a different race is probably the least risky. While visiting our school, Ruby Bridges pretended to be the White governor of Louisiana. How might she have portrayed one of her White classmates in 1960? Caity, a White student, pretended to be Ruby Bridges as a 1st-grader. How would she have portrayed one of her African American friends in our class? Historic representations are more like performing a play to tell a story from the past—a worthwhile learning experience, but not as difficult as imagining oneself in the present as a person of a different race.

Choosing a race not represented in the class gives everyone an opportunity to discuss the stereotyping or misinformation that they notice without risking offense to a class member. That, too, is useful. Yet it is when we are brave or curious enough to ask someone of another race questions that we begin to break down stereotypes and honor each other as different but equal human beings.

If a project is so difficult for adults, is it appropriate to assign it to children? Is its usefulness worth the discomfort? I think this is another example of the way adults can learn from children. The students in our class gave each other advice, asked each other questions, and talked about stereotypes. Sometimes they were silly, and sometimes they needed a little prodding from an adult, but they ultimately made images and had conversations they will remember.

I frequently remind my students that experiencing discomfort when considering a new idea is a sign of learning, so it would be unfortunate to avoid uncomfortable assignments regarding race. For such a critical topic I try to push the boundaries of my comfort zone, help students feel safe, and trust that our meaningful and memorable conversations help reduce racism and prejudice in the future.

Katie Hyde
Through a Sociologist's Lens

I REMEMBER OVER A DECADE AGO and around the time I'd first heard of Wendy's *Black Self/White Self* project, recognizing myself in Ruth Frankenberg's (1993) poignant analysis of progressive White women's struggle to see or understand the meaning of race in their own lives. Since we (Whites) often associate race with people of color and not ourselves, our Whiteness remains unmarked and unexamined. Frankenberg's ethnography, *White Women, Race Matters: The Social Construction of Whiteness* (1993), pushed me to see the need to recognize and articulate the ways race shapes my life experiences, interests, opportunities, and everyday reality.

While Frankenberg refers to the detrimental consequences of color blindness and power-evasive talk about race, Mica Pollock (2004) uses the term "colormute" to refer to our silences and avoidances around race. Her book, *Colormute: Race Talk Dilemmas in an American School*, offers a nuanced analysis of the paradoxes and dilemmas surrounding race talk within a California high school. She begins by examining the paradoxical ways that students' talk exposes race as both fictional and real. She calls this seeming paradox "race bending" and suggests that educators use the practice of race bending strategically; in other words, educators should continue using race labels (for example, in discussions about disparities in resources and achievement among racial groups) while also helping students understand how race is socially and historically constructed. She urges educators to "ask provocative questions"; "navigate predictable debates"; and "talk more about talking" (pp. 224–25). By getting students talking about identity and experimenting with representation, the *Black Self/White Self* project offers a way in.

I am drawn to the *Black Self/White Self* project's potential to foster self-discovery and understanding. Looking at the collection of students' self-portraits, I am impressed by three things—the exquisite care students took in framing their photographs, the compelling details and depth of their writings inspired by their photographs, and the diversity in students' representations of self. From Caity's determined look on the soccer field to Chris's intense absorption in his book, from Tray proudly kneeling in his baseball uniform to Jessica leaping happily and carelessly with her hands in the air—their photographs reveal the students' individuality. Students cherished this opportunity to look at themselves.

I am also drawn to the way the project promotes introspection as well as awareness of social and historical identities and stereotypes. Looking at their other-self portraits, I see several paths students took toward valuable discoveries about race and identity. Some portraits, like that of Lillie's shackled hands, are reminders of the past. Whether or not students were fully cognizant of the relationship between the past and present, the process of enacting their own version of the past undoubtedly stirred up new ideas and insights. For some students the crucial moment of discovery occurred when they recognized their uncertainty about how to portray "others." Mario, for instance, realized he'd never considered what it would be like to have a different racial identity. Others are stumped as to how to verbalize and portray such a shift. With unassuming comments like Alex's, "What would a White person look like? You're White," students acknowledge their own ignorance and open themselves to classmates' viewpoints and experiences. Along with several fellow African American classmates, Talisha creates two portraits that are nearly interchangeable—both demonstrate yoga poses—implying that that one's interior sense of self doesn't necessarily shift according to racial identity. Finally, students make important realizations concerning their own power to create representations. Neil's writing warns us to think twice about the strong messages that images convey. This is the kind of awareness we hope will prepare students to deconstruct racialized images in the media and popular culture and even history books.

In revising and embellishing their other-self portraits, students play with and disrupt the idea of fixed identities. They learn to look more carefully and beneath the surface to question what is appearance versus reality. Their mindful observation deepens their visual literacy, while engaging them with the meaningful and nuanced practice of communicating their stories and impressions with words and images. They discover the limitations and challenges of visual representation. Their insights arise from the process of constructing images, as opposed to simply deconstructing images, an activity to which some visual literacy programs are limited.

Lesson Plans | *Black Self/White Self*

Reading and Understanding Photographic Portraits

TIME NEEDED: 50 MINUTES

1. Select six to eight photographic portraits with a range of subjects and backgrounds.
2. Using a computer or slide projector, project the images one by one. This allows students to focus together on the same image and discuss it as a group.
3. Spend about 5 to 10 minutes on each image. Begin by showing the photograph with the simplest background—ideally one with a plain backdrop. Ask the students to say or write down concrete details that they see in the photograph, such as the subject's gender, age, ethnicity, clothing, and other physical features.
4. Ask questions about other characteristics of the portrait, including background, props, gesture, expression, and point of view/angle.
5. After discussing the details visible in the photograph, allow students to make inferences about the photograph's subject. Is this a businessperson? A mother? A student? Pose such questions as, "What can we say about this person from what we can observe in the photograph?" or "What might be the story of this photograph?" Follow these questions up by asking, "How can you tell?" Ask the students to support their hypotheses with evidence from the picture.
6. Referring back to the images, discuss with students how photographers make use of certain tools, such as background, timing, point of view, gesture, expression, and props, in order to tell a story.

Planning Self-Portraits

TIME NEEDED: 50 MINUTES

1. Look at examples of authors' portraits in classroom books to reiterate the variety of ways portraits are made. You might choose some examples with the subject in action—for example, throwing a ball or making a speech. Other photographs might be formal portraits where the author is posing in a studio and looking at the camera with a smile or serious expression. Some pictures might show an author at home on her front porch.
2. Work with your students to generate a list of staging choices for consideration in making their photographic self-portraits. As students give examples of such elements as "background" and "camera angle," write their ideas down as a list on the blackboard.
3. Discuss a hypothetical example such as, "How would I make a portrait of myself? What would I wear? What would I be doing? What props might I include in my picture?"
4. Give students 5 minutes to write plans for making their self-portraits. Ask them to make notes for their portrait using the list on the blackboard as a guide.
5. As their homework assignment, ask students to bring in whatever clothing and other props they will need for their self-portrait.

Making Portraits Together

1. Give a 10- to 20-minute demonstration on how to use the camera—any camera can be used for this project, including simple point-and-shoot digital cameras.
2. If possible, enlist a few parents or community volunteers to work with small groups of students outside the classroom.
3. Group students into pairs. Working with one pair of students at a time, review their written plans and gather the necessary materials, including the students' props and the camera.
4. Have each student carefully direct his or her partner on how to compose the shot—how to position and angle the camera, what to capture in the photograph.
5. Before making the exposure, allow partners to switch places so they can double-check whether the angle and distance are right and ensure that there is nothing unwanted in the viewfinder.
6. If using digital cameras or Polaroid instant cameras, allow the student to assess the photograph once it's made. Allow students to choose whether to re-shoot. Each student should be allowed two to three shots.

Delving Deeper— Reading and Writing About Portraits

TIME NEEDED: 50 MINUTES (A 40-MINUTE SESSION PLUS A 10-MINUTE SESSION)

1. Prepare for the following writing activity by printing students' images before class. (If using digital cameras and printers, it will take less than 30 minutes to print one image for each student in an average class.) Group students into new pairs and give them a few minutes to share their self-portrait photographs. If students have shot more than one photograph, ask them to select only one for this activity.
2. Allow students to choose whether they'd like to read their own photograph or their partner's.
3. Ask students to spend 10 minutes writing down the concrete details they see in the picture in front of them. Challenge them to list as many as 30 details.
4. Allow a few minutes for sharing between partners.
5. Ask students to use their list as a starting point for writing about the person in the photograph. Tell them to introduce this person by writing in the third person, even if they're writing about themselves. Allow the students 5 minutes for writing, and remind them to draw upon the details that are visible to any viewer—the same ones they referred to in their list.
6. The following day, ask students to expand upon their writing for 10 minutes. This time, invite students to use their imagination by speculating about things that cannot be seen directly in the photographs. Suggest that students consider questions like: "What might the person be thinking?" or "What is important to the person in this photograph?" Remind the students that they don't have to "get it right."

Imagining Another Self

TIME NEEDED: 50 MINUTES

1. Read aloud or assign for individual reading *Through My Eyes (*Bridges, 1999) and/or *The Story of Ruby Bridges* (Coles & Ford, 2004).
2. Ask for two volunteers to take part in a role-playing activity based on Bridges's story. The activity can be done in small groups of four to six students or with the entire class. Ask one student to play the part of Louisiana's White governor and another to play the part of Ruby Bridges. Tell the remaining students to play the role of Bridges's classmates from either her old or new school.
3. Allow 10 minutes for a dialogue/debate between these historical characters. Encourage everyone's participation.
4. As a group, discuss the challenges and discoveries associated with the role-play.

Planning Other-Self Portraits

TIME NEEDED: 25 MINUTES

1. Explain to students that their next assignment is to make a portrait of themselves as someone of a different race. Tell students that this person can be imaginary rather than someone they know or someone they've read or learned about in school or on TV. Allow students time to respond to this idea—asking questions and putting the assignment into their own words.
2. Ask students to spend 5 minutes writing about their idea. Present them with a planning worksheet with two questions: "What will your portrait show?" and "What symbol will you include to communicate your idea?" The planning worksheet also should provide space where students can sketch their portrait ideas.
3. Ask for volunteers to share their ideas. Allow students the chance to provide one another with feedback.

Talking About and Making Other-Self Portraits

TIME NEEDED: 30 TO 40 MINUTES PER PAIR OF STUDENTS

1. Follow the same steps as in the Making Portraits Together lesson plan above, but allow even more time for dialogue among students. As students ask questions of one another and discuss their ideas, they may choose to revise their plans. Allow time for improvisation. Partners should help each other experiment as they prepare to shoot their photographs.
2. If possible, enlist a few parents or community volunteers to work with small groups of students outside the classroom.
3. Working with one pair of students at a time, gather the necessary materials, including the students' props and the camera, and carry them to the locations chosen for making the photographs.
4. Allow each student to carefully direct his or her partner on how to compose the shot—how to position and angle the camera, what to capture in the photograph.
5. Before making the exposure, allow partners to switch places so they can double-check whether the angle and distance are right and ensure that there is nothing unwanted in the viewfinder.
6. If using digital cameras or Polaroid instant cameras, allow the student to assess the photograph once it's made. Allow students to choose whether to re-shoot. Each student should be allowed two to three shots.

Reconsidering Other-Self Portraits—
Altering, Writing, and Reflecting

TIME NEEDED: TWO 1-HOUR SESSIONS

Session 1

1. Whether the students use Polaroid 600s, 35mm film, or digital format, provide each student with prints of each of their two or three other-self photographs. Tell students to choose their favorite image.
2. Ask students to think about how they'd like to change or add to their photo to more clearly show themselves as another person. For example, students may want to draw on the image to change the way their hair, clothes, or skin looks. They may decide to add words to their picture or draw something in the background to help establish context.
3. Provide students with markers as well as a sheet of acetate, which they can place over their print and draw/write on as practice. This allows students to experiment and observe how their portrait changes.
4. Next, ask students to draw and/or write on their actual photographs.

Session 2

5. Again, group students into pairs and give them a few minutes to share their other-self portrait photographs. Ask students to choose whether they'd like to read their own photograph or their partner's.
6. Ask students to carefully read their own or their partner's photo and write about the person they see in the image. Allow 10 minutes for writing. Remind students to pay attention to the concrete details visible in the photograph, while encouraging them to use their imagination by considering elements that are not shown in the photographs.
7. Ask students to gather all their *Black Self/White Self* work—their self- and other-self portraits as well as the writing that accompanies each picture.
8. Ask students to review their first drafts in order to polish the spelling and grammar for presentation in the book. Also consider whether the finished pieces should be handwritten or typed.
9. Provide each student with an 8.5 x 11-inch sheet of paper, which will be their designated page in the class book. Allow students to arrange their work on this page. Each student should present both portraits of him- or herself.
10. Ask for a volunteer or volunteers to design the book's cover.
11. Assemble the pages into a book and make one copy for each student.

THREE | American Alphabets

Picturing Words from the Language of Home

THE *AMERICAN ALPHABETS* PROJECT is a written and photographic exploration of personal language and culture. Initial writing activities focus on the concept of home. While brainstorming alphabetical lists of words and writing dialogues and poems about home, students discover how the words we know and use depend on where and who we are. Next, students use their alphabetized lists of words as a guide for shooting pictures at home. They make one picture to portray each of the 26 "home" words on their lists. Students then assemble and label their pictures within alphabet books. These activities honor children's choices and expressions—in the variety of words chosen and the distinct ways students decide to represent words, the alphabet books highlight students' individuality and their personal experience of home. In a final activity, students work together to make a collaborative visual alphabet about home. In doing so, they learn about people of different cultural heritages and appreciate the connections between language and culture. Students curate and design a public exhibition of their collective vision, which defies racial and class stereotypes related to experience and language.

The alphabet project suits such literacy goals as writing dialogue, writing specific descriptions, writing poetry, understanding setting and character in reading and writing, and improving conventions of writing. The project also addresses objectives in social studies class, especially learning about people of different backgrounds and appreciating connections between language and culture. With slight changes in instructions and emphases, teachers can use the project to teach the vocabulary and concepts of math and science.

Wendy Ewald
An Artist's Frame

LIKE MOST EVERYONE I know, I first encountered written language in children's alphabet primers. Looking back, I now see that the words and visual examples used to represent letters reinforced the worldview of the middle-class White girl I happened to be. A picture of a shiny new car illustrated the letter C. My father ran a Chevrolet dealership in Detroit, so I thought this example had been dreamed up with me in mind. I assumed that the congruence between written expression and one's own experience of the world held true for all children.

Since then, the role of language in our culture has undergone several mutations, many of them brought on by the mass media. From McLuhan to Spielberg to MTV to PowerPoint to rap to the Internet, people have oscillated between thinking about communication as "technique" or "substance." Evolution in media technology has made text, except in its most rudimentary form, into a dialect most accessible to a powerful but culturally narrow elite.

In contemporary times, language is supposed to be democratic, available for all to use; and writing is one of its most important uses.

Impostor, Spanish
alphabet word, 1998

But while the United States has become increasingly diverse, the culture of our schools has remained much the same as in my childhood: White middle class. And the language sanctioned in the classroom is, as it was in the 1950s, an extension of a White middle-class ideal. The words taught in school constitute our society's official language, and unless we master the intricacies of it, our chances of making more than a marginal living are alarmingly small. Too many children, including those who speak English as a second language, are excluded from or condescended to by the current system.

A few years ago, for example, after my husband and I adopted a baby boy in Colombia, I began to hear disturbing stories from the English as a Second Language teachers I know. They talked about the bad treatment their students sometimes received from other teachers, who assumed that because the children didn't speak English well, they were stupid. Those stories prompted me to think about using photographs to teach language. With the students' help, I would make pictures to illustrate the alphabet so children could influence the images and meaning of a primer—in effect, make it their own. I wanted not just to mend an educational system, but to see our language(s) and our children as they actually are in the world, without the haze of conventional rhetoric.

Talk, African American
alphabet word, 2000

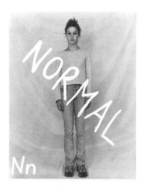

Normal, White girl alphabet word, 2002

For many years, North Carolina has been a stop on the Central America–to–North America migrant stream. Some of the migrants have "settled out"—taken up permanent residence in the United States. Many of them don't speak English and many are not citizens.

I created an alphabet with the Spanish-speaking children of these immigrants. We began by discussing how language itself migrates (Spanish from Spain to the Americas, for example) and where in the world different languages are spoken. I asked them to think of a word in their own language for each letter of the alphabet, and to assign these words visual signs specific to their culture. I photographed the signs, objects, or scenes they selected. When the negatives were developed, the children altered them with Magic Markers, adding the letter and word they were illustrating.

The Latino children said their English-speaking peers were mistrustful when the Latinos spoke Spanish. They were happy to work on a project in their own language that they could share with their schoolmates without fear of hostility. The words they used—like *nervioso* or *impostor*—were symptomatic of their uprooted way of life. Taken as a whole, their lists of words amounted to a kind of cultural self-portrait.

Raas (head), Arabic
alphabet word, 2003

Arabic alphabet exhibit
opening at the Queens
Museum, New York, 2003

Making the Arabic
alphabet, Queens Mu-
seum, New York, 2003

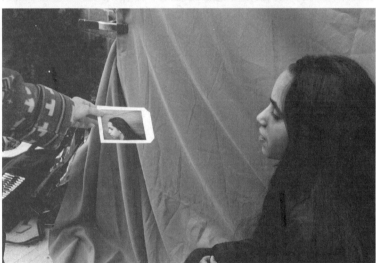

A couple of years after working with the Latino children, I made an "African American Alphabet" with students at Central Intermediate School, a historically important Black high school in Cleveland, Ohio, that had produced important leaders like Stokely Carmichael. Like the alphabet created by Spanish-speaking children, the terms for this alphabet represented the thoughts and values that African American children consider an integral part of their lives.

The students started their alphabet by reading aloud writings by John Edgar Wideman and Toni Morrison that incorporated African American vernacular. Eventually I also made an alphabet with White high school girls in Andover, Massachusetts, that highlighted their culture, and an alphabet with Arabic middle schoolers in Queens, New York.

The Arabic students had previously never had the opportunity to meet as a group in their school. We eventually turned their alphabet into huge silk banners and hung them from the second floor of the Queens Museum. We invited the students' parents and other members of the Arabic community to attend an opening celebration. As they watched the banners sway above them in the air-conditioning, they talked about how important it was to see their language honored in this way. Out of these alphabets, I put together a book called *American Alphabets* (Ewald, 2005), which I hoped would allow us Americans to see ourselves, and the issues of race and culture, in a fresh light.

Setting the Stage

IN THE FIRST PART of the *American Alphabets* project, students look at their own use of language. We first ask them to write three different alphabetical lists of words. In writing a list of school words, home words, and words they know but do not use, students recognize that words can be personal and specific to place and context. Next, we ask students to explore in more detail their home words by writing dialogues and poems about home scenes and conversations. By developing three separate lists, students can see that they are fluent in three different languages, not counting words they may be learning in Spanish, or other languages such as Hebrew, French, or Korean. We hope they will recognize the school language as their common language. Home alphabet lists then begin to reveal our diversity and our unique ways of communicating.

Word Lists for Three Different Alphabets

When we led this project in 2002, our class included African American and White children of both well-educated, middle-class families and families that struggled financially, as well as immigrants from Honduras, Nigeria, and Zimbabwe. Everyone spoke English and participated in an introductory Spanish class. Some studied Hebrew outside of school, and some spoke a native language other than English at home. One child was the only English speaker in his home.

We start by pulling as many alphabet books off our bookshelves as possible. Letting students know that they will soon be creating alphabet books, we give them time to browse through the books and show their friends their favorite discoveries in the books. If anyone thought alphabet books are for beginners, they soon recognize the richness of language, the depth of knowledge, and the creativity of the illustrations. Helpful examples are *Eating the Alphabet* (Ehlert, 1989), *The Icky Bug Alphabet Book* (Pallotta, 1986), and *G is for Googol: A Math Alphabet Book* (Schwartz, 1998). There are, in fact, many other alphabet books associated with every topic in the curriculum and many informative texts organized according to the alphabet.

For the first writing activity, we ask students to make three word lists that represent different "languages" in their lives. Looking around the classroom and thinking about how we spend our time at school, leads us to the first list—a school alphabet. Next to each letter, students write what they consider important "school" words. They record the first words that pop into their heads. The students work individually but inspire others with their suggestions.

We ask the students to write their school alphabet lists while sitting among their classmates in the classroom. They are surrounded by references to our shared language. It is easy to recognize how individual students constructed their lists. Alex clearly has read the print on the walls. His list includes Benjamin Franklin, Colonial Times, and Intolerable Acts, and resembles the week's social studies lessons, to which he'd clearly paid attention. Caity's list is more varied and refers to multiple school subjects—art, technology, gym, Español, math, music, and writing. She also includes specific topics (harmony and universe), tools (iMac and AlphaSmart), and learning strategies (listen and study). The school lists include many common and predictable words: history, homework, friends, pencils, and books. But they also include words describing materials and methods of instruction not found in every class, such as pattern blocks, linear units, and "Money Bait." Although the words point to routine parts of our math lessons, outsiders might not know that red trapezoid-shaped pattern blocks equal half the area of yellow hexagons, or that we prove that three green triangles are equivalent to one trapezoid, and thus three-sixths of a hexagon. Students quickly notice that word choices sometimes exclude others from meaningful conversation.

Next we ask students to list important words spoken in their homes. Without the opportunity to look around one's home while composing this second list of alphabetized words, students have to rely on memories. To trigger the memories, we suggest the students might envision touring their home or seeing each member of their family. They might revisit the last conversation they had as they left for school that morning. As the students brainstorm the lists, we ask them to record the first words coming to their minds, to avoid getting stuck on letters for which they can't think of a word, and not to overthink their choices. They can fill in the blanks and make selections of their favorite words later. We encourage silent, individual writing during this writing time. Students coming from homes where English isn't the dominant language may include words from whatever language is spoken at home.

Some students follow our advice and include words and phrases heard at home, such as "just want to know," "leave me alone," "yakkety, yakkety, yak," and "you be nice." One student's first word for N is "No!" Lisa recalls hearing her own mother saying, "What in the world?!" as a question and an exclamation.

While most lists have words that might describe almost any home—bathroom, door, porch, furniture—the lists are personalized with the names of family members and an impressive level of specificity, including unpredictable details like "kitty litter," "chocolate syrup," "Jamaica," "ferrets," and "quality time."

Some of the students take the approach of listing many words for any given letter. Next to the letter B, for instance, Lillie writes "birds, Barney, books, bed, Brother," and D stands for "doors, dad, dog, and Dictionary." Lillie includes mostly common and proper nouns in her list, whereas Nytrepa includes both verbs and adjectives evoking emotions, in addition to naming family members and friends. In general, the students include many more adjectives—caring, encouraging, wise, naughty—and verbs—flip, meow, know, smile, see—than one usually finds in alphabet books. Many include verbs connected with favorite sports and hobbies, such as dunking, jumping, dancing, reading a book, and drawing.

With two lists in hand, students begin to see how their language is specific to setting. Students can recognize how we use many versions of English depending on the formality of social settings and the dialects and colloquialisms of our families and communities. While there is some overlap across the home and school lists, there is more variety. For both her home and school list, Lillie uses the same approach of listing several words, mostly nouns, for each letter. But the actual words differ. At home J stands for "Juice" and "Jacket," while at school J words include "John Hancock" and "jump." Lillie's home words for L are: "Lillie, labrador black, light switch, loud," whereas "linear units, lunch, liturature" are words related to school.

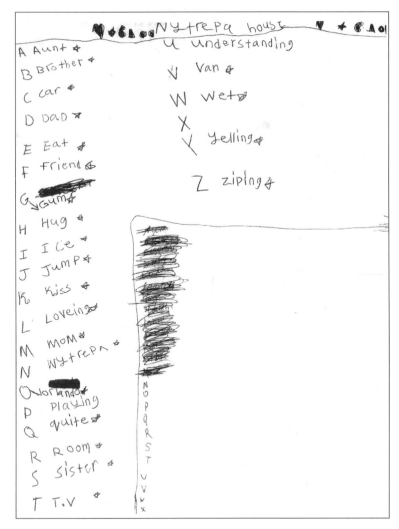

Nytrepa's home list, 2002

P stands for "puppy, Pickle, phone, piano" at home versus "perimetar, pencils, paper, poetry, piano" at school.

We ask the students to review their school and home word lists and prepare a third list: words they know but never use. The example we provide is "eminent domain," a legal term Lisa learned from her attorney father. She shares how she experienced this term as difficult and alienating, but as she speaks, raised eyebrows and smirks appear on faces of some students who wonder aloud, "You mean, we can put bad words on the list?" Another responds, "I don't want to get in trouble!" We assure them that even though they are brainstorming these "never used" words—including "bad" words—they won't say them aloud or publish them in a book. The idea is to see how they learned these words and why they don't use them.

Students write an interesting assortment of spellings of four-letter words. We notice that students need to work on words with silent *w* and words with digraphs such as *tch,* but choose not to use these lists for spelling practice! They list phrases like "come on you punk"

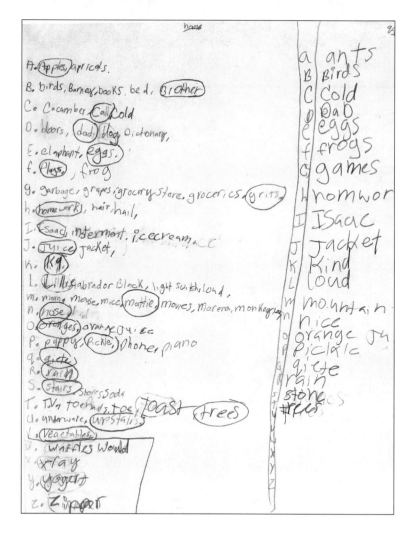

Lillie's home list and school list (opposite), 2002

and derogatory names—"geek," "freek," "crackhead," and "idiot," which they know they're not supposed to say. Many pursue the idea of difficult words they know but don't ever need to say. They write challenging vocabulary words like "authoritative," "navigational," "negligent," "valenvitoria," and so forth. Even with the mischievous listing of X-rated words and the ostentatious and inventive listing of multisyllabic words like "antidisistablishmenterism," the students are noticing the power and possibilities in their use of language.

Exploring One Alphabet: Writing About Home

Next, we turn our attention back to the home alphabet lists, with the intention of finding depth, liveliness, and uniqueness in our ways of representing our home language. We want students to discover how "home language" conjures up a specific setting and reveals the special spirit of particular people. Drawing on their home alphabet lists, we ask the students to use dialogue and poetry to write personal stories set in their homes.

We read aloud short excerpts from *Shiloh* (Naylor, 1991, pp. 1–2),

A. alphebet, Art, animals. At G-Arthurs
B. board, books, birds. birthdays,
C. crayons. colord pencils. Cafeterias. class room. Computer,

D. dance, drumes,
E. enemies.
f. friends, Aractions, feild day
g. garden.

h. history. heights.
I. that up I'll read dance.
J. John hancock. Jump,
K. Kind
L. linear units. lunch literature
m. markers, math, msat ord. ms.
N. notbook, noise.
O. over heads
p. perimetar, Pencils, Paper, poetry, piano,
q. qiete
r. reading. roller couster
S. Stalk, Science,
T. table. teacher,
U. umbrella
V. violence. Vocabalary
W. writing, war, Working, Tickeria
X. xytophone Cnitr
Y. Yodel, yucky, yong, malika, Lillie
Z. Zipper

Roll of Thunder, Hear My Cry (Taylor, 1976, pp. 154–155), and *Caramelo* (Cisneros, 2002, pp. 55–56). We ask students to visualize what they hear in the selected passages, which portray at-home, family conversations about a universal topic: food.

Inspired by the passages they'd heard and equipped with their home alphabets, the students begin writing conversations to capture the distinct quality of mealtime conversations in each of their own homes. They write quietly and independently. Their written dialogues, full of informal speech, are vignettes of family experience, windows on casual, spontaneous conversations.

Some students immediately write about their family's conversations about food itself; others write about the nightly rituals alluded to in titles like "Before Dinner," "Dinner Talk," and "Cleaning up." Dialogues titled "Oh please Mom," "No haircuts," and "What I would do to get ice cream" feature realistic, persuasive debates with parents. Some writings portray yearly celebrations at Thanksgiving or Sukkot, while others, such as one called "Love in the kitchen," expressed appreciation for mothers and their cooking.

Tanaka's never-used word list, 2002

DINNER TALK

"Come on Rick,
come on Jeddy,
dinners ready."
That's my step
mom. I hope dinners
good tonight.
Maybe hamburgers.
or maybe burritos
mmmmmmmmmm.
"David turn off the
T.V."
"I don't want to."
"I'm going to count
to three."
"O.K. I will."
David is the most
reluctant T.V. turn off
person I have ever
seen.
Here it goes into the
kitchen. O man, it's Quiche.
—*Justin*

CLEANING UP

"It is time to get to
work and clean up your
    room!"
mom said.
"But I am drinking my
orange juice" I said
"Then do it after you drink
your orange juice"
"But I don't want to"
"Please go to your room
and clean up before I
count to ten One, two, three"
"Okay I will do it but first
I haf to get done drinking my
orange juice"
"four, five, six, seven, eight,
nine, ten!"
"I'm going to my room for
    real now mom"
"I bet you could get your
room cleaned up in just an
hour"
"Don't worry I will get it
    cleaned
and why do I haf to clean
it anyway?"
"Because it's good to clean up
your room and also people are
coming over tonight"
"But why can't I just
let them not come
In my room because
They don't haf to see
My room"
"But it would be nice
if they saw your room"
"Well Okay I guess I will
clean up my room"
"Now get to work!"
I wounder what people are
coming over to night, and
I wounder why they haf
To see my room.
—*Alix*

During writers' workshop our students gather in a circle to listen to volunteers read their work. In this sharing of their stories, they recognize familiar themes within homes—tedious or incomprehensible adult rules, special nicknames family members give us, the process of negotiating with parents, and the teasing and pestering students often endure from siblings. Emphasis on home conversations brings out specific settings and language, informal talk, and greater intensity of emotion.

For the next day's writing workshop activity, we challenge students to develop poems based on their written dialogues. Once again, we begin with a few examples of poems that include mealtime images and family themes. Nikki Grimes's "My Own Man" (Grimes, 1999) and Mimi Chapra's "Mi Mamá Cubana" (Mora, 2001) include the kind of specific imagery and dialogue we have talked about. In addition, Grimes's and Chapra's poems elevate themes of individuality and family pride.

Rather than emphasizing the use of particular rhyme schemes or rhythm patterns, we focus on content—scenes and language from home. Building on their list of words, as well as their written dialogues, we ask students to write poems that home in on a precise, often affecting, theme. In the following example, Neil's poem titled "Privacy" draws on five words from his home alphabet list: "annoying," "dancing," "fights," "magazines," and "room."

PRIVACY
I'm all relaxed.
Reading my favorite book.
Guess who comes in my sister acting like
the star.
Dancing here, singing there.
What the heck is wrong with her?
Picks up my magazines throws them down.
I get up and say to her please leave.
And then she walks away.
But I'm sure it will happen
again!

Whereas Tanaka resigned himself to his mother and sister's teasing affection in a poem about words (specifically, family nicknames), "Embarassing Names," Terrence defended the way he cherishes his mother in the poem that starts with "Beat."

EMBARASSING NAMES
I can't help but notice
all the embarassing moments
all the times . . .
that she embarassed me
but not just one she
two shes
and their names are mom and
    sister
they call me embarassing names
mostly in public
to be more spicific
they call me Tee or Chip-dip
I don't know if it on purpose
or by accident
they must know it's embarassing
if it's on purpose
they must never get tired of it.

"BEAT"
"Beat"
"Beat"
I like my Momy
people say
"dad do" but I
say
"Height" Height if you
don't
like it then make me

write it because I am not
going
to hide it my Mom knows
it and she knows I love her
with
all my "heart" and I am not
going to hide it
from no one they'll
just have to lose
it
and face the music!

TALKING ABOUT LANGUAGE AND HOME

The American Alphabets *project weaves together an exploration of language with an investigation of home. Below are suggestions that highlight the complexity of these overlapping topics—suggestions that allow students to consider how these topics of language and home are simultaneously personal and social, private and public.*

Support English language learners. *Many teachers have immigrant or international students whose command of and comfort with the English language may be limited. When students brainstorm lists of expressions and objects from home, allow them to include words and phrases in their native language and then share treasured examples with the class. More important, help all students recognize the prevalence of prejudice and misunderstandings tied to language. Discuss the struggles of students and families who are assimilating to life in the United States. Useful pictures books featuring young protagonists emigrating from Argentina, Hong Kong, and Italy, respectively, are Jacqueline Jules's* No English *(2008);* I Hate English! *by Ellen Levine (1989); and Josephine Nobisso's* In English, of Course *(2003). For middle and high school students, we recommend selecting vignettes such as "My Name" and "No Speak English" from Sandra Cisneros's* The House on Mango Street *(1984) to discuss the isolation and intimidation experienced at times by non-native English speakers in this country. Julia Alvarez's* How the Garcia Girls Lost Their Accents *(1991) works well in tandem, as it reveals that middle- and upper-class immigrants also struggle with language and cultural assimilation.*

Question the "standardness" of English or any language. *Teachers also should be mindful that cultural and language differences among teachers and students affect classroom culture and practices, and in turn students' capacity to learn and excel, as discussed in Lisa Delpit's* Other People's Children: Cultural Conflict in the Classroom *(1995).*

We also highly recommend the essay "Nobody Mean More to Me Than You and The Future Life of Willie Jordan" in Some of Us Did Not Die: New and Selected Essays of June Jordan *(Jordan, 2002). Jordan describes her college students' translation of texts from Black English to Standard English, and vice versa, and in the process summarizes guidelines of Black English such as, "Never use the –ed suffix to indicate the past tense of a verb" (p. 165), and underscores the "presence of life, voice and clarity" as central to the value system of Black English (p. 163). Jordan recounts her students' tactical decision to use Black English in protesting the death of a classmate's brother, which occurred during the semester and at the hands of Brooklyn police. Her words bear witness to the ever-present racism in her students' lives and the urgent relevance of the politics of language. In his essay "Everyone Has an Accent," linguist Walt Wolfram (2000) stresses the importance of raising students' awareness about dialects, especially the ways dialect variations—related to accents, grammar, and colloquialisms—are natural and inevitable.*

Encourage a curiosity about words. *The* American Alphabets *project will pique students' curiosity about words and help them recognize their already complex command of language. When asking students to create lists of words they use in different contexts such as school and home, we suggest that all students are multilingual, even when each of their lists is written in one language. Let students be the experts by asking for volunteers to create alphabetical lists of words in Spanish, Arabic, or any other language spoken among the students. Invite students to interview their grandparents about favorite colloquialisms, and then ask students to compose yet another list of words.*

Students of any age can investigate the visual dimension of language with Ed Young's Voices of the Heart *(1997), which illustrates 26 Chinese characters that contain the symbol for heart and represent emotion words such as "joy" and "sorrow." Young explains how these characters derived from paintings of emotional scenes—paintings made to show the emotional quality of places and activities. Looking at examples of a pictorial language can inspire students as they make their own visual representations of concepts related to home, presumably concepts close to their hearts.*

Define home and family in broad, inclusive terms. *As the word lists and photographs shared in this chapter reveal—"home" is a wide-reaching theme—one that invites students to think about the people with whom they live, the physical space in which they live (whether their home is a house, apartment, or trailer), the tangible stuff within their homes—toys, furniture, clothes—as well as the intangible moods associated with home and family life. Students may think about how family members get along or not, loved ones who have gone away, the* *ways family members spend their time together and apart, favorite and dreaded activities, household chores, and parents' jobs or struggles with unemployment. The* American Alphabets *project gives teachers a personal and nuanced tour of their students' lives. Although teachers can relax knowing students, themselves, possess a great deal of control and authority as the tour guides, they also should expect that students' words and photographs may highlight how students' home lives differ along the lines of family customs, family structure, and economics.*

Since these differences can stir up discomfort or even shame, we recommend choosing a unifying theme for initial conversations about home. In addition to the theme of food suggested in this chapter, other possibilities might be music, pets, siblings/cousins, and names. Furthermore, there are countless examples of children's literature that will foster dialogue about universal and intimately personal elements of home.

We recommend that teachers share at least one story with the intention of reminding students that "home" and "family" are broadly defined, so that students living with adoptive or foster parents, single parents, lesbian parents, or grandparents can embrace the chance to share their home lives with classmates and teachers. Patricia Pollaco's storybook In Our Mothers' House *(2009) is one of many dealing with lesbian or gay parents. Defining home in broad, inclusive terms means acknowledging all types of family structures, as well as recognizing that family experiences range from joyful to painful. We recommend Katherine Paterson's classic,* The Great Gilly Hopkins *(1978), in which feisty, 11-year-old Gilly struggles to adjust to her latest foster home and comes to terms with the absence of her biological mother. Students who have experienced being separated from their loved ones will relate to Sharon Creech's* Walk Two Moons *(1994) in which the protagonist travels the country with her grandparents in search of her mother.*

Other poignant stories about transience and the experience of being uprooted or homeless include Christopher Paul Curtis's Bud, Not Buddy *(1999) about a 10-year-old orphan living on his own in the time of the Great Depression. A contemporary story of homelessness,* Fly Away Home *by Eve Bunting (1991), portrays a father and son living in an airport. Many students can relate to the experience of being caught between two worlds—whether it's because they move from one parent's home to the other's, they come from a multiracial or multilingual family, or they have moved from one part of the country or world to another. To deal with this theme, we recommend stories such as Pam Munoz Ryan's* Esperanza Rising *(2000), about a family's fall from fortune when they must leave Mexico and resettle in California during the 1920s, and Allen Say's* Grandfather's Journey *(1993), about a Japanese man's journey between and love for two faraway places.*

Finally, because of its amazing range of stories related to the themes of language and home, we again suggest that teachers select age-appropriate passages from The House on Mango Street *(Cisneros, 1984). Esperanza's autobiographical stories deal with class and ethnicity, instability and loss, loneliness and dreams, houses, neighborhoods and belonging, laughter and tears, and so on—in short, almost any topic that arises in students' portrayals of home during the* American Alphabets *project.*

LISTING WORDS FROM HOME and writing richly detailed dialogues and poems about home life set the stage for making visual portraits of home. In the next part of the *American Alphabets* project, each student creates a visual alphabet by photographing 26 words from A to Z, using the home alphabet list already created. Combining abstract words like "journey" with concrete words such as "living room," students make literal and symbolic representations of their personal home lives. After taking pictures, we ask students to assemble their photographs in books, labeling and designing each page. Next they read one another's books, asking questions and discovering similarities and differences.

Students' conversations about similarities and differences in one another's books model the intent of many curricular literacy and social studies goals that can seem dry and boring when addressed through textbook assignments. Students are enthusiastic about recognizing what they have in common, inquisitive about differences, and tolerant and appreciative of one another's choices, perhaps because they admire the amount of careful work they've all done.

Photographing Home Alphabets

Immersing themselves in scenes from home pushes students to consider the uniqueness and significance of the language they use and hear at home. Students' next assignment is to make a visual home alphabet by photographing 26 home words. Before taking home a camera, we expect students to make written plans for their photography. We ask them to retrieve their brainstormed lists of words. They now need to narrow their long lists and select just one word for each letter of the alphabet.

We suggest that the students carefully choose words that characterize their own families and homes. As Justin planned his pictures, he coded the words on his list with *M*'s and *D*'s to indicate which ones—such as "soccer," "rug," and "mom"—he could shoot at his mother's house and which ones, like "tree house" and "order," at his dad's. Students also need to think carefully about how best to represent or communicate their ideas with pictures—something they've already

Creating a Community Language: Home Alphabet Books

practiced in other LTP assignments. When their selected words are objects such as "TV" and "quilt," the pictures' main subjects will be straightforward. However, we encourage the students to be as specific as possible in their planning. On her A to Z list of home words, Caity noted her intended strategy for taking pictures. Next to "G: Groceries" she wrote, "after my mom comes back from the grocery store," and next to "T: TV," she wrote, "my TV while it is on." Students also need to think creatively about how to represent verbs and adjectives. We remind students they can act out ideas, use props, and create make-believe scenes. Caity's plan for representing "Z: Zany" says, "me jumping up and down, running around." She planned to illustrate the word "warm" with "me sitting near the fire place with my dog."

We give the students point-and-shoot cameras to take home for 3 or 4 days, when possible over a weekend. If you have 14 cameras, for example, you can send them home in two rounds. The shooting then takes 2 weeks to complete. When taking pictures, students bring along their lists, and with checkmarks and highlighting devise a system for tracking their progress. We assure students that they can revise their plans once they are at home and begin to notice objects and settings that will improve their ideas. We also encourage them to invite family members to participate.

Our students make pictures about the things they do at home, such as eat, sleep, dance, dunk, help, jump, wake up, play, hug, yell, and talk. They photograph the rooms they live in and the everyday things around them—a pillow, an umbrella, a lamp. Students portray family members in their pictures of "brother," "mom," and "pet" and the adjectives they associate with their family members and homes—quiet, quick, loving, mad, loud, annoying, and warm.

Whether consciously or not on the part of students, the objects featured in some pictures reference a family's cultural background as well as their values. For "N is for newspaper," Tanaka photographs an edition of the *Wall Street Journal*. For the letter "M" Keinan photographs a photograph of Malcolm X. Mario chooses a large living room banner of the Virgin of Guadalupe to represent "G." Another student represents "O" for order with a photograph of a neatly arranged shelf of Bibles and religious books. Along with family idols and heroes, students' pictures of "basketball," "aquarium," "video games," "TV," and "art" reveal their favorite hobbies. Katharine's pictures of "telescope," "nature cabinet," and "map" highlight her family's interest in exploration, as do the photographs Lillie takes on a family trip to the mountains.

As impressive as the variety of words chosen to represent the people, places, possessions, and activities associated with home, are the

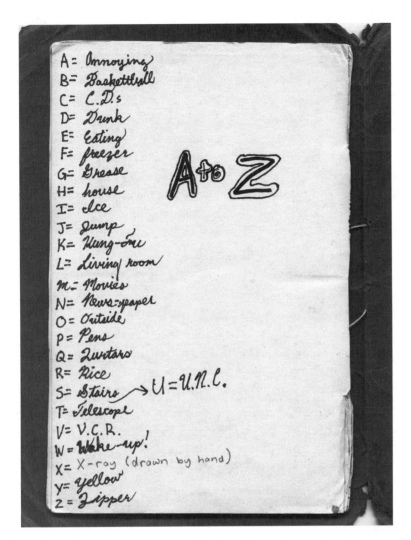

different picture-making styles utilized by students. For instance, students' portrayals of "H for home" range from a drawing of simple houses and trees, to a playhouse, to an actual house—one with two ladder-back chairs resting on the front porch. Some pictures include clever word plays as in Katharine's "U for underdog" photograph that captures her dog underneath the kitchen table.

Students often insert themselves into their pictures, even when their selected words are objects as opposed to verbs or adjectives. In his picture of "tree house," Justin appears mid-air, swinging from a rope attached to a two-story tree house, and in his picture of "videos" he lies on the floor with ten videos covering his chest and arms and a scared look on his face, as though he's been assaulted. In contrast, Chareese's photos don't include any people. She uses her Barbie dolls to set up scenes and activities.

Chareese aside, many students like to turn this project into a family collaboration. If students want to appear in their pictures, they need a helper to operate the camera. They also invite family members or friends to act out the words and scenes they want to photograph. Since Jamond's family had a history of doing LTP projects over the years, his mother and sister are ready to help him set up scenes and role-play various actions and emotions. We see Jamond's mother scolding in a picture of "annoying," another parent hiking in a photograph of "quick," and a father pouting and looking "angry." Other collaborators are seen jumping rope, demonstrating ninja or kung fu moves, and sitting quietly studying a math book. In these photographs, which capture the people, pets, and activities that constitute home life, we also see family as a vital, prominent part of students' lives.

Making Home Alphabet Books

The next activity ties back to our initial look at the classroom's variety of alphabet books. Now we ask the students to make their own alphabet books. This involves three steps: assembling books, labeling and designing the pages, and creating title pages and word indexes. So far students have concentrated on one single letter, word, and image at a time. Now they have to piece together their 26 chosen words and home photographs to make a book that other people can read. This process helps them visualize their work in more complex ways as they consider how others might understand their ideas.

We ask the students to make simple booklets by folding four sheets of paper in half (we use 9 x 12-inch paper). Once each piece of paper is folded in half, there are 16 "pages" to work with. This allows them 13 pages for their 26 photographs (two per page), in addition to three extra pages for writing (a title page, an alphabetized list of all the words, and a poem).

Before attaching any photographs to the book's pages, the students lay out their entire book—placing the pictures in alphabetical order and deciding how two photographs will fit on each page. When they realize that vertical photographs don't fit easily and need to be cropped to fit the page, they have to make their first revision. We also allow the students to crop any photograph if they feel doing so will emphasize the main idea of the image. Jamond cropped the width of two vertical pictures in order to place them side by side on a page. The pictures' tall, narrow shape exaggerates the height of the slender, upright CD rack in the "C for CDs" picture, and Jamond appears taller in his "D for dunk" action shot.

Once students attach their photographs with double-sided tape, they design the rest of the pages. We ask them to include the letter and the word, written on the photograph or on the book margins. Beyond this standard labeling, students can draw in objects and scenery with permanent markers. Extra writing on photographs

Tanaka's "W: Wake Up" and Jamond's "G = games, H = helping," 2002

integrates instructions for the reader (such as sound effects), conversation bubbles for talking pets, and editorial comments. On Alex's "D for dance" picture, he wrote, "Everybody loves me." Sarah's "K" stood for "kids racing," represented by two sisters chasing each other. The sister who's ahead says, "I'm beating you," and the other answers, "not for long." On the same page Sarah added "Vrooom Vrooom" next to a motor bike in a photograph representing "L/loud." Her picture for "M/mouse" on the next page featured Sarah's cat named Mouse asking, "What are you looking at?"

Katharine's "U: under-
dog," 2002

Katharine's "U: under-
dog," 2002

With the understanding that they would share their books with
other readers, the students are motivated to check one another's spelling, use dictionaries, and ask for help. Since they use permanent markers, we emphasize how important it is for them to use care. In spite of
all their efforts to get it right, there are some spelling and handwriting
errors. Yet, even with errors, the pictures themselves help convey the
meaning of the chosen words. One student spelled "journey," *jornei,*
and wrote the letter *J* to look like an *F*. But her meaning is clear; in her
photograph she's standing on a path leading out of the picture. At this
stage of the project, the primary emphasis is on communicating ideas
with photographs, rather than on spelling and writing.

Once students have assembled and labeled each page of pictures,
they design title pages by combining cutouts and lettering, drawing
and pieces of extra photographs. Kara's book is titled "From African
Baskets to Zig-Zag," and "Z" is represented by a photograph of six
pairs of alternating black-and-white shoes arranged in zig-zag fashion. In the center of Trevan's book cover is a picture of three brothers
standing in a line from shortest to tallest. Underneath, Trevan added
a credit line for his collaborators: "Help by: family and friends."

Reading Alphabet Books and
Writing Reflections on an Alphabet Word

Working side by side in the classroom as they assemble their home
alphabet books, the students share their photographs with one another, ask questions, and draw conclusions. Even when students
work on their personal alphabet books, the classroom is noisy with
students' comments and enthusiasm regarding their friends' work.
Now they have the chance to read even more deliberately their own
and classmates' final sequence of alphabet images. As always, the
process of reading photographs requires paying close attention to

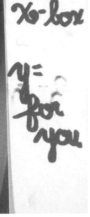

details. Working in small groups, students affirm the ideas behind a classmate's photograph by noticing relevant details in the pictures. They quiz one another by asking classmates to explain their interpretations of pictures with identifiable details.

We ask students as they share their books to consider how their words and pictures, taken together, create new or different meanings. There are endless questions, such as: What is that? Why did you show that part? We pose even more questions: Do you hear these words at home? Whom could you interview to collect other ideas and stories attached to these words? What are the concrete versus abstract words in the list?

For a closing writing assignment we ask the students to write a poem, rhyme, or rap related to a word and inspired by the matching images in the alphabet books. The students can decide whether they want to write about one image or a series of images. We ask them to add their poem to the last remaining page in their books.

The sequence of events in Jamond's poem reflects the scenes he portrays in his images. In his self-portrait "J for Jamond" we see Jamond in a basketball jersey, "heading down the court," in this case the sidewalk

Katharine's "A: angry," Tanaka's "K: Kung Fu," and Jamond's "Q = quiet" and "Y = for you," 2002

Jamond's A, B, C, D book
pages, 2002

Katharine's title page and
index for her alphabet
book, 2002

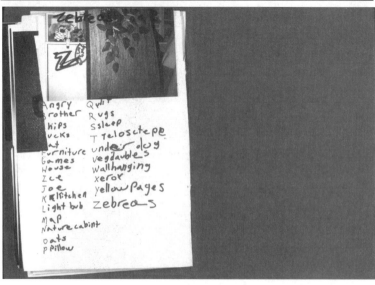

in his neighborhood. The preceding image, with its trophies, awards, and NBA gear, is named for a favorite NBA star "I/Iverson" and symbolizes the glory of hitting the game's winning shot at the buzzer.

B IS FOR BASKETBALL
I got the rock
I'm
  bringing
    it
      down
so you better watch the clock
I'm scoring any
second now
dude trying to trap
me but it don't
really matter cause
today thats not happening
yo your shot is blocked
that's a rejection
the balls headed in
my direction
go down the court
make a shot
and I hit one
while I'm hot my
man's cold so I
still the ball
and head down the court
down by one one
second left the
buzer rings the
shot is in the hole

AFTER SHARING THEIR HOME ALPHABET BOOKS with one another, students plan and create a second visual alphabet. This time they will collaborate in making a single home alphabet that integrates everyone's individual ideas about home language and imagery. In this part of the project students also will have the opportunity to present their collaborative home alphabet to a public audience. The final outcome will be a school-based exhibition of photography and writing about home. Each student curates and designs a poster for the exhibition. In curating this exhibition, students are challenged to look at and weave together diverse representations of home. Having students negotiate the selection of words for each part of the alphabet and then produce a variety of images to represent each word demonstrates how language continually evolves.

Creating Public Portraits of Home

Selecting Words and Shooting Photographs for a Collaborative Home Alphabet

The first step in creating a collaborative visual alphabet is to come up with a new list of alphabetized words. We divide the class into six groups (four students per group) and assign each group part of the alphabet—*A* through *D*; *E* through *H*; *I* through *L,* and so on. We ask each group to choose one word for every assigned letter. As kids work within their groups to brainstorm words for their assigned letters, they consult their individual home alphabet books for ideas. They discuss and debate their favorite possibilities considering the words they've seen in one another's books, as well as entirely new words.

Jamond's I and J book page, 2002

Some groups choose words by recognizing things they have in common—annoying big sisters, love of basketball. Others gravitate toward words they've seen pictured in distinct ways. For example, one group noticed how Sarah's photograph of a small TV hidden within a packed bookshelf contrasted with a picture of Anthony standing next to a TV set taller than him. Looking back at their individual alphabet books fuels students' curiosity about where their classmates live and what their rooms and animals, and so on, look like. Once each group settles upon on a single word for each of their four or five letters, we use a class chart to record the alphabetical list of home words: "annoying," "basketball," "CDs," "dunk," "eating," "furniture," "games," "home," "ice," "jump," "kisses," "loving," "mad," "night," "order," "pets," "quarters," "rugs," "sisters" "TV," "unique," "VCR," "warm," "xtra special," "yogurt," and "zany."

We ask the students to take the cameras home for a second time. This time instead of shooting pictures of all 26 words in the collaborative alphabet, the students photograph only the four or five words chosen by their group. For instance, the *M* through *P* group would make pictures about "mad," "night," "order," and "pets." The result would be representations of these four words made in four students' homes.

Curating and Designing Posters
for a Classroom Exhibition

The next activity involves curating posters for an exhibition featuring students' collective ideas and representations of home. The exhibit will consist of 26 posters, each poster displaying photographs and writing pertaining to one letter/word within the collaborative alphabet. Each poster has one student curator/designer. To begin, each group decides which member will curate and then design the poster for each of the group's assigned letters. On the class chart we record a student's name next to each word. For example, our 2002 chart indicated that Justin would be responsible for curating and designing the "P/pets" poster. (When the class size is less than 26, it's necessary to ask a few students to curate two posters; when the class size exceeds 26, two students can work together on some of the posters.)

Each student curator/designer begins by collecting fellow group members' photographs pertaining to their word. For instance, Justin gathered four pictures of pets, including his own picture. Curators also have the option to include the photographs they've seen in classmates' individual alphabet books. (We make sure duplicate prints from the students' individual alphabet pictures are available for the posters.) Since students have spent time reading and responding to one another's individual work, they are already quite familiar with classmates' pictures. Justin remembers seeing many photographs of pets in his classmates' work. It doesn't matter that the photograph of Sarah's cat appears on the *M* page of Sarah's book (her cat's name is Mouse) or that Katharine's dog is featured in the "U for underdog" photograph. Any of these pet pictures can be incorporated into Justin's "P for pets" poster. Having many materials (new photographs and old ones) makes the process more complex and creative.

Students' curatorial work involves thoughtful organizing and decision making. Once they've gathered all relevant images, the student curators decide which images to include, how many to include, and whether to crop any of the photographs. We ask them to carefully study the array of pictures. Our students recognize some redundancy—for

Alix's "M: Mad" poster, 2002

instance, there is only one pet picture that doesn't feature a cat or dog. Yet, they notice that other words are captured with unexpected variety—students' photographs of basketball include both action shots and still lifes; some pictures reference professional stars, and others favorite college teams. Likewise, their photographs of CDs range from a close-up of five favorite CD covers to an entire wall of neatly arranged record albums to a Discman resting on a checkered tablecloth.

On her "M for mad" poster Alix included only three photographs but chose them well—each picture is a unique representation of the word "mad." In one picture we see Katharine's father's contorted face (his expression could be interpreted as angry or crazy), while another shows a different student's father reading *MAD Magazine*. The third photograph shows two brothers arguing.

Each student works as both a curator and a designer. Poster design entails arranging pictures on the poster board (the posters themselves can be oriented vertically or horizontally), labeling the posters with drawing and writing that tie together the images, and writing. The posters' written elements include a poem, a definition, and a sample sentence using the featured word. We ask students not to write a typical dictionary definition but an explanation of the meaning of the word as the student understands it.

Jamond was responsible for curating the "B for basketball" poster, on which he featured the pictures seen above from his individual booklet, and this definition:

Definition:
Basketball is a very popular sport. You play it with a orange ball with black stripes. It's a team sport. You're trying to get the ball in the basket but watch out there are people trying to get the ball and score. There are different positions point guard, shooting guard, small forward, power forward, center. You can play it indoor and outdoor. It can be 12 or 13 people on a team.

Sentence: Ya'll ready to play some basketball.

In contrast with the sparse arrangement of pictures on Alix's "M for mad" poster, over a dozen photographs dominated Justin's "Pet" poster. While his orderly arrangement of 12 horizontal pictures into a grid (three columns and four rows) might imply that pet ownership is common or regular, Justin's poem emphasizes what makes pets special.

PETS
Stroking my cat
makes me and her
feel great.
The way she
sticks up her
tail and raises
her back in
appreciation.
The way she
snuggles up
next to me and
stays there
until I move.
She comforts me
My cat is a
great friend, to
me she seems
to know my
feelings.
All cats can
be like this
if you want them
to be.

In designing the "E for eating" poster Mario effectively shows how a single word or idea can be represented visually in a number of ways. In the top half of the poster, we see signed pictures of classmates eating in different contexts—Alix leans against a car as she munches on a snack; Justin shares an evening meal on the back porch with his brother and father; Neil, looking hungry and ready to eat, waits at the table with a tight grip on his fork and knife. On the bottom half of his poster, Mario cut the edges of photographs to isolate specific foods and dishes—a tiny box of gelatin, a pan of eggs, a plate full of pasta and vegetables, juice and junk food on a countertop. Mario's sample sentence says, "I eat at lunch, dinner, and dessert. I eat night and day."

Kara and Sarah worked together to design the poster for "U for unique." Each of their poster's eight photographs are cropped and placed on top of bright construction paper cut into a different shape such as a star, a heart, and a flower. Sarah's poem springs directly from their selection of photographs.

UNIQUE
A pig sitting on a table
wearing sunglasses and lipstick,
A pair of one-of-a kind
green sunglasses in the
newly cut grass,
A very weird double
jointed thumb on your sisters
hand,
A plant that dies one day,
and comes alive the next.
Those are all *Unique*.
Unique is a word unlike another
it's the word that means different.

Sarah's poem reminds us that the *American Alphabets* project is about language itself, as well as respecting differences and seeing connections.

Installing and Sharing the Collaborative Exhibition

As they receive feedback from their classmates, students appreciate the need to make the work coherent to others. They take the time to step back to "read" each poster and the entire exhibit before presenting it to the public. Students consider the individual voices of each poster's curator/designer, respond to the multiple photographs represented on each poster, and appreciate all the decision making. They hope to foster with the viewers the same kinds of conversations they've had with one another during the book-making process. Our students want viewers to be surprised by the variety and the similarity of images from different homes and to appreciate all the decisions students made in creating *Annoying to Zany: A Class Alphabet About Our Lives at Home*.

When we are ready to present the *Annoying to Zany* alphabet to a larger audience, we find a space large enough to display 26 posters on a wall just inside the entrance to our school. Students measure the space to determine how to arrange the posters, make a title poster for the whole show, and work to neatly attach the posters to the wall. Later, we ask the students to take turns being "tour guides" to help one another view the whole show. Many students comment on how hard they worked and how pleased they are with the final products. They also mention the unity of the class as they work together and discover similarities in their images related to their home language. They are effusive in their compliments about one another's photographs.

While reviewing their finished work, we ask students to jot down the alphabet one last time and write reflections about the posters from A to Z. This final writing activity gives students another opportunity to think about language and visual representations of home. Looking again encourages students to see details they may have missed before. For instance, next to "R for rugs," a student wrote, "designs, diamonds, shapes, colorful." Students highlight their personal favorites with comments like, "I like how he drew a basketball"; "I like how he cut out the pictures [in "E for eat"]"; "I like the double jointed thumb"; or "I like the design with me in the basketball." This closing activity requires students to think about the meanings implied within the home scenes. For instance, next to "F for furniture," a student writes, "Some furniture has plastic to keep it from getting dirty." Looking again encouraged students to think and write about the words themselves—next to "N for night" students write: "Night falls after day" and "Night is darkness. Bedtime." The exercise brought to mind personal associations with words: Next to "A for annoying" were comments like, "Lots of little people are annoying" and "Annoying is just like my little brother." Finally, in reviewing their work students make interesting comparisons between different posters—"I noticed that the pets poster has the most pictures"—and within individual posters—"It's unique, nothing looks the same, every [picture's] background is different" or "Some houses are new, old, big, small."

A few students comment on the exhibition as a whole. Sarah writes, "I noticed that if we put all of our posters together it will give our class's personality." Malikah observes that "our work showed our own thinking about a certain topic." Kara writes, "We all can and do all sorts of things. We all have certain things, like houses. They're lots of unique things about us. Everyone in the whole entire class could take a picture of at least four of these things. Lots of people in our class have at least one pet."

We invite the rest of our school to participate in our discussion about words and photographs that represent home. The exhibit stays on display for several weeks, and we notice there are almost always children and adults examining the photographs very closely and reading the students' writing. During the weeks of the exhibit no one asks, "Why study the alphabet in 4th and 5th grade?" Observers can see the importance of the students' work: letters as building blocks of words; words as suggestions of a variety of images; words combined to make sentences and poems expressing feelings and ideas about *home*. Observers appreciate the similarities and differences in images chosen by class photographers.

Lisa Lord
A Teacher's Reflection

WHEN I WALKED DOWN A STREET in Athens, Greece, and saw print on a street sign, I couldn't read a word. I wasn't completely certain the sign wasn't upside down. I enjoyed a restaurant meal more when I pointed to a fish in a cooler instead of a word on a menu. When I taught in South Carolina a sea island student asked, "We cuss up K yet?" I answered, "Huh?" I needed repetition and elaboration before I knew she was asking whether I had shown her how to write the letter *K* in cursive yet. Those are obvious lessons in the importance of understanding language.

Working with students on the *American Alphabets* project reminded me of the many times we think we understand one another's language, when in fact we would benefit from pointing out an object or asking for repetition and clarification. We would communicate better if we didn't assume we pictured the same idea as someone else.

In our class A is not for "apple," or for "aardvark." In our culture, for the sake of teaching the letters of the alphabet to preschoolers, we buy toys and books filled with pictures and words to go with each letter. For older children, thousands of so-called alphabet books are in print, displaying a variety of insects, reptiles, sights to see, foods to eat, facts about states, poetry terms, and so forth. My 4th- and 5th-graders already know the alphabet and lots of words that begin with each letter when they enter my classroom.

My question was, could my students study the alphabet in a new, personal way that would engage their curiosity and imaginations and build writing skills and vocabulary? Would the words chosen reflect the diversity of the classroom? Would different definitions of family emerge? Would choosing words and planning images prompt us to appreciate our common language and how we understand one another?

As teachers, we should do the *American Alphabets* project as a celebration of the language we share in the classroom. We also should do this project as a celebration of the language that sounds the same when we read and speak it but conjures different ideas and meanings, depending on our varied experiences. We need to set and develop a stage for students to recognize their similarities and to comfortably ask for clarification and explanation about differences—to realize they aren't necessarily thinking the same things when they use the same words.

And we should do this project for the sake of the processes that are involved. In *American Alphabets*, students examine lots of letters, words, and images. They make innumerable decisions, often negotiating choices of words and images, not to mention photographic choices about framing, point of view, symbols, and timing. Other classmates and audience members, too, question and elaborate on layers of meanings and their significance.

Perhaps it takes a lifetime of practice to gain the habit of thinking that we might not understand another person or a situation as well as we think we do—continual practice to not jump to conclusions and lock into our own understanding of a word or an image. The *American Alphabets* project helped me open my mind. As a teacher I realized, "Oh, yeah, this is their alphabet, not mine. This is kid language, not teacher talk." Once again, my understanding was prodded and grew in just the way that I wished for—to help me to remember not to assume I understand. A is for "appreciation" of the power of language. Once my eyes were opened, I rejoiced in the theme of Tanaka's pieces that celebrate individuality among kids and music—they don't all like the same CDs! I breathed a sigh of relief in the tenderness of Justin's poem about his cat, a recognition that some things don't change. As teachers we can enjoy our students' self-expression; we can learn about their culture with as much enthusiasm as we would give to learning about a more obviously "foreign" culture.

STUDENTS' ALPHABETIZED LISTS of home words are peppered with misspellings: Kichin. Grocries. Friendlieness. Qwelt. Medatation. Loveing. Inoying sister. Yet, there is no shortage of wisdom, not to mention warmth, behind the word choices. These 4th- and 5th-graders fashion a knowing portrait of home as a place and a concept. This wouldn't have been possible without the chance to carry cameras into the distinctive worlds of their respective lives. Giving students the opportunity to take cameras home with them, which is crucial in this project, is admittedly complicated since the range of possible subject matter multiplies—some students have unhappy and unsafe home lives, and pictures sometimes expose differences related to class, culture, and family composition. But again and again, we've seen students cherish this kind of freedom and handle the responsibility well.

Katie Hyde
Through a Sociologist's Lens

It is likely that students have already noticed what their classmates are wearing and picked up on what their friends' parents "do" and where (and whether) families vacation, but they haven't been privy to the kind of details that appear in the photographs made in the course of this project, like the posters on classmates' bedroom walls or their pets' favorite place to sleep. Our students took pride in sharing pictures of "x-tra special" toys and belongings, the artwork above the mantel, the content of their bookshelves, and the front steps of their home. They took pride in their families and the love they have for them.

For years my Literacy Through Photography colleagues and I have treasured and continued to talk about a remarkable piece made in a 4th-grade, community-themed LTP assignment. To accompany his photograph of street graffiti in front of a boarded-up house and littered yard, Sherman wrote a poem that begins, "Names spray painted on the street/Bottles crashing on the ground, scaring you every time/People filled with fright every time there is a fight/Even though you hear people shooting, you still hear people hooting/But everything in my community is not bad." He goes on to catalog the neighborhood's special qualities—the pretty houses, a big tree, the shop owner at his favorite store across the street. After naming each person in his family, Sherman concludes, "They are the part of my community I love the most. So don't judge my community by first sight. My community is all right. If you lived in my community, you'd understand."

Sherman's words are a poignant and pointed reminder of the complexity of photographs and the difference between insiders' and outsiders' points of view. These are two vital concepts that all the projects in this book hit upon. Sherman's poem, like all the examples presented here, speaks to the value in allowing young people to frame and showcase their world as they see it. With encouragement from his teacher, who was humbled by his insightful grasp of the politics of representation, Sherman shared his work with the local paper in response to their one-sided, unfavorable portrayal of his neighborhood. Within the right framework—careful parameters for a respectful, open-minded, and inquisitive reading of one another's pictures and words—students' portrayals of mundane and idiosyncratic objects and moments allow them to teach and learn from one another. Teachers have just as much, if not more, to learn about what is important to students and how they see their lives. During the *American Alphabets* project described in this chapter, Lisa provided students a frame inside which they placed one home alphabet picture to give to their family. Seeing their careful choices—such as

Keinan's picture of framed family photos—was like peeking at an intimate visual letter from the student to his or her loved ones.

Apart from the visual and emotional depth of students' *American Alphabets* work, another appeal of the project is its versatility. The alphabet can be used as an organizational framework to plunge into an in-depth consideration of virtually any topic, whether a specific theme like "home" or a broad area of the curricula, such as American history or science. Reminiscent of the beautiful illustrations in Lisa's extensive set of alphabet books, I hold in my mind a collection of word-inspired images made for a variety of visual alphabets by teachers and students in the United States as well as in Tanzania. A 4th-grade student smiled while posing as Abraham Lincoln in an American history alphabet, and one of my college students showed her Indian passport to represent "immigration" in another alphabet about America. Teachers in Tanzania acted out scenes to represent the "Maji Maji rebellion" in a history alphabet, "illiteracy" and "pain" in a gender alphabet, and "protection" and "counseling" in an HIV alphabet. An environment alphabet made by American middle school students included pictures of "waste," "mechanical weathering," and "outer space," while Tanzanian high school students made an entire alphabet about homeostasis, featuring words like "hibernation."

In addition to the critical and creative thinking involved in making still pictures to represent abstract ideas or intangible nouns—such as "order," "questions," "journey," and "undoing"—another exciting feature of the *American Alphabets* project is the opportunity to discover entirely new meanings, surprises, and questions as a final alphabet, combining the visions of an entire class, appears. Students can and should study the synergy of the 26 words strung together in a collaborative alphabet (or the hundreds of words included in a class set of individual alphabet books). Together, students can investigate vocabulary, parts of speech, the sound and the visual rhythm in the sequence of words. They can think about what words are missing and which ones are culturally specific, and compare the visual and written communication of words and ideas. They can imagine how the alphabet might have looked different in the past or might look different in the future, and in doing so think about the ways in which they have been framing language through the use of symbols to stand for abstract concepts. Even after working on this project for months, students will have plenty to see and discover and say when considering their work as a whole.

Lesson Plans | *American Alphabets*

Word Lists for Three Different Alphabets

TIME NEEDED: 1 HOUR

1. Share a variety of alphabet books. Let your students know they will be making their own alphabet books in the future.
2. Have your students make three alphabetical lists—words they consider to be important school words, words related to their homes, and words they know but never use. Looking at all three word lists, help your students see three different "languages" they know, in addition to other languages they are learning, such as Spanish, French, and Hebrew.
3. Your students can further explore their alphabets/languages by asking such questions as: What are the similarities and differences among the words on my three lists? What words are missing? Which words are concrete and which ones abstract? Which words are nouns, verbs, and adjectives?

Exploring One Alphabet: Writing About Home

TIME NEEDED: 2 HOURS

1. Read excerpts from literature that present at-home, family conversations related to food. Discuss what mealtime conversations are like in each home.
2. Ask students to write dialogue related to mealtime that might occur in their home, using words from their home alphabet lists if possible. Ask volunteers to read portions of the dialogues they have written.
3. Begin a mini-lesson with some poems that include mealtime images and family themes, such as "My Own Man" by Nikki Grimes and "Mi Mamá Cubana" by Mimi Chapra.
4. Ask students to re-read the dialogues they have written and incorporate some of the dialogue in a poem about their home. These poems will be published in their individual alphabet books and perhaps the collaborative home alphabet.

Photographing Home Alphabets

TIME NEEDED: HALF AN HOUR IN CLASS (IF STUDENTS HAVE EXPERIENCE WITH USING CAMERAS AND PLANNING PHOTOGRAPHS; 90 MINUTES, IF NOT); 1 WEEK OUTSIDE OF CLASS

1. Distribute cameras. Each student should place a piece of masking tape on the camera and label it with his or her name.
2. Ask each student to make one photograph to represent each of the 26 words on his or her original list of home words. Ask students to keep notes of the photographs they make. Having the cameras over the weekend is helpful to many families.
3. Download the pictures from each camera. Using the USB cable provided with the camera, connect the camera to the computer. When using a Mac computer, iPhoto will open automatically. Click on "import all." Once images are imported, create a new folder (either within iPhoto, or on the computer's desktop or hard drive). Name the folder with the appropriate student's name. Copy all the images into the folder, by highlighting the images and then dragging them into the folder. Make a backup of each student's folder on a DVD, flash drive, or external hard drive.

Making Home Alphabet Books

TIME NEEDED: 2 HOURS

1. Have students make a booklet for their home alphabet photographs using cardstock or construction paper (9 x 12-inch, 4 sheets per student). Students may stitch, staple, use comb-binding machines, or punch holes and use brads in order to make a book.

2. Give students double-sided tape to affix the prints to the pages of the book. Allow students to use ordinary scissors as well as ones with patterned edges to crop the photographs—something that is necessary for vertical photographs, and desirable when the students want to increase the emphasis on certain components of their photographs. Students also may use permanent markers to accentuate and alter images.

3. Require everyone to write the letter and its associated word on or near each photograph in the book. Ask students to complete their books by including their completed poem, a list of all 26 words in the book, and a title page.

Reading Alphabet Books
and Writing Reflections on an Alphabet Word

TIME NEEDED: 1 HOUR

1. Ask your students to work in pairs, with partners exchanging their alphabet books. Consider posing specific questions for your students to think about as they read their partners' alphabet photographs. For example:

    What are your favorite and least favorite words within the alphabet?
    What words are difficult to understand?
    Are there words in this alphabet you wish did not exist?
    What are the concrete versus abstract words in the list?
    Are there similarities and differences among the words?
    What sentences would you write using these words?
    Do you notice a visual rhythm among the words?
    Do these words belong to any particular group of people or culture?
    Do you use or hear these words at home?
    What words are missing? What stories are not told?

2. Inspired by these photographs, the student should prepare three pieces of writing: a poem, rhyme, or rap inspired by the photographs; a definition of the word composed in the student's own words; and a sentence demonstrating the use of the word.

Selecting Words and Shooting Photographs
or a Collaborative Home Alphabet

TIME NEEDED: 1 HOUR IN CLASS AND 1 WEEK OUTSIDE OF CLASS

1. Assemble students in small groups and assign each group four or five different letters of the alphabet. Ask the students, by referring to their individual home alphabet lists for ideas, to agree on one "home" word for each of the letters the group is assigned. Record the words chosen by each group on chart paper to make a class home alphabet list.

2. Redistribute the point-and-shoot cameras. Ask your students to make photographs representing each of the words their group agreed on. (Students should make about three photographs representing each of their group's words.) This process will result in about 12 photographs of each of the words photographed in different homes).

Curating and Designing Posters for a Classroom Exhibition

TIME NEEDED: 3 HOURS

1. Use the class's home alphabet chart as the starting point for making an exhibit of 26 collective posters. Working in small groups, ask each student to claim the one word that he or she will be responsible for curating and designing. Give each student a standard-sized piece of poster board for exhibiting the images and writing and his or her set of collaborative alphabet prints. Ask students to write their names on the back of the photographs and to give them to the person responsible for exhibiting the word shown in the photograph.
2. Select and gather writings to be included (the poem written for the assigned word, the definition, and the sample sentence).
3. As a group, develop a model of how the posters will be organized. For example, our students oriented their posters vertically and marked off a 6-inch strip at the bottom for writing the assigned letter in upper- and lowercase and the chosen word; they used the upper part for displaying photographs, a poem, the definition of the word, and a sample sentence using the word. Students give credit to their fellow photographers by indicating on their posters who made each picture.

Installing and Sharing the Collaborative Exhibition

TIME NEEDED: 2 HOURS

1. Divide students into three volunteer groups. Ask one group to write a letter to the school principal to gain permission to install the exhibit in a prominent place in the school. Ask the second group to write an exhibition introduction, which will be displayed along with the posters, and to give the exhibit a title. Our title was *Annoying to Zany: A Class Alphabet About Our Lives at Home*. Ask the third group to arrange the 26 posters in the exhibit area, using measuring tape for spacing, and Velcro tape to secure the posters well.
2. Take the class to see their own work. For about 20 minutes have half the class serve as tour guides for their own poster and one other student's poster, and have the other half of the class tour all the posters, taking notes on their clipboards about what they notice. "Tour guides" prompt "viewers" to look closely at their work and answer questions. Students switch tourist and tour guide roles for another 20-minute session of examining one another's work. Back in class, ask students to write silently about the exhibit and what they've learned about one another.
3. Students, teachers, and parents from the entire school community view the exhibit as they walk along the hallway, and they can be invited more formally to celebrate the opening of the exhibit. Students may invite the members of another class to a guided tour of the exhibit and may share their personal alphabet books with other students.

FOUR | Memories from Past Centuries

Performing History, Thinking About Everyday Choices

THE *MEMORIES FROM PAST CENTURIES* PROJECT begins with a careful study of archival photographs and case histories of children who survived the Holocaust. After learning background information and discussing the context of the images and histories, each student is asked to select a photograph of a child survivor and then write about him or her from various points of view—as the child, a witness, a Nazi soldier. As the project progresses, students develop attachments to "their" children and their circumstances, while also making connections between events and individuals' beliefs and behaviors during World War II and those of the present. After writing from the perspective of Holocaust survivors, witnesses, and Nazis, students speak and act out these roles—pretending to *be* someone who lived during this time. The students make videos of one another's performances, and finally students collaborate in groups to incorporate their writings and video clips into finished art pieces. The *Memories from Past Centuries* project entails authentic and meaningful writing, reading, research, and social studies lessons. At each stage of the project, the students' work is about understanding and empathy.

Students also feel empowered to make a statement. In *Memories from Past Centuries*, students recognize the cruelty and weakness of people who follow the crowd and refuse to speak out against injustice or evil. The morals in students' stories often concern making choices and are thus relevant to kids' everyday lives at home and at school. By extending lessons beyond the particulars of one historical time period, students learn something about bullying, peer pressure, and intolerance of many kinds. Likewise, there are wider messages in this project about the meaning of active citizenship, freedom, compassion, and responsibility. The students' stories are often about critical moments and turning points; they point to the truth that the decisions they make, that we all make, *matter*. Appropriately, the final part of *Memories from Past Centuries* is all about choices—choices students make together in creating a finished piece of art, a multimedia movie.

Wendy Ewald
An Artist's Frame

IN 1998 I WAS COMMISSIONED by curators Marvin Heiferman and Carole Kismaric to produce a new work for the group exhibition *To the Rescue: Seven Artists in an Archive,* which opened at the International Center of Photography in New York. The artists were two photographers, a video maker, two painters, and three installation artists. Each of us was asked to use the American Jewish Joint Distribution Committee (JDC) archive as a starting point.

The JDC is the world's leading Jewish humanitarian assistance organization and was created during World War I to send aid to

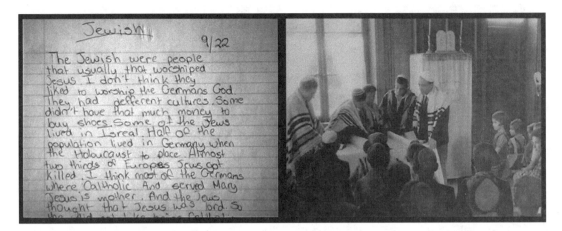

the suffering Jews of Palestine and Eastern Europe. Today, the JDC works in more than 70 countries and in Israel to alleviate hunger and hardship, rescue Jews in danger, create lasting connections to Jewish life, and provide immediate relief and long-term development support for victims of natural and man-made disasters. The JDC Archives contains photographs, documents, films, and videos, many dating back to World War I.

The archive's general aim is to document how a Jewish community takes care of itself. The curators believed that our work could create a dialogue about the JDC's efforts as well as the role of art in communicating humanitarian values and creating a socially concerned voice. (For more information about the JDC, see the resource list in this book or visit the JDC online at www.jdc.org.)

I felt that the archive demonstrated, first of all, our responsibility to one another. And since it was the archive of an organization that has reached out to people displaced by war and persecuted for their religious, political, or social convictions, I decided to pose questions that would help me understand how we see one another: how we look different, and how we look the same—how we *are* different, and how we *are* the same.

I began looking for photographs that would resonate with the elementary and middle school students I'd be working with. Two other teachers in the Durham Public Schools, Lisa Lord and Robert Hunter, worked with me from the outset of the project. The students, I assumed, had little or no knowledge of what had happened to the Jews. I selected photographs taken during World War II of children who had survived the Holocaust. It was startling to see that many of the kids in those pictures were smiling. Then I realized that the photographer *had* to make the children appealing so people would want to care for them now that they were homeless and, in many cases, without families. But the pictures themselves didn't provide

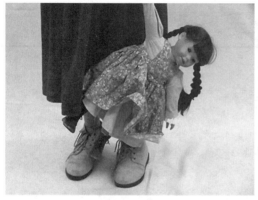 

Video still from *Memories from the Past Centuries* with JDC photograph and Grace Ann's doll, 1998

enough information about the children's experiences. Fortunately, there were case histories attached to the photographs—stories to fill in the blanks.

My concern was to help my 5th- and 8th-grade collaborators make some part of World War II real for themselves. I hit on the idea of matching the students with their historical counterparts—I gave each student a photograph and case history of a Jewish child of the same gender and roughly the same age. Some of the students started to swap the pictures among themselves. What evolved was a recognition of the striking similarities between the students and the children whose likenesses and stories they would take on.

But first I wanted to ascertain just how much the children knew about the war. It wasn't clear how much, if anything at all, they'd learned from their families and their communities, or from books or movies. The situation provided lots of room for imagination, so I asked the students to write about what they knew about Jews and Nazis. Indeed, they knew virtually nothing. One of the students thought Nazis were American Indians, another believed that Catholics were Jews. What part of our history was being lost? How might an archive be used to counter that loss?

I showed the students a picture of a little boy, Sacha S. (a pseudonym), in his concentration camp clothes. They laughed; one said, "He's got big ears." Then, very slowly, I read them Sacha's case history. They listened in complete silence.

> On their arrival at a concentration camp, Jews were separated into two lines: one for those who were going to be exterminated, the other for people designated for hard labor. Sacha's parents were put in the line for hard labor. Sacha, who was two-and-a-half years old at the time, was shunted toward the extermination line. His father picked up a sack, grabbed the boy, stuffed him in the sack, and whispered, "Don't be afraid." Mother, father, and son survived the war.

I gave each student a photograph and a case history. I asked them to read through the histories and look for words they didn't know. Their vocabulary expanded to include words like *tragedy* and *extinction*.

I asked the students to write about the child in their picture in the first person, as if they were writing about themselves. They also were asked to write two more pieces: one as if they were a witness to their child's experience, and another as if their parents were Nazi sympathizers. I wanted them to consider the historical sweep of the situation. I felt if I asked the kids to imagine just one part of the story, the project would be incomplete as an artwork and as a learning experience.

The students were passionate about learning more about their children. They wanted to know what the war was like for the person whose picture they held in their hands. They were studying a history of persecution, crimes, and injustice—things they encountered in their own lives, today. They were absorbing history by rooting it in the personal. It is hard to imagine them learning about it in a way that would have more meaning.

The children in the photographs had no power to change their situations. Many of the kids looking at these archival images were African Americans who had less power than other kids in this country. I wanted to clarify these power relationships. It seemed to me that I needed to make an installation that would place these students and the children they were portraying in the same room at the same time. The way to do this, I decided, was to make a two-screen video installation that involved them both.

Each student and I picked one piece of the student's writings to dramatize. I tried to balance it between the three types of voices (the voice of the student, of the child in the picture, and of the Nazi-sympathizer parents). The students memorized their pieces and practiced their delivery. Some parents told me that their children practiced at home in secret.

My cameraman husband and I constructed a simple set with different-colored backdrops that could be changed with each performance. The students brought props and costumes. Grace Ann portrayed Ita K. holding a doll, which she imagined that Ita had tried to keep with her. Grace Ann brought her own doll, and we filmed her dialogue focused solely on the doll dangling at her side.

Many of the children tried to dress in the same way as their historical partner. Patrick wore a blue-and-white striped polo shirt to mirror the concentration camp uniform of Sacha S. As soon as I began editing the video, I could see Sacha's portrait on one screen and the image of Patrick on the other, holding the picture of Sacha. The connection between the boys was clear. Patrick delivered a performance

For more information about the American Jewish Joint Distribution Committee (JDC), see the Recommended Websites section in the References and Additional Classroom Resources for Teachers and Students or visit the JDC online at ww.jdc.org.

Patrick viewing his *Memories from the Past Centuries* video performance, 1998

Jessie's rap, "Holocaust," 1998

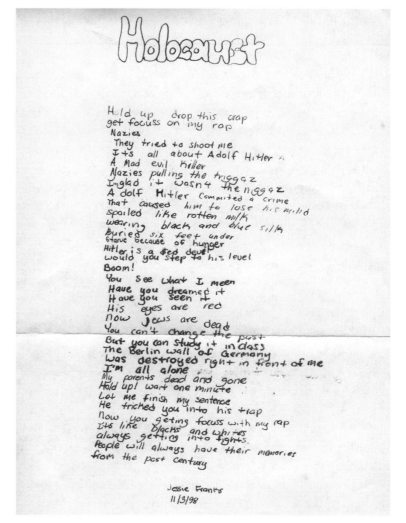

that conveyed a remarkable echo of Sacha's horrific experiences, as well as the injustices he had experienced in his own life.

Sean, one of the 8th-graders, performed his Nazi piece in front of a fire-red cloth with his hands and legs spread apart, wearing a Yankee cap. In the editing room, with historical photos of Nazis on one screen and Sean's performance on the other, I could see the similarity between the Nazi symbol and the lettering on the ball cap.

One of the African American students, Jessie, had a hard time getting into the project. At last he wrote a rap about Hitler "a mad evil killer" as well as "fights between blacks and whites." His rap closes with the line "People will always have their *memories from the past century,*" which inspired the name for this project about the Holocaust. Jessie was too shy to deliver the rap so Sean, one of the other students, performed it for him. I used Sean's voice over drawings made by other students and photographs of the Holocaust from the archive.

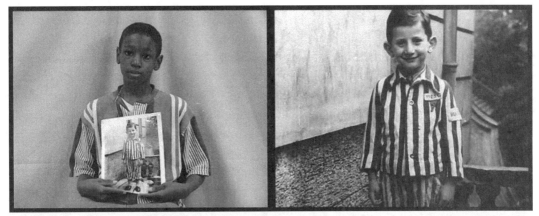

In the edited video, the students were introduced by their own names and the names of the Jewish children they were portraying. They spoke to the camera in the persona of the child in the JDC photograph. The editing stressed two contrapuntal ideas: one, the student's performance side-by-side with the image of his or her Jewish counterpart; and two, the writings of the students *before* they'd studied the war alongside photos from the archive—illustrating a poignant and somewhat eerie tension between imagined history and historical reality.

Naturally, I was nervous about taking on the stories of victims, perpetrators, and witnesses so directly in a public video about the Holocaust. At the initial screening of *Memories from the Past Centuries* for the JDC, I took a seat, trembling, next to Marshall Weinberg, the JDC's liaison for the project. The lights went up. Marshall hugged me and said he loved it.

Lisa Lord and Robert Hunter raised money to bring their students to New York to see the exhibition at the International Center of Photography and to visit the Holocaust Museum in Washington, DC. Parents talked about how important the project had been to their children and how they considered it something that was their own. As for the students, they wondered what became of their "children" after the war.

Video still from *Memories from the Past Centuries* with Patrick and JDC photograph of Sacha S., 1998

Video still from *Memories from the Past Centuries* with Crystal and JDC photograph of Essie Z., 1998

It happened that Sacha S., now living on Manhattan's Upper East Side after early retirement from AT&T, came across a story about the exhibition in the *New York Daily News* and got in touch with Marshall Weinberg. Sacha had never talked with his own children about the war. After seeing the installation and the images of himself as a child, the memories started coming back. "Time doesn't mean anything," he said. "To this day I can't be in the dark."

Setting the Stage

THE FIRST PART of the *Memories from Past Centuries* project involves four background activities that set the stage for students' own creative work. First, we delve into students' preconceptions about Jews. Realizing that students' knowledge of the Holocaust, and even Judaism, varies widely, we want students to have a chance to write down and then talk about what they think they know about Jews. They record their preliminary thoughts in personal diaries, which we introduce as a means of personal reflection and exploration. Students return to their diaries throughout the *Memories from Past Centuries* project. Second, we briefly introduce students to a website about Anne Frank's diary in order to expose them to the history of the Holocaust and to introduce them to the power of sharing personal stories through print and the web. Third, students have the opportunity to investigate primary historical documents to learn about Jewish children who were rescued during the Holocaust. Each student comes to know the circumstances of one individual child's survival. As a fourth activity, we read aloud children's books to provide additional historical background related to the Holocaust.

Exploring Preconception—
What (We Think) We Know About Jews

We describe diaries as a place for personal reflections, questions, expressions of feelings, and records of events. We explain that diary writing is not necessarily meant for an audience beyond oneself, although some writers' diaries eventually are published. At this stage in the project, students can choose to share diary entries or keep them private. Students revisit their diaries throughout the month-long *Memories from Past Centuries* project.

Working privately in the spirit of communicating within personal diaries for the first time, we ask students to write about "Jews." Wanting to discover what they know about the word, we are purposely vague. Some of the students in our group thought we'd said "juice" or "jewel," so we wrote "Jews" on the board. Only three of the students in that class were Jewish; most were Christian or non-affiliated. That year some students needed help getting started; some protested and grumbled at first. Their reluctance faded when a non-

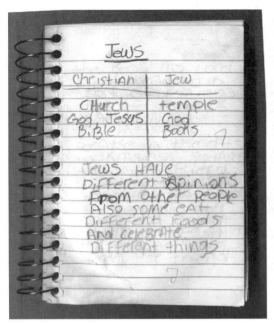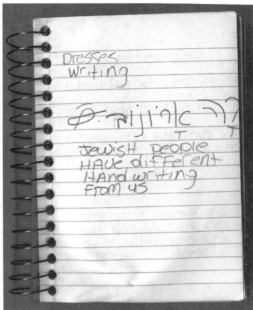

Jewish classmate reminded them about parents bringing dreidels, latkes, menorahs, and Hanukkah stories to class.

On this day, and most days, the *Memories from Past Centuries* project fit into the day's writing workshop. Students faced one another at their work tables but focused on their own notebooks. They decorated their journal pages with symbols and drawings such as a flag or a Star of David. Mostly, they filled their diary pages with words, some of which eventually were crossed out, rearranged with a complicated system of arrows, or highlighted with boxes and stars. In responding to the open-ended prompt written on the board, some students confessed to having "no clue," while others listed historical events, people (Judah Maccabee, Anne Frank), cultural symbols of Judaism, Jewish holidays and rites, and geographical points of reference such as Israel. Several students mentioned one of their classmates (Jessica, whose mother had come to speak with the class during Hanukkah), and two mentioned participating in a school play that dealt with Judaism. Erin made a list of three things she knew: "good things about Jews: 1) they are fun; 2) they can teach us things; 3) they celebrate hannukah." (Teachers, of course, also should be prepared to address students' cruel or intolerant statements about Jews firmly and discreetly.)

Cherica, an African American student, writes "different" four times in her diary entry, which includes a chart mapping differences between Christians and Jews and an attempt to illustrate Hebrew script. Elijah, a White student, takes a different approach. In addition to explicit references to places (Jerusalem, a synagogue) and people (Anne Frank, his classmate Jessica), Elijah's writing implicitly

Left: Elijah's diary entry about "Jews," 2005

Right: Cherica's diary entries about "Jews," 2005

downplays differences among Jews and himself. He describes Jews as having white skin color, originally from Europe, and among his friends.

As hoped, our students are honest in this initial reflection. (Of course, teachers should address any cruel statements firmly and discreetly). Javonte, an African American student, writes:

> I don't get it when she says Jews. I think she means like Jewitch people, as in people who wear little small tight hats that fit on the back of the men's heads like it is stuck to it. That are Jewitch people that come from Jerewsalem and I think about Jessica and Jacob [two Jewish classmates] and I think of Jewda Macabe that Jessica's mom told us. The batle when the Jews fought and they lit candles for eight days for light to protect them through the batle.

Now sitting close to one another on the classroom rug, Javonte and other volunteers share from their diary entries, revealing bits of truth, some stereotypes, as well as misinformation. One student says that Hitler was a Jew. When Hitler's name comes up, another student mentions killing Jews and that Hitler wanted to take over the world. Jacob, one of three Jewish students in the class, announces to everyone that he is offended by the assignment.

> JEWS
> I am a Jew and I don't like writing about this because it makes me feel like we are a completely sepreate group of people. I don't think a lot of people know what a Jew is. I'm kind of offended that people don't know. I think *everyone* except me and Jessica in this class is Christian.

This is the only occasion during the *Memories from Past Centuries* project when students talk openly and as a group about their own religion. (Jacob later adds Zoe to the list of Jews in the class.) We ask if Jacob thinks it would help for classmates to know more about his religion, and he agrees. Possibly trying to lighten the mood, Sam offers, "No one knows of my religion either—Universalist Unitarian." Alfranzia points out that Christians not knowing about Jews must seem as shocking to Jacob and other Jewish students as someone not knowing about Jesus would seem to her. Jessica's comment serves as an appropriate conclusion to our initial conversation, "When I think of Jews, I think of myself." In this conversation a few students volunteer their religious affiliation, but this isn't required or even solicited. The project thus begins with recognition of both the religious diversity in the class and the possibility of students' sensitivity and pride in having others know about their heritage and beliefs.

A Famous Diary and a Modern Genre

In our second lesson, students begin to learn about the history of the Holocaust. Linking through the educator's website, www.learnnc.org, we look at the Holocaust Memorial Museum's website pages about Anne Frank. Specifically, we look together at the section "Anne Frank the Writer/An Unfinished Story," which features an online exhibition of Frank's original writings from age 13 to 15. In the section called "First Entries," students hear a young girl reading Anne Frank's words as they appear on the screen, "I know that I can write, a couple of my stories are good. My descriptions of 'The Secret Annex' are humorous, there's a lot in my diary that speaks, but whether I have real talent remains to be seen. . . ." Another section, "Going into Hiding," begins with the words, "Anti-Jewish decrees followed each other in quick succession. Jews must wear yellow stars. Jews must turn in their bicycles. Jews are banned from trams and are forbidden to drive. . . ." Students also look at the way the exhibition presents artifacts and photographs together to share Anne Frank's story.

As students experience words, photographs, videos, and music, we encourage them to notice how various kinds of information are combined to tell stories and give personal viewpoints. Students explore the website in groups of four, taking turns in selecting pages to view. They click through the site—at times talking more about whose turn it is to move the mouse or whether they are ready to click on a new subtopic about Anne Frank. "Go back to that part." "I want to see that picture." "Is that her sister?" Even so, the students are taken by the physical demands, the danger, the bravery, the impossibility of staying quiet and cloistered for so long.

While discovering Frank's famous diary, students continue their immersion in their own diaries. We want this brief exposure to her story (and the website as a means of sharing her story) to provide context for the remaining stages of the project and introduce students to primary documents—the study of which we devote much time to later. Furthermore, this activity shows students an example of a multimedia website designed to preserve history. Finally, we hope this introduction to Frank's diary serves as inspiration. We want students to discover that one person's story (even a young girl's) can teach the world about history and morality, and can stir people's consciousness to bring about action and change.

The students' journal entries attest to the strong impression made by this brief exposure to Anne Frank's life. Students' reflections and questions home in on her diary as well as the fact of her and her family having been in hiding. One student wrote, "Hiding was very important to not get caught if you were a Jew." Another remembered the exact date—June 12, 1942—that she'd been given her diary.

Screenshot from the U.S. Holocaust Memorial Museum's Anne Frank website

Another student noted that, upon receiving her first diary on her 13th birthday, Anne asked herself whether she would "be able to do great in writing." Students were also impressed with Anne's integrity, commenting on her bravery and the absence of anger.

Studying Documents and Getting to Know Children's Survival Stories

With the stark backdrop of Anne Frank's story, we shift our attention to stories of children who *survived* the Holocaust. We make it clear that most children did not survive, but explain that our focus will be on the courage of rescuers. The American Jewish Joint Distribution Committee (JDC) supported numerous organizations that saved the lives of tens of thousands of children during the Nazi era. After the war, JDC photos of child survivors, with attached case histories, helped make the public aware of the plight of these young refugees and other displaced persons. We began our work with a thorough and thoughtful study of a particularly rich collection of these photos and their accompanying data housed in the JDC archives. Eventually, the JDC photographs and case histories will be the source for creative work that we hope will remind others of the lessons of history. Readers can access JDC archival materials by e-mailing archives@jdc.org.

Photographs of Rescued Children

Instead of presenting all this information at once, we first give each student a photograph of a child who survived. The black-and-white JDC photographs, themselves, contain layers of information. Some of the children are pictured with one or two siblings; others stand alone facing the camera with a smile or a serious expression. We usually match students with rescued children of the same gender and close in age, but otherwise the matches are made randomly.

We ask students to "read" the photographs. In this first activity with JDC documents, students have no idea what the children have been through. We suspect it is easier for students to identify with an image (as opposed to a written statement) of a child who appears similar in terms of gender and age, although some are older or younger. The photographs require students to be careful observers and kindle their curiosity and imagination.

Students study the photos with a spirit of discovering clues. They list in their diaries all the details they can. Most students record the child's gender, guess at his or her age, describe clothing, and mention items in the background of the portrait. Some note such details as "number tag" and "jail clothes," which gave important clues about the setting. Others speculate about the feelings of the child photographed, basing their ideas on facial expressions and postures. Jessica writes:

March 16, 2005
My child
Not happy
Striped short sleeved shirt
Long braided hair
Stern look
Looking down
Doesn't want to look at camera
She's white
She looks older, 14? 15?
It's sunny outside
Shadow
Big nose (like most Jewish kids)

We ask students to write a second entry about their photograph, this time listing questions. Jessica's thorough list shows her sharp thinking:

JDC photograph of Essie Z.

Questions about my kid:
How old is she?
What's her name?
How did she survive?
Did she have any other family?
Who rescued her?
How old was she when the holocaust started?
Did all of her family die?
Where was she rescued?
Did Christian's or Jews rescue her?
Did she escape or hide?
Was she taken to a concentration came before she survived?

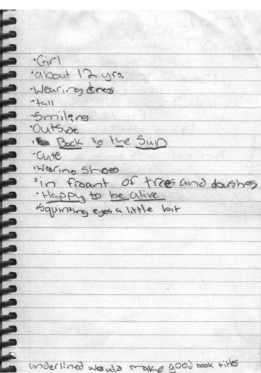

JDC photograph of Jola C. and Erin's list of details, 2005

The handwritten list reads:
- Girl
- about 12 yrs.
- wearing dress
- tall
- Smiling
- Outside
- Back to the Sun
- Cute
- wearing shoes
- in froant of trees and doushes
- Happy to be alive
- Squinting eyes a little bit

underlined would make good book title

Alfranzia, an African American student, continues to think of her notebook as a diary, probably influenced by seeing Anne Frank's diary. She writes:

> Dear Diary,
> Guess what. I just met a new friend. Exaly she is "my child." Yes, she is a Jew and she has on a checkerboard dress. She has medium sized hair, and it is black. She looks pretty happy. She looks like she is 9 or 10 years old. Her dress has about 5 or 6 different dezings. She looks very healthy. She looks either Spanish or white. I think she is either 4 ft. 2 or taller or maybe shorter. I think this was a fun fun fun picture, not like a school picture. I can imagine her in 5th grade. By the way she look it seems that she is a nice person/friend.

Alfranzia's second entry continues as follows:

> Dear Diary,
> Things I want to know about my child.
> 1. What's her name?
> 2. Her age when she was rescued.
> 3. Where she was born? When did she get rescued and what year?
> 4. Where did she live after she got rescued?
> 5. Did she have any siblings?

6. Did her siblings get rescued also? If they did, how old were they and their names?

7. Who was the person who rescued them?

JDC case history and photograph of Dina J.

Students become increasingly invested in the lives of the children in their photographs. Alfranzia calls the girl in her photograph "my child" and tells her diary that she's met a new friend who she imagines to be in 5th grade, like herself. Zoe asks, "Was she scared?" and "Did she confront the Nazis and still get away?" Gabby writes, "I really do hope my person is alive. God Bless." As a whole, students are eager for more information, asking all the important questions: Who helped them? When were they rescued? How did they escape? What were they feeling? Most students want to know more details about how the child had managed to survive and are also concerned about whether the children's family members had been as fortunate. Students also started asking, "Why?" Domineck's writing was sparse but poignant: "Why didn't the Nazis like kids?"

Case Histories of Rescued Children

We ask students to add to or revise their diary entries after reading the children's case histories, which were written by the JDC. These case histories are one or two pages in length and are photocopied reproductions of the original documents. They provide basic biographical information—the child's name, age, nationality, and ethnicity—and also describe the child's appearance and personality.

They also provide any information available regarding the fate of the child's parents, the child's whereabouts during and following the war, as well as information regarding the people responsible for rescuing the child and the sometimes miraculous turn of events that helped spare the child.

Some students find answers to their questions within the case histories. For example, Alfranzia labeled this section of her diary, "Answers: 1) Dina J. 2) 7 1/2 years old 3) Paris." At the bottom of a journal page, another student revealed that the asterisk she'd written next to Warsaw stood for "a real place!"

In closely reading both the photographs and case histories, students appreciate more and more how significant the children's survival was, and the unimaginable hardships they had endured. Compared with Anne Frank and so many others, however, these children were the lucky ones. We don't want students to stop at being awed; we want them to imagine the courage and inventiveness necessary for rescuing the Jewish children.

Reading Aloud Children's Literature on the Holocaust

To reinforce what the students have learned and to encourage them to think further about ideas of rescue, daily choices, social action, and altruism, we read *The Cats in Krasinski Square* (Hesse, 2004), a picture book of historic fiction about brave children who use their wits to sneak essential supplies to Jews sequestered in the Warsaw ghetto in Poland. Again going back to their diaries, students reflect on the story. By reading this story while the students are studying the photographs and case histories, we hope to emphasize stories of individuals' power to make a difference rather than stories of Nazi atrocities. We want students to wonder how people assessed risks and then summoned the courage to act. Students also make meaningful connections between the project and modern-day references to the Holocaust. For example, in his diary Elijah wrote:

> Yesterday, we visited a Anne Frank website. I read some of her stories. They were very good. I also saw a 10-second movie that she was in. Today we read a book called *The Cats of Berkeley Square.* It was about Ghetto people. And cats sneaking food. In the end it was happy, opposed to the real story of the Holocaust. Today in the newspaper there was an article about the Holocaust.

We read another children's book, *My Secret Camera: Life in the Lodz Ghetto* by Frank Dabba Smith (2000). This book tells the true story of a young photographer, Mendel Grossman, who documented the lives of thousands of children and adults held captive in Jewish ghettos. The story provides more historical context as well as an example of how photography can be used to promote social change. Like *The Cats in Krasinski Square* (Hesse, 2004), this book looks at the ways that Nazis branded Jews and held them captive. The photos create an even starker portrait, showing parents and children separated from each other, lines of weary people with their possessions on their backs, groups of Nazi guards, and the face of a solitary Jewish boy looking fearful and confused. In listening to the story and looking at the photographs, our students make connections to "their" children, remarking, for instance, "My person lived in the same ghetto as in the story." The story prompted other insights: "It was because they're different," and probing questions such as, "Is a ghetto a concentration camp?" Another question thrown out was, "Did this take place before or after slavery?" And someone asked, "I'm a Christian; would I die?"

TALKING ABOUT THE HOLOCAUST

Neither the Holocaust nor general European history is part of most elementary level curricula, although some 3rd-, 4th-, or 5th-grade students may already know something about the history from family conversations, news media and television programs, and/or children's literature. Recognizing the difficulty of teaching young students about the Holocaust, here are a few suggestions for implementing the Memories from Past Centuries *project.*

Build on a classroom environment in which students explore the real world. *Many of the students in our classes are not new to hardship and tragedy, or heroism. Many of the students' families have endured struggles related to illness or death, displacement, and/or economic instability. One way that our students become comfortable with investigating and sharing their personal stories—the good and the bad—is through foundational LTP projects, such as making self-, family, and community portraits (described in Wendy's book* I Wanna Take Me a Picture *[Ewald & Lightfoot, 2001]).*

Another classroom activity that develops students' awareness of and sensitivity to the world around them is reading the local newspaper each day. Lisa steers her students away from stories of heinous local crimes (she will tear out a page reporting a murder or rape), but she generally leaves the activity open-ended. This means students' exploration may focus on almost anything they want to read—even if it's related to American soldiers at war or the physical devastation and human suffering brought about by recent earthquakes. The goal is to allow students to know and talk about what's going on in the world.

Carefully select the Holocaust photographs students will see.

While Grossman's images from the Lodz ghetto present students with a startling reality, there are many kinds of terrible realities students don't see. In the drawings and photographs presented in the aforementioned books, students see ghetto walls but not wire fences around concentration camps. They also don't see enslaved people laboring in work camps, prisoners' emaciated bodies, or the camps' crematoriums. Students understand that the camps meant death for many, many Jews, but knowing this and seeing it are quite different. When implementing the project at the middle school level, a different set of photographs may be acceptable to use.

For the 4th- and 5th-grade project, we felt it was important to focus on survivors. In this sense, studying the JDC photographs of rescued children is more age-appropriate than studying Anne Frank's life through her diary and other primary documents. There are a number of children's books telling the story of children that survived (see the References section at the back for a list of recommended readings).

Choose a central piece of children's literature for context.

Although the students are fascinated with the JDC case histories, they are sometimes cumbersome for students to read because of the advanced vocabulary and the unfamiliar European places and names. By contrast, Lois Lowry's Number the Stars *(1989), a work of historical fiction set in Nazi-occupied Denmark, provides context about World War II that is appropriate for the students. Also compelling for students is connecting with a protagonist of their own age. Lowry presents the story of 10-year-old Annemarie Johansen, who becomes involved in the resistance when she and her family attempt to rescue her best friend, a Jewish child named Ellen. Furthermore, Lowry's book presents perspectives that are considered in the* Memories from Past Centuries *project—those of Nazi soldiers, Jewish children, and young people and adults who risk their lives to help Jews survive.*

Writing Historical Fiction

IN CONTRAST TO the quick viewing of the Anne Frank website, students begin digging deeper into the stories of the children who survived the Holocaust. Students are getting to know their child as they speculate on the dire circumstances and complicated emotions children experienced—with their imaginations they fill in missing information. In the next part of the *Memories from Past Centuries* project, we present students with a new challenge: telling the child's story from three different points of view. In this stage of the project, students draw on what they've learned from their study of the primary documents and what they imagine to create three voices and three characters.

A Child's Story

To introduce the idea of telling a story in the first person, we read an excerpt from *Voices of the Alamo* by Sherry Garland (2000). When asked what they noticed about the way it was written, one of our students responded that he could tell what the characters felt—whether they were mad about something or cared a lot. Another student said, "Davey Crockett talks like he's in real life." We wanted students to notice how first-person stories communicate emotions, give life and particularity to historic events, and make readers wonder about what else is happening for the character.

We hope that in shifting back to "their" children, the students will create voices that convey emotion and draw upon any background and/or contextual information they have learned.

First, we ask students to write diary entries in the voice of the child in their photo as if they are telling the story of the child's experience. "Be your person. Write about where you are hiding, how you feel, what happened." Someone asks, "Should we write with 'I'?" We explain that we read passages from *Voices from the Alamo* so that students would realize that they could write that way. Another student asks if she can get the book she recently read in our research class to help her write the child's story, while another asks if it is OK to use the case study to remember names and facts. We reassure students that their writing doesn't have to be perfect, that they may include information from the case studies in their own words. The idea is to be accurate but also to add in feelings and events as they imagine them.

Since students have studied their photo, listed observations, wondered about details of the child's life, researched answers in case histories, and identified with characters in fictional picture books, the next step of writing a first-person account comes naturally. Some students rely heavily on the details of the JDC case history, even copying it verbatim. Others, like Jessica, whose account about Essie Z. is both grim and hopeful, took the opportunity to embellish the facts with rich and invented details of sounds, places, actions, and feelings.

> Before the war I lived with my Mom, Dad, and two brothers on a farm near Barnow. I was 6 when the Germans invaded. My father managed to keep us in a neighbors farm. I remember one night hearing the door open, seeing the neighbor, and my mother picking me up and running with me. I heard a blow as we ran, faster and faster. We hid in the woods, and slept during the day. At night we would look for food. Later

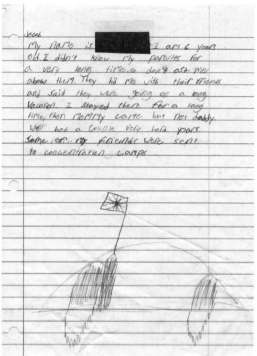

JDC photograph of Simon
K. and Jacob's writing and
drawing, 2005

my older brother and I found shelter on a farm, we had to
pretend to be Poles so we wouldn't get caught. For 3 years
we worked caring for the farmers baby. My dad joined the
partisans and fought in the forests. We saw him again after
we were freed by advancing Russians. Then we heard Mommy
had been caught and murdered. I'm now 14, I live in a DP
camp in the US zone of Germany with daddy, my brothers, and my step-mother. I get scared from all these years of
frightful experience. But the American Joint distribution
comettie treats me well and I hope to stay. I love sewing,
cooking, and knitting. I also want to become a dress maker.

Mary's succinct entry about Jola C. speaks to the painful but necessary act of keeping a record of horrific events.

> Dear Diary,
> I just recieved this Diary from my sister. She said its for what
> all we went through. I would rather not remember any of it.
> And besides, I haven't had enough schooling yet.
> Sincerely, Jola

Students share their diary entries with a partner. Looking at the
photograph of Hannah B., who looks tall, thin, and confident, a
student tells her African American classmate, "You look like her."
Another chimes in, "Yeah, you do." The idea of pretending to be
the rescued child is a smooth transition for everyone: Students write

with first-person pronouns and past tense verbs (hid, pretended, caught, murdered, found shelter, and so on) when telling what happened. Most, like Zoe, who wrote about Sonia G., allude to a sense of relief that the past is behind them.

> Finnally I have found peace, in Italy. At a Jewish children's training center. I am 12 years old, the road to a bad end has stopped. At a fork in the road, I took the good side.

Some students, like Tray, focus on the facts of survival and causes of death. In his diary writing about Itzik B., Tray doesn't have all the facts right and his "mistakes" reflect the limits of a typical 5th-grader's knowledge of European geography and history, as well as his struggles as a reader. Yet he still captures the truth of struggle. Having to write about a particular event in the first person helped him understand history as a matter of life and death. He wrote:

> My name is Itzik. My Mom and Dad was killed. The German captured my hometown. The only reason my mom and dad was killed is because: mom: was killed of malnutrition (which means bad food). Father because my father volunteered to fight with the red Army. But he died. I have travel a lot of places, like from Poland to Russia because the Germans made us run away too. Then I move to Kasakstan. When the war ended I moved back to Poland and then I have moved with these people to Palestine. But I couldn't go any farther so I stop at Italy. So the AJDC toke care of me here. and I hope for the future I can move with my uncle to New York.

The rescued children were moved from place to place, making the twists and turns of their journeys hard to follow. A number of our students are confused about geography and vocabulary, as well as the pronunciation of words within the case histories, which were written with an adult audience in mind. Many underline unfamiliar words or phrases in the case studies. But none of this confusion matters as much as their concern for the children they are pretending to be. They get the big idea: People were in danger, in danger because of their identity. Students easily identify with the plight of fellow children. They understand that the children's reality is full of fear and suffering, and that there were heroes who took great risks to save people's lives.

A Friend's Story

After the students have "become" the child in their photos, we ask them to pretend to be a friend of the child—perhaps someone from school or the neighborhood, perhaps someone who is not Jewish. We

Mary's writing from the
perspective of a friend of
Jola C., 2005

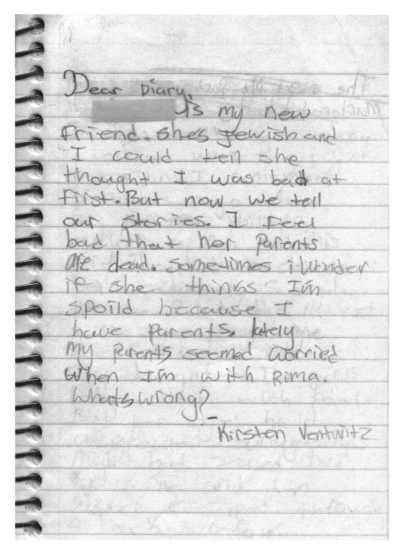

Dear Diary,
_____ is my new
friend. She's Jewish and
I could tell she
thought I was bad at
first. But now we tell
our stories. I feel
bad that her parents
are dead. Sometimes i wonder
if she thinks I'm
spoild because I
have parents. lately
My parents seemed worried
when I'm with Rima.
Whats wrong?
                    — Kirsten Vantwitz

ask them to tell as much of the story as they can from the friend's perspective and remind them to continue writing with "I." They are again to build their writings on the information provided in the case histories and the photographs.

Students realize the friend will be completely imaginary. They also realize the friend cannot possibly know what happened to the Jewish child—the friend could know only that the other child, who happened to be Jewish, was gone and no one knew where. Someone asks, "Could we say, 'I wonder what happened?'" Someone else suggests she'll pretend to be a friend talking to her mom about possible reasons she hasn't heard from the missing friend in so many days. Another idea involved being interviewed about the friend who had disappeared, so as to have a chance to report memories and feelings about the friend.

Students' characters are brilliantly realistic. Their writings allude to a widespread sense of fear and distrust, the powerful reach of Nazism, and an awareness of guilt by association. In these accounts, we're presented with children who are trying to figure things out. In a sense, these writings let the students express what they would do and say, how they might respond. We see the simultaneous gentleness and piercing wakefulness of children. Their imaginary stories mention what they've overheard or sensed from their parents—the information intended to be kept from children—and awareness of adults' feelings and fears. They're suspicious and worried that something's "wrong" and that there is "something else" their parents aren't telling them.

Jacob writes about "his" child, Simon K., from the perspective of a little boy.

> Today a new kid came to our house. His name is Simon. He is nice, but he's a Jew and Mommy said we shouldn't trust him. He was sad this morning because his parents left, but now he's not as sad because Mommy gave him a cookie. He's still very nerveous and very scared. I overheard Mommy and Daddy saying that he didn't really ever know his parents. Daddy doesn't think they'll come back, but I'm more hopeful than him. I think they will come back a really long time later.

Brandon's diary entry, which refers to his rescued child, Paul S., is written as a memory.

> I remember when Paul used to come over my house all the time after school until one day he wasn't at school and he never came back. So I wonder what happen to him. I wonder if he transford to another school. He's a jew and I heard that Jews and ansis don't like each other, so maybe he was taken or recude and got sent off were none of this would happen.

Jessica writes an imaginary conversation between the imagined friend and her mother, expressing concern about Essie Z.

> "Hey Mommy where's Essie?" My mom had been quiet for the last few days. I've been wondering where my best friend Essie is, I haven't heard from her in months. "Sarah be quiet you'll wake the others." My mother and I live in one of the many Ghettoes in Barrow. "Mommy, what's wrong" She seemed afraid to tell me, scared. "Essie's mother was captured by the Germans, we have yet to know more." My Mommy and Essie's were best friends before Essie and I were born.

"What's gonna happen to her Mommy, what?" I was now crying and tugging on my mothers dress. I knew there was something else, I just knew it!"

When students share these entries at the end of this class, we sit back and let a conversation unfold in which students pose meaningful, necessary, and poignant questions. For instance, one child asks, "Did all the Germans not like Jews?" A Jewish student answers that some of the Jews themselves were Germans and couldn't hate themselves. Someone else remembers Anne Frank's story and *The Cats in Krasinski Square* (Hesse, 2004) when pointing out that people who weren't Jews took risks to help the Jews. Another student leaps to a different time in history when he remarks, "I'll answer with another question—did all the people in the South own slaves?"

We felt this discussion marked the moment when students began realizing how widespread hatred is and that what happened to these Jewish children is not an isolated event. Students were beginning to wonder how they might avoid hating or being hated. Another student brought us back to empathizing with the rescued children's reality by asking us to imagine having to hide in a bag for days when we were only 2 years old. Students were creating voices for the child survivors and for people who cared about them. The more they gave a voice to the children in the photographs, the more those photographs came to life. We felt the strength of the students' writing came from the emotional connections forged as a result of beginning with a photograph of a person, a character—using a technique often employed by writers. From students' first diary entries about the JDC photographs, they claimed the children as their own.

A Nazi's Story

When we are discussing the idea of telling the stories from a friend's point of view, one student speculates that it would be very difficult to tell the same story from a Nazi's perspective, having no idea they would be asked to do just that. In creating a third voice, we want students to stand in the shoes of Nazis. Tapping into the Nazi mentality helps students see that Nazis, too, were people making choices; it reminds students that day-to-day decisions ultimately can have monumental consequences. So far, the students' writings stressed turning points; Zoe, for example, wrote, "I am 12 years old, the road to a bad end has stopped. At a fork in the road, I took the good side." We believe this kind of thinking will permeate the next lesson as well. We hope that a larger lesson in this activity will be the realization that anyone can be pulled into a gang, a movement, a system of violence, destruction, and hatred. In fact, students' writings do contain moral lessons about making choices and, accordingly, are relevant to kids' everyday lives at home and at school.

To begin this challenging lesson, we read the first few pages of Lois Lowry's *Number the Stars* (1989). In this scene, two friends—one Jewish and one non-Jewish—encounter some soldiers on a city street in Nazi-occupied Copenhagen. As this group of students listen to Lowry's description of the soldiers, one murmurs, "Nazis." We ask students how the Nazi characters make them feel. One student replies, "It was scary. They're staring at you and they got rifles." Others comment, "I wondered if they'd ask if they were Jews" and "I thought they were about to kill them." Another student explains, "It was like the soldiers were acting and playing a part because they were laughing and they had a heart and said [to the girls] 'go home.'" From Lowry's novel, students sense the girls' fear of the Nazis, but also notice the soldiers' humanity—how one soldier mentions his own daughter.

When we ask students to again write in their diaries, this time taking on a Nazi attitude, more than one respond with "that's hard." One student asks what the connection was between the Nazis and his child. We respond that this is exactly what he and the other students have to think about. When some claim that their child never interacted with a Nazi, we remind them that the Nazis had indeed shaped the lives of the rescued children. From the case histories and children's stories, we hear about families forced into hiding, families struggling to survive under Nazi occupation, families being separated, and both adults and children being taken away by Nazis and sometimes killed. Students are still trying to make sense of the history they are learning about. Dessa whispered to Danielle, "Why did they hate the *Jews*?," his intonation suggesting this was something he couldn't wrap his head around.

As we expect, this assignment is a stretch for our students. Although some students are more comfortable than others, by the time they share their story from a Nazi perspective, many of the accounts include some admission of guilt and reflection on the heartlessness of their deeds. We try to simultaneously recognize the discomfort of this writing assignment and honor the creative license students are accustomed to in writers' workshop, while reminding them that most Nazis were not necessarily repentant about their atrocities. Some of our students' Nazi characters notice the look of fear or tears in the eyes of their Jewish prey. They find ways to make exceptions and risk getting in trouble as they let Jews escape. The emotion in the students' stories sometimes comes across in their penmanship. For instance, Zoe suddenly switches to all capitals when writing in the

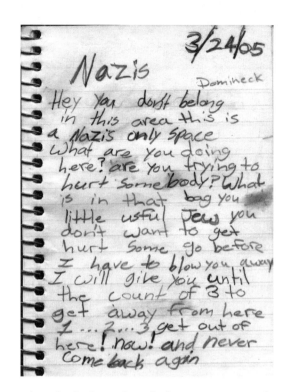

DanPelle   March 24

Hult you are not aloud
on the primises I said
patroling the town the
little girl told me
she was a non jew
I went to get a drink
and a bunch of little
girls playing double dutch outside
I put down my coffee and
Yelled Hult What are
you doing here you need
to go home now and this
is just a warning if I
catch here agian you
are in big trouble
yes ser and they ran
off into the distance
Some times I think to
myself why did I
become a Nazi? was
this ment to be
my future here?   *

Nazis
                    Domineck   3/24/05

Hey You don't belong
in this area this is
a Nazis only space
What are you doing
here? are you trying to
hurt somebody? What
is in that bag you
little usful Jew you
don't want to get
hurt Some go before
I have to blow you away
I will gike you until
the count of 3 to
get away from here
1 ...2...3 get out of
here! now! and never
come back again

Danielle and Domineck's
writing from a Nazi per-
spective, 2005

Nazi voice in her journal, and it looks as though she is pressing much
harder with her pencil.

Some of our students draw upon the familiar language of kids
complaining about rivals or foes. For instance, Breonna's journal entry contains a Nazi's private thoughts about Holocaust survivor Dina
J. We see a digression into the kind of thoughts that might swirl
inside the head of a child who's lost her temper—exaggerated and
impulsive ill feelings toward a peer.

Dear Diary,
Hi. My name is Naya. I'm a Nazi person. It's a little girl name
Dina. I think she's either 7 or 6. I want to kill her so bad.
I can't stand her. She is always looking at me like I'm the
dumbest person on earth. And I'm always yelling at her saying. What the huck are you looking at me for. Is something
wrong with my face. Don't get scared tell me. . . .

Gabby's writing also suggests an anger bubbling up inside her Nazi
persona.

I'm a nazi who kill Jew people. I'm a nazi who servied that
day I'm a nazi who will stay alive these days. Nazi are out-
standing. I don't want this person Fella to stay alive I want
her to die. Jews are bad, bad news. They make want to kick.
Stick'em, Sock'em, bit'em. Everything.

Like other classmates, Domineck skillfully includes in his writing details of his rescued child, Sacha S., whose parents kept him hidden in a bag.

NAZIS

Hey you don't belong in this area this is a Nazis only space. What are you doing here? Are you trying to hurt somebody? What is in that bag you little useful Jew you don't wan to get hurt some go before I have to blow you away. I will give you until the count of 3 to get away from here. 1 . . . 2 . . . 3 get out of here! now! And never come back again.

We ask for volunteers to share with the entire class their writings from the Nazi point of view. Mary reads her piece to everyone gathered close together on the floor.

Sometimes I wonder if becoming a soldier was a good idea. I miss my wife and kids. I remember 3 nights ago when my partner, Phillepe, murdered a couple. As I looked around I noticed that there were two girls watching, scared in the corner. The littlest girl's eyes met with mine. They were swollen from crying but some showed a spark of courage. The daughters crept out the back window. I could have stoped them, but I didn't. Have I disobeyed my order or saved their lives?

We comment that Mary's writing resembles a diary entry in which one privately grapples with difficult questions. She points out how her Nazi character explored two different paths/possibilities. After reading his Nazi story, Elijah speaks to the visceral nature of his new level of understanding, saying, "I felt like I was a Jew," and that he could feel the life spurting out of every Jew he'd killed (as an imaginary Nazi).

In depicting the fear and suffering, exhaustion, and desperation of Jews, the case histories and literature make clear that Nazis hated Jews. However, the reasons for this hatred are not well defined. Although the opening scene of *Number the Stars* provides a glimpse into a Nazi's humanity, none of our sources provide a deep understanding of the historical and economic context that fostered the rise and power of Nazism. This doesn't become a focus in our project, although some students' writings reveal a blind following of Hitler himself or of other Nazi generals. The following writings imply an understanding of Nazi actions as rooted in fear and desperation:

Frece I said you'r Mom and Dad are now died because there Jews now . . . I saw the back door close. Oh my gosh did I just let some Jews ecape. I can't let Hitler find out or he will fire me. Or mabe he will kill me. I have to cepe this a cecret too. This is bad!

That book that Ms. Lord read to our class was amzing. It really made me feel sad about what anunsees did to Jews. People was just scared to stand up and say your crazy to the leader of the anunsees. They were scared to die and just joined him on his killingspree.

In Jacob's Nazi journal entry, he draws four swastikas and writes of both a hatred of Jews as well as soldiers' need to follow Hitler's obsessive orders.

Jews, Jew, Jews, all Hitler was intrested in. Find them, kill them, find them, kill them. I hated them as much as you like, but night-time raids? Filthy Jews. If it wasn't for them I wouldn't even have to do this.

As a group we talk about how one answer to the question of why Nazis hated Jews was that German children were taught to hate Jews. One student brought historic documents to class. He shared Nazi fairy tales that were used to indoctrinate German children. If stories for children could be used to teach hate, then perhaps our stories could be used to teach resistance. We explain that the next step is to make videos of the students *being* the characters they created, and that students eventually will incorporate their writings and videos into finished art pieces. As a rationale, we explain that writers and actors have a chance to make the world a better place, and that others will have a chance to see their work.

Creating Multimedia Art with a Message

IN THE FINAL PART of our *Memories from Past Centuries* project, students work together to create multimedia art that integrates the historical materials and their own imagined characters. The process involves three main steps: First, students record themselves performing their scripted stories; second, they work in teams to plan a larger story that integrates the stories of several rescued children *and* leaves readers/viewers with a powerful message about history; third, they work on school computers to create multimedia movies to be shared with one another and with family and friends.

Trying Out a Part—Performing and Recording Stories About Rescued Children

We start by asking: How could our work help make the world a better place? The students give heartfelt responses. One answers that her work will allow people to see how things are different now. Someone added that the school has both Jewish and Christian kids and they are all treated well. Another student makes a connection to the present—"People doing bad things now should listen and see what it looks like when people get hurt." Yet another student makes a connection to museum displays that help people understand what others have gone through. We remind students that even now there are people joining hate groups such as neo-Nazis. A student recalls a recent newspaper article reporting that the "Indian kid who killed all those people was a Nazi." Adding that Jews are not the only target of hatred and violence, we point to other places in the world where people are being hurt or killed for being different. We also take the opportunity to say that while there are close-minded and hateful people, there are also those bystanders who might disagree with injustices or atrocities but neglect to take action. We let the students know they will have a chance to make art to open people's minds and make a difference.

It's one thing to pretend to be someone you're not and express that person's ideas in writing, even when you're leaping across decades of time and unfathomable differences of opinion; it's quite another thing to pretend *to be* that other person and *speak* the ideas. In the next part of our project, we ask students to perform as one of the characters they've envisioned. They have to know the story of their child survivor by heart, not in the sense of knowing a script verbatim but in the sense of understanding and play acting someone else's per-spective. Like the scripting of different voices, this assignment also builds on students' comfort with and interest in play. We liken this activity to taking a field trip—touching something or walking down the road where something happened.

Students choose any of the three versions of their survivor's story: the one told from the child's perspective, the one told from a friend's point of view, or the one told by a Nazi. Working in pairs, students help each other rehearse the stories and then they video record each other telling the stories. The most useful form of rehearsal is having one's partner ask interview questions: "What's your name?" "How old are you?" "Where are your parents?" Without being reminded to do so, students naturally address each other as the characters they are portraying. They answer questions using the first person, elabo-rating on real and imagined events and circumstances. In the pro-cess of rehearsing, students learn their partner's story well enough to prompt their partner as needed once the recording begins. After rehearsing their parts two or three times, each pair is responsible for video recording each other using a Flip or other small camera. (Flip cameras are small and easy to operate—they have only one main button that starts and stops recording, and can be plugged directly

Wendy filming India, 1998

into a classroom computer to upload video files and recharge the battery. See the Resources section at the back of the book for more technical notes and details.)

The videotaping requires a relatively quiet space where small groups can work one at a time. We make use of the two available options—a corner of the media center and a small cluttered room usually occupied by special resource teachers. Rather than letting this be an adult-directed project, we want students to direct one another. Many choices are left to the students.

For example, after setting up a digital video camera on a tripod, we allow students to position the camera, determining its height and distance from the performer. In moving the camera, students can create a frame that excludes some of the background distractions, such as students milling around the library. After students learn how to start and stop the recording, they designate and follow their own cues for starting and stopping. Students also decide how to begin their recording—will they appear on screen the moment the taping begins (and if so, will they be looking at the camera?) or will they walk into the scene? Will students sit down with their arms folded or will they stand and make a bold gesture, such as a Nazi salute?

Once they begin, students are expected to keep the camera recording. We have realized that without any limits, students want to make endless re-takes; we set the limit at two takes per student. The camera person at times will interview the speaker if he or she gets stuck. For example, one partner might ask, "How old were you?" when her partner pauses and seems lost. These brief exchanges seem natural, resembling any other interview. Plus, students know they eventually can edit out any long pauses or fumbling false starts.

As we watch partners telling the stories, becoming Holocaust survivors, friends, and Nazis, we notice that the students who seem to struggle the most to understand and remember the stories are, in fact, the most believable characters. Their pauses and stammers look like a struggle to tell a painful story.

On the other hand, we have noticed students speaking most confidently about the portions of stories that somehow resonate with their personal lives. The family lives of many of the students are unstable, some tragic. One boy whose father has never played a role in his life elaborates on what the survivor's father did to keep the child safe. Another student whose own father is terminally ill emphasizes this parallel in the story of her survivor, when she remarks two times that "my dad was too sick to take care of me and my brother." A student whose mother had been murdered just a few years before sadly recounts how the same thing happened to the Jewish child. We come to realize we've mistakenly assumed that our students' lives would be completely different from those of the survivors. As a writing and reading comprehension strategy, we often promote making connections to one's own life; some students put this into practice, whether they realized it or not.

Students don't worry about coolness. They get into their parts and for the most part seem relaxed as they perform. In fact, for some, this acting is so much about playing that they don't recognize the "school" elements. None of the students try to memorize their parts in the *Memories from Past Centuries* project. Instead, they grow to be comfortable with taking on different roles after getting to know their rescued child and imagining their characters through historical documents and the process of their own creative writing.

Collaborating to Make a Larger Story with a Lasting Message

Next, we ask the pairs of students who have recorded each other to join with another pair, making teams of four. The teams first familiarize themselves with each member's story—they share their JDC photographs and case histories and talk about their videotaped performances as survivors, witnesses, or Nazis. We then ask teams to begin thinking about how to fit their four stories together to make one larger story. We explain that each team will use a school computer to create a digital movie featuring their performances, JDC photographs, and any writing they can produce to introduce and integrate the pieces. We invite students to apply their skills as writers to a new medium by considering what to cut and what to keep and how to create a sequence. Above all, each team needs to consider

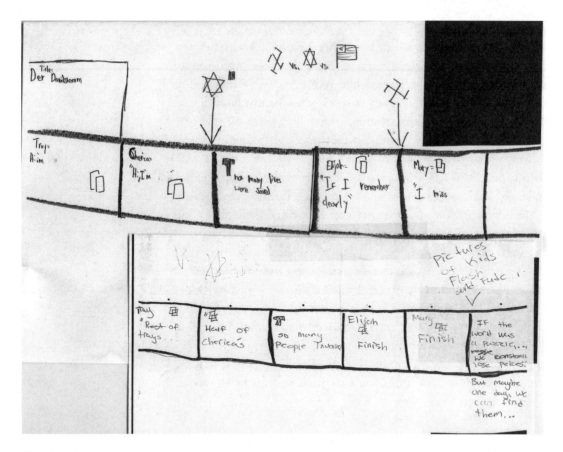

Storyboard, 2005

the message it wants to convey with its work. We expect teams to plan an engaging, thought-provoking story, something people will choose to watch all the way through and, we hope, over and over again. We want students to have the opportunity to present something unforgettable, believable, and inspiring.

The next step, creating storyboards, pushes students to plan more concretely. Students tape two pieces of construction paper side by side and draw frames corresponding to the intended parts of their movie. Students use symbols for Text, Video, Title, and Photo to label the frames of their storyboards. As teams plan how to sequence the various parts, they also think about what text they can write to move from the voice of a survivor to that of a friend/witness or a Nazi. What text will introduce and close their piece? How can writing help set the stage for their historical fiction? We explain that the objective is to sketch the main sequence on paper, while considering the larger message of the piece. We tell students they can write on their storyboard panels any other notes that will help guide them during their computer work.

Elijah, Tray, Mary, and Cherica realize immediately they can split each person's video performance into parts. As seen in their storyboard, they plan to briefly introduce each voice with a short video clip and then include more details from each story during the second half of the movie. On their storyboard, they imagine an 11-part sequence: Title, Video, Video, Text, Video, Video, Text, Video, Video, Photos, Text. They include notes about effects—such as flashing and fading photos—and draw a Star of David to designate the two Jewish voices and a Swastika to denote the Nazi counterparts.

In developing storyboards, students rely on several habits of good writers. Students work together to make careful choices about beginnings and conclusions. For example, one group reviews each person's film clips, searching for a quotation that will serve as a catchy opening line. Knowing the effectiveness of repetition, Elijah suggests that his group use as a conclusion a repeated line from his teammate Mary's story: "Saved two lives, saved two lives, saved two lives." Recalling the importance of details, students refer to their diaries again and again. By the time they finish their storyboards, it becomes more apparent to the groups what big ideas they want their audiences to get from their story.

Making Movies and Going Public

As their final assignment, each team of four students uses the storyboard as a foundation for creating the digital movie. This involves the following steps: importing digital files; sequencing the photograph and video files at the bottom of the digital movie window (the files appear as frames resembling students' handwritten storyboards); editing video clips; writing text; adding transitions (for example, to overlap a picture and text panel or to have a photograph fade into a video clip); adding sounds; and finally, exporting digital movies as QuickTime files that can be saved on a CD or DVD, or uploaded onto the web. (We use iMovie as this application is readily available on the school's iMac computers. Readers using other movie-making software—such as Windows Movie Maker—can follow the same basic steps outlined here, although some of the terminology and software icons differ.

Mary, the only child in the class who has ever used this application, helps us move around the computer lab to teach each group iMovie basics. As we import digital files (video files and scanned JDC photographs) into each team's digital movie project, students can see that the imported files are called "clips" and appear on the right half of the screen. (The clip file looks like a digital photo album.) Each team consults its storyboard as the students drag their clips into the digital version of the storyboard, running along the bottom of the screen. They arrange their four members' video clips and scanned JDC photographs into the proper sequence. At this point, and throughout their computer work, we remind students to save their movie projects.

Elijah, iMovie still, 2005

The process of combining the JDC photographs of their children with their own creative presentations is an exciting part of the project. Students wholeheartedly embrace the work of choosing what and how to communicate with an audience. They have a lot of information to consider, but even more, they sense their power to do something. They have an opportunity to tell the stories they've envisioned in a way that might remind other people of the lessons from history. The storyboard helps the movie-making teams get started; even more changes and decisions about the final product are made as teams work at the computer.

The video editing is the most time-consuming task as students enjoy previewing their cuts again and again. They make subtle changes to their individual video segments, which last anywhere from 3 seconds to a few minutes. While the editing is time-consuming, each team quickly masters the process. Students scroll through their video footage (using fast forward to save time once they are familiar with the clips) and simply move the digital movie crop markers to decide which parts to cut and keep. It's easy to preview a cut and to revert to the original clip when students change their minds or make mistakes.

Next students add text—usually at the beginning, the middle, and the end of their movies. Their text provides context and helps teams transition from one person's story to the next. The process of adding text involves choosing the size, font, color, and the speed with which the words will scroll across the screen. Students have fun experimenting with all the ways to include text—it can "fly" across the screen or it can appear as typewritten words with each letter appearing one by one. The final touches include sound effects and transitions—for instance, a still photograph of a survivor might fade into a video clip of a student performing as a survivor or witness. Students spend hours creating movies that turn out to be anywhere from 3 to 10 minutes long.

The creativity and originality of the students' finished work is striking. Elijah, Cherica, Tray, and Mary's group borrowed the video camera to make a new piece of video for the opening scene of their movie: The camera zooms in on a hand writing the name *Der Davidstemm* on a piece of paper that also contains a drawing of a Star of David. As planned in their storyboard, their movie quickly introduces all four of their characters with short video clips: Tray says, "They call me Shi for short. My mom and dad was killed." Cherica then says, "Hi, I'm Sarah, and I'm going to tell you about when I was younger." Playing a Nazi, Elijah continues, "Well, now that literally everyone in Germany believes that the Nazis were wrong, I feel like I have sinned. I would say that my greatest influence to be a

Nazi came from my childhood." Also playing a Nazi, Mary says, "I miss my wife and daughter." After these succinct introductions, they return to each character and present more details of their stories. Tray tells about when "the Germans captured our town. . . ." And Elijah goes on to explain that he became "legible" to be a Nazi and was "taught to hate Jews." In Mary's piece she wonders if she made the right decision in becoming a soldier. Her question, "Have I disobeyed my order or saved two lives?" is repeated as the film moves to its conclusion.

At the very end we see the four JDC photographs quickly appear on the screen followed by the words, "If the world was a puzzle . . . we constantly lose pieces but maybe one day we can find them." As these photos and words flash and fade from the screen, there is an ominous siren blaring. These students tell us that hatred is not inherent. They remind us that hatred is taught and show Nazi characters agonizing over their choices and actions. They leave us with the message that things can be different.

Each 5th-grade team produces a movie with a gripping sequence and a provocative message. Like the group above, the others use several effective strategies in their movie making. For instance, the teams experiment successfully with the use of text—making interesting choices in terms of font and size, as well as the timing, placement, and movement of text on the screen. Students have to choose whether their words will scroll across the screen from left to right or from the top to the bottom (or bottom to top). One group decides to play with the brightness of the text for effect—as the closing words "we are survivors" appear on the screen, they became brighter and brighter.

Students use text to present titles, conclusions, captions (such as the names of the rescued children), and transitions between video clips. For instance, as a sequence moves from one person's story to another's, groups insert transition phrases such as, "A different perspective" or "Some Nazis killed because they thought it was right. Then they saw how wrong they were." While often missing the reality of Nazi thoughts and actions, the content of the text often provides commentary. In another movie, seven sentences scroll from the bottom to the top of the screen one at a time, each sentence separated by an empty black screen.

> What you have just seen are the faces of children that survived the Holocaust.
> They survived after hiding or being adopted by Christian families.
> Some parents were taken to concentration camps and killed.

Austin, JDC photograph of Dina J., and Eric, iMovie stills with text, 2005

Danielle, Breonna, and Dessa, iMovie stills with visual transitions, 2005

> Others left their children alone to hide.
> Some, like Renata and Luthar, got to stay with siblings for a
>   while.
> Others got to stay with a parent.
> Either way, these four children survived and most are still
>   alive now, happy, healthy, and safe.

Furthermore, the students came up with worthwhile titles, such as "Remembering World War II, The Holocaust," "We Are Survivors," and "I Survived" (the letters of this last title appeared one by one on the screen).

Along with their thoughtful use of text, students refine their sequences by adding effective visual and audio transitions. For example, they experiment with the sound of a clacking old-fashioned typewriter (which was appropriate given the decades-old JDC case histories); a train whistle or siren, which reminds them of concentration camps; or a spinning film reel. In one movie, the shift from one student's story to another's story lasts only a few seconds but contains nine subtle transitions: Danielle finishes her story as a survivor with these words, ". . . I got put in a Ukraine family and lived there, until liberation." She stops talking, but continues to rock back and forth and looks away from the camera. As the name Dina appears on the screen, just below Danielle's face, we hear a typewriter. The screen then becomes black except for *Dina* in bright white letters. Next, a photo of Dina appears while the typewriter ceases and the movie zooms in on the archived photograph. Before the image fades completely, we hear the voice of Breonna, ". . . name is Erica." Once

Breonna appears on the screen, she continues with, "and I am Dina's friend. Dina was born in Paris to a worker's wife. . . ."

Later in the same movie, students choose to blend the image of a student posing as a Nazi with the photograph of a survivor. Dessa, posing as a Nazi, stands facing the camera, then looks down and turns away. A photograph of Joseph, a rescued child, then appears. When Dessa turns around again and says, "Man, I can't believe I actually thought about killing all those Jews . . . at the concentration camp. . . . That's not concentration. That's maybe murder." With an emphatic "hmmph" Dessa crosses his arms, shakes his head, and looks down. The screen then shows Joseph once more.

As a final effective strategy, students make wise editing choices by including video clips that are full of emotion. The scenes convey anger, disbelief, confusion, sadness, conviction, and doubt. In a convincing performance as a Nazi, Sam says:

A woman and child were running. I raised my gun, aimed, and was about to fire when a little voice inside me said, "what are you doing!" It's like the fire, fire had been extinguished. I dropped the gun and watched.

He pauses dramatically before asking himself, "What are you doing?" and abruptly smashes down the imaginary gun held in his hands.

Students don't censor the clips where they pretend to be crying or move nervously in front of the camera (one student commented, "I was twitching a lot," when watching himself on the screen). The students' gestures and fidgets also seem natural. Bonica looks up as though searching for the right word or a memory. Erin twirls her hair and pushes it behind her ear. Elijah scratches his head, and Michael earnestly holds his chin between his forefinger and thumb as he begins his story.

As the students, in teams of four, follow a story map and work to combine archival photographs, their own video material, and digital movie embellishments, they continue to ponder and refine the overall message they are presenting. We overhear the students in one team discussing ideas for the title of their piece. They each say something about the efforts various people have made in order to save a child's life. One group member says, "We want to thank our parents for what they did for us." Another responds, "But we're not only talking about parents." Searching for the right one-word title, someone suggests "thanksome." Finally, they agree on "I Appreciate You." Their choice of the first-person pronoun shows how much they identified with their rescued children as well as how much they recognize the difference the rescuers have made.

`ed` ⸨⸩ QT 602Kbps 4:19/10:29

`ed` 561Kbps 5:49/7:47

Above and opposite, left to right: Sam, Michael, Bonica, Alfranzia, and Erin, iMovie stills with emotional performances, 2005

Aside from the affecting, powerful messages that can be gleaned from the final products, we are also impressed with all the learning that happens throughout the movie-making process. In addition to the computer skills that students hone, this final phase of the *Memories from Past Centuries* project challenges students with complex higher order thinking. Each group adopts ideas from other groups as they overhear trials and decisions being made. We hadn't expected them to view their work over and over again, but now we see how essential this repetition is to their ability to draw powerful conclusions. They are engrossed in their editing partly because they are seeing themselves.

Finally, we burn the digital movies onto DVDs and watch them over and over. Each student goes home for the summer with a DVD of his or her team's movie. (Digital movies also can be easily exported to classroom blogs or websites like youtube.com.) We hoped the DVDs would be passed around and seen by people who had not participated in or were unaware of our project.

PROJECT VARIATION
American Indian Boarding Schools

IN AN ADAPTATION OF *Memories from Past Centuries*, we ask another classroom of students to study the before and after pictures of Native American youth who were forcibly taken from their homes at the turn of the 20th century and placed in Indian Boarding Schools to be "saved, civilized and Americanized." As in *Memories from Past Centuries*, students study school portraits and other primary documents such as school records and then write about their own version of a particular child's story from three perspectives—his or her own perspective before and after internment and the perspective of a school headmaster, teacher, or guard. In students' emotional performances, which we again videotape, it is obvious that the plight of these children resonates with the students.

When we show a selection of the video performances to Lisa's class the following year, we are amazed by their thoughtful responses. We expect the initial comments to be evaluations about the performances themselves. But from the very first comment, we see that students view their fellow students' work as a legitimate and important source of information on a topic they themselves find incredible. Just before showing the videos, Lisa provides students with background by reading Eve Bunting's story *Cheyenne Again* (1995), which she describes as historical fiction—she says that, in other words, Bunting's story, like the students' stories, is an invention, but was created by an author who had checked her facts. As if the performances are a continuation of Bunting's story, right away students demand to know more. One student asks, "Why didn't they take everyone, why just the kids?" As students reflect on this question, we wonder whether the same indignation, surprise, wisdom, and honesty surface in most conversations about children's vulnerability and potential. Would conversations about bullying or gangs, for example, be as effective? Students recognize immediately the boarding school's actions for what they were: kidnapping. They name the injustice; they call it "illegal." Even more important, they draw on parallels—"That's like what happened to the Jews!" "That's segregation." Their strong reactions and passionate dialogue underscore not only the power of creatively blending historical and personal voices, but the power of using children's own work as curricular material.

HOW MUCH LOVE and how much hate have children learned by the time they are in school? I imagine humans begin learning to love from the early relationships that are necessary for our survival as babies. How do we learn to hate? In *The Swallows of Kabul*, a novel for adults, Yasmina Khadra (2005) writes of characters who see public executions daily and become unsettled if one doesn't occur. She writes of "the light of conscience gone out" (p. 9).

Lisa Lord
A Teacher's Reflection

I wondered if the *Memories from Past Centuries* project, which focuses on the Holocaust and thus deals with matters of hatred, violence, and conscience, would be my students' first recognition of the possibility of genocide. I don't think they had ever considered the murder of a whole group of people, but they *had* been learning to love and to hate. Their hate lessons were learned through cruel events in local news or from fights at school or in their neighborhoods. I also wondered about explicit teaching in homes, schools, churches, and neighborhoods about what is holy and right regarding violence. I wondered too about the feeling that sometimes cruelty is justified or even something one is bound to do. How many times have I heard students justify fighting by saying, "My mama told me I have to hit him back if he hits me?" Home teaching trumps school rules that forbid fighting. Adding to the power of lessons from families and neighbors, my students are saturated with ideas and images from TV, movies, music videos, video games, advertisements, and computer games. For the sake of entertainment and commercialism, they see and hear violence every day. What if students could create their own stories and art to resist the pervasive violence of their world? Along with its authentic and meaningful writing, reading, research, and social studies lessons, this project is also about just that—helping students recognize their own capacity to make a difference, and giving students the chance to create their own artwork with a message powerful enough to kindle a flame of resistance to prejudice and cruelty.

In creating their artwork, students saw and heard themselves speaking as someone other than themselves. Students were repeating the imaginary experience of being another person, of being enemies. Is this a way to *practice* empathy? And how much practice is needed to slow down long-rehearsed, hit-him-back responses? Can stories from history and participation in creating art about resisting violence teach children a new habit of placing themselves in someone else's shoes? Can these lessons in empathy stand up to lessons in hate and re-sensitize students to the horror of violent acts in the world?

One of my students reminded me of the Nazis' effective technique for indoctrinating children—they used *altered* fairy tales and nursery rhymes, propaganda-filled literature, in a time when stories were the most common amusement for children. For a long time in the United States, every child knew the traditional versions of "Little Red Riding Hood," "Cinderella," and "The Three Little Pigs" because those stories had been repeated so often. What were German children learning from Nazi fairy tales? Prejudice? Hatred? What do

Americans learn from "Little Red Riding Hood" and "Cinderella"? Obedience? Cleverness in outsmarting the Big Bad Wolf? What are the lessons available in jingles and TV theme songs? What else is repeated often enough to be embedded in our hearts and minds, in our sense of identity and values?

If I had thought about how many times my students would read the one-page case histories or examine the single black-and-white photo of a Holocaust survivor in their assignment, I would have called it excessive and unnecessary. If I had known how many times they would reverse and replay the segments of their video pieces, I would have planned directions to move to a new project. (I didn't realize at first that the redundancy would be productive and would enrich students' understanding instead of causing them to lose focus.)

But when I noticed the questions that arose throughout this project, such as, "Why did the Nazis hate the Jews?" and "Were all Germans Nazis?" and "How can a videotape make the world a better place?" I was thankful that the portraits of survivors and the stories of resistance and bravery captivated students. I was grateful they could tirelessly watch themselves take on different historic roles. Showing this experience to be more powerful than fairy tales, television, video games, and jingles, Domineck added this afterthought in his video, " . . . and it really happened."

SOME OF THE MOST POWERFUL and haunting voices in *Memories from Past Centuries* are those that reveal the hidden doubts and internal struggles of students' Nazi personas before, during, and after their acts of violence. For instance, speaking as a Nazi, Sam says, "I raised my gun, aimed, and was about to fire when a little voice inside me said, 'What are you doing!' It's like the fire, fire had been extinguished." Their emotionally charged writings suggest the students' personal stake in confronting disturbing realities, and their willingness to try to understand.

I thought about the challenge and complexity of writing from the Nazi perspective when, by chance, I heard on a March 2009 *New Yorker* podcast a reading of Eudora Welty's short story "Where Is the Voice Coming From?" (1963)—another story told from the unusual point of view of a murderer. Welty wrote this story, about the killing of a Black civil rights activist, in the immediate aftermath of the murder of Medgar Evers in her hometown of Jackson, Mississippi. Reflecting on Welty's enigmatic title, the podcast discussion considers whether she refers to her own voice—her own ability to write the chilling story the same night of the murder—or to the voice of

Katie Hyde
Through a Sociologist's Lens

the narrator, as if grappling with the question of "who is this voice, this person, where does he come from?" The podcast shared Welty's own reflection that "whoever the murderer is, I know him, not his identity, but his coming about in this time and place. . . . I should have known by now what such a man had going on in his head." This risky and rare assignment in *Memories from Past Centuries* asks students to consider where the voice is coming from.

In their stories, students search for the meaning behind Nazi violence. When their voices refer to themselves, they often allude to doubt, guilt, and unease. Danielle's persona asks, "Sometimes I think to myself, why did I become a Nazi? Was this meant to be my future?" As in Welty's story, the emotions of students' voices are palpable; the power of their writing, and of their understanding, is enhanced through their use of voice.

Today's elementary school lessons about the civil rights movement and middle school curricula on the Holocaust are set against the backdrop of the occasional KKK rally or religious leader intent on burning the Koran. They're set off against the more widespread expression of anti-immigrant and nativist sentiments. The rhetoric of mistrust, exclusion, hatred, and fear underlying White racism is still alive today. This serendipitous chance to listen to Welty's story reminded me that hearing and creating voices from multiple standpoints, even from the perspective of an evildoer, can lead to a deeper understanding of the historical and sociological underpinnings and implications of hatred. I am reminded that one group of students ended their movie by likening the world to a puzzle and suggesting that "we constantly lose the pieces but maybe one day we can find them." Imagining multiple perspectives helps students piece together the puzzle. This project allowed students to stare in the face the evil of some, to appreciate the exceptional bravery and strength of others, and to recognize their own voices and agency.

Lesson Plans | *Memories from Past Centuries*

Exploring Preconceptions—
What (We Think) We Know About Jews

TIME NEEDED: 1 HOUR

1. Make or buy small notebooks to serve as diaries. Introduce students to the idea of diary writing.
2. Without discussion beforehand, ask students to write about "Jews."
3. Invite volunteers to share their diary entries and allow group discussion of the ideas shared.
4. Introduce the idea that the class will be working on a project to learn stories from the past and teach lessons for the future.

A Famous Diary and a Modern Genre

TIME NEEDED: 1 HOUR

1. Locate websites related to Anne Frank and her diary. We suggest the section of the Holocaust Memorial Museum's site "Anne Frank the Writer/An Unfinished Story," which includes an online exhibition of Anne Frank's original writings from ages 13 to 15.
2. Ask groups of four students to explore the selected website. Encourage students to learn about Anne Frank's story while also noticing the component parts of the website, such as sound recordings, archival photographs, artwork, captions, and so on.
3. Allow 10 minutes for quiet writing of diary entries following the website exploration.

Studying Documents and Getting
to Know Children's Survival Stories

TIME NEEDED: 2 HOURS

Photographs of Rescued Children

1. Readers can access JDC archival photographs of children who survived the Holocaust by contacting the American Jewish Joint Distribution Committee Archives at archives@jdc.org. Ideally, provide each student with a different photograph; if necessary, print multiple copies of children's photographs.
2. Distribute one photograph to each student.
3. Ask students to read their photograph and write down observations in their diaries. Students should focus first on the concrete details they see in their picture, such as the rescued child's expression, gender, possible age, ethnicity, clothing, and other physical features. Students also should notice details within the background of the photograph.
4. Next, ask students to write down questions they have regarding the child. Explain that the students' second diary entry should list or describe things about the child that they wonder about.

Case Histories of Rescued Children

1. Print and distribute case histories that match the JDC photographs. The case histories for JDC photographs can be obtained by writing to the American Jewish Joint Distribution Committee Archives at archives@jdc.org.

2. Ask students to read the case history, allowing 10 to 15 minutes for this. Explain to students that once they've read through the case history, they may consult a classmate, teacher, or the dictionary to understand unfamiliar words.
3. Ask students to return to their diaries to add notes about what they've learned from the case histories. Students should write any answers they've found to their questions. They also can write new questions and observations that arose while reading the case histories.
4. Allow time for students to discuss what they've discovered in reading the photographs and case histories. Encourage them to share their child's story with classmates.

Reading Aloud Children's Literature on the Holocaust

TIME NEEDED: 1 HOUR PER BOOK

1. Read *The Cats in Krasinski Square* by Karen Hesse (2004), *The Yellow Star* by Jennifer Roy (2006), or another short selection about people who helped Jews survive during the Holocaust.
2. Allow time for discussion of students' impressions and their questions regarding Holocaust history.
3. Read *My Secret Camera: Life in the Lodz Ghetto* by Frank Dabba Smith (2000) to provide more historical context and to show students how photography can be used to promote change.
4. Again, allow time for discussion of students' impressions and their questions regarding Holocaust history.

The Child's Story

TIME NEEDED: 1 HOUR

1. Read excerpts from *Voices of the Alamo* by Sherry Garland (2000) or another children's book in which different characters tell the same story from different points of view.
2. Explain to students that you'd like them to pretend to be the child in their photograph and to write that child's story in the first person. Explain that they can draw on their imagination while consulting the photograph and case history, and all the details and questions written in their diaries.
3. Allow students 20 minutes to write in their diaries about what happened to their child, reminding them to explain events as if they were the child.
4. Ask for volunteers to share their diary entries and allow time for class discussion.

A Friend's Story

TIME NEEDED: 30 MINUTES TO 1 HOUR

1. Discuss the concept of changing point of view. Refer to *Voices of the Alamo*.
2. Explain to students that they will now consider the child's story from a friend's perspective.
3. Allow students 20 minutes to write about what happened to their child while pretending to be the child's friend. Ask students to continue writing in the first person. Remind them that they are telling the same story as in the previous lesson but this time they are writing it the way another child would understand it.
4. Ask for volunteers to read entries. Allow time for class discussion.

A Nazi's Story

TIME NEEDED: 1 HOUR

1. Read Chapter 1 of *Number the Stars* by Lois Lowry (1989).
2. During group discussion about the chapter, ask students what they noticed about the young girls in the story as well as the Nazi soldiers. Ask students how the characters *felt*. Allow time for questions, comments, and dialogue.
3. Explain to students that their next assignment is to write the story of the child the way a Nazi would tell it, and that they should again write in the first person.
4. Ask for volunteers to share their entries. Allow time for class discussion about the stories and the feelings students experienced in writing their stories and in listening to one another.

Trying Out a Part—Performing and Recording Stories About Rescued Children

TIME NEEDED: MINIMUM OF 30 MINUTES FOR EACH PAIR OF STUDENTS

1. Explain to students that the next activity will involve playing one of the parts they've created. Ask them to choose one of the three voices/stories they've created.
2. Designate pairs of students who will work together on performing and recording the stories they have written.
3. Ask the partners to rehearse their parts. Encourage students to get to know their own story and that of their partner well enough to speak it without reading from their diaries.
4. Find a quiet space in the school where the video recording will take place. Each pair of student actors/photographers will need at least 30 minutes with the digital video camera. Schedule pairs of students to take turns with the camera and tripod at 30-minute intervals throughout 1 or more school days or during reading/writing time over the course of a week or 2.
5. Set up the digital video camera on a tripod and then let students determine the height and distance of the camera from the person being filmed.
6. Explain to students how to start and stop the recording, and let them know that they should keep talking once the recording begins even if they make mistakes or get stuck. Encourage partners to work as a team, allowing the partner to give cues when needed.
7. Encourage students to think about what gestures and movements they'll make during the recording. Remind them to speak in a loud and clear voice. Allow each student one or two takes to tell their story.
8. At the end of each period/day, upload the digital files onto a computer and save each individual file with the appropriate student's name. Do not delete the files from the video camera.

Collaborating to Make a Larger Story with a Lasting Message

TIME NEEDED: 1 HOUR

1. Group two sets of partners together to establish teams of four students.
2. Explain that each team will design a digital movie that combines their different stories using the videos, the original photographs, and new text.

3. Introduce students to the storyboard concept. Explain that the storyboard will help students think about the larger message of their movie and will help them sequence the pieces.

4. Give each team a few sheets of construction paper that they will tape together to make a long rectangular strip for their storyboard.

5. Show students the symbols for Text, Video, Photograph, and Title. Tell them they will draw boxes/rectangles on their paper to designate each frame of their movie.

6. Remind students of all the materials each team has to work with—four video clips, four JDC photographs, four diary entries. Ask students to discuss which materials will go into their digital movies. Encourage students to also decide what additional text they might add in order to tell the group story.

7. Once students know which pieces they will include, ask them to decide on the sequence.

8. Ask students to use their storyboard to represent the components/frames of their movie in the correct sequence.

Making Movies and Going Public

TIME NEEDED: I HOUR MINIMUM PER GROUP OF FOUR STUDENTS

1. Each team of four students will need at least an hour to collaborate at the computer to create a digital movie. Schedule this time throughout the school day for a few days or during reading/writing time for a few weeks.

2. For each team, create a computer folder that includes the video footage and scanned JDC photographs. (Students will include text by typing it into digital movie frames instead of using scanned copies of their diary writings or the case histories.)

3. Spend time with each team to teach them digital movie-making basics. The first steps will involve importing video files and photographs and then arranging these files in the proper order. In effect, students create a digital storyboard in their digital movie project that mirrors their handwritten storyboard.

4. Once the files have been imported, students should name and save their movie project (and continue to save it every few minutes).

5. Next, students will follow their storyboard plan and begin using text options for digital movies. They will insert a text panel in the appropriate places (title and end pages and transitions) and make decisions about the appearance of the text (font, size, scrolling or still text, the length of time the text remains on the screen, etc.).

6. Show students how to experiment with sound effects.

7. Finally, explain to students that they should determine how to move from one storyboard frame to another—in other words, what the transitions will look like. For example, students will decide whether or not consecutive frames will overlap (as a video ends, a still photograph appears momentarily on top of the video).

8. After saving the movie project, export the file and burn it to a disk for each team member.

9. When all groups are finished with their projects, organize a premiere screening of all the movies.

References and Additional Classroom Resources for Teachers and Students

Daily Literacy Workshop in the Classroom

Atwell, N. (1998). *In the middle: New understandings about writing, reading, and learning.* Portsmouth, NH: Boynton/Cook.

Atwell, N. (2007). *The reading zone: How to help kids become skilled, passionate, habitual, critical readers.* New York: Scholastic.

Calkins, L. (1994). *The art of teaching writing.* Portsmouth, NH: Heinemann.

Calkins, L. (2000). *The art of teaching reading* (2nd ed.). Boston: Allyn & Bacon.

Graves, D. (1991). *Build a literate classroom.* Portsmouth, NH: Heinemann.

Graves, D. (2001). *The energy to teach.* Portsmouth, NH: Heinemann.

Classroom Expectations

Charney, R. (2002). *Teaching children to care.* Greenfield, MA: Northeast Foundation for Children.

Denton, P., & Kriete, R. (2000). *The first six weeks of school.* Greenfield, MA: Northeast Foundation for Children.

Social Justice and Anti-Bias Education

Delpit, L. (1995). *Other people's children: Cultural conflict in the classroom.* New York: New Press.

Derman-Sparks, L., & Edwards, J. (2010). *Anti-bias education for young children and ourselves.* Washington, DC: National Association for the Education of Young Children (NAEYC) Books.

Derman-Sparks, L., & Ramsey, P. (2011). *What if all the kids are White: Anti-bias multicultural education with young children and families* (2nd ed.). New York: Teachers College Press.

Ferguson, A. (2000). *Bad boys: Public schools in the making of Black masculinity.* Ann Arbor: University of Michigan.

hooks, b. (1994). *Teaching to transgress: Education as the practice of freedom.* New York: Routledge.

Lee, E., Menkart, D., & Okazawa-Rey, M. (Eds.). (1998). *Beyond heroes and holidays: A practical guide to K–12 anti-racist, multi-cultural education and staff development.* Washington, DC: Teaching for Change.

Pollock, M. (2004). *Colormute: Race talk dilemmas in an American school.* Princeton: Princeton University Press.

Pollock, M. (Ed.) (2008). *Everyday anti-racism: Getting real about race in school.* New York: New Press.

Sadker, D., Sadker, M., & Zittleman, K. (2009). *Still failing at fairness: How gender bias cheats boys and girls in schools and what we can do about it.* New York: Scribner.

Singleton, G., & Linton, C. (2006). *Courageous conversations about race: A field guide for achieving equity in schools.* Thousand Oaks, CA: Corwin Press.

Other Literature and Films for Discussions About Social Issues

Alvarez, J. (1991). *How the Garcia girls lost their accents.* Chapel Hill, NC: Algonquin Books of Chapel Hill.

Cisneros, S. (2002). *Caramelo.* New York: Knopf.

Frankenberg, R. (1993). *White women, race matters: The social construction of whiteness.* Minneapolis: University of Minnesota Press.

Goldblatt, D. (1989). *The transported of Kwandebele: A South African odyssey.* New York: Aperture.

Greenfield, L. (2002). *Girl culture.* San Francisco: Chronicle Books.

Greenfield, L. (2006). *Thin.* San Francisco: Chronicle Books.

Jordan, J. (2002). *Some of us did not die: New and selected essays of June Jordan.* New York: Basic Books.

Khadra, Y. (2005). *The swallows of Kabul.* New York: Anchor Books.

Martinez, D. (1994). *Mother tongue.* New York: Ballantine Books.

Oates, J. (2009, March 9). Hearing voices: Joyce Carol Oates reads Eudora Welty's "Where is the voice coming from?" On *The fiction podcast: A monthly reading and conversation with* The New Yorker's *fiction editor, Deborah Treisman.* http://www.newyorker.com/online/2009/03/16/090316on_audio_oates.

Peters, W. (Producer and director). (1970). *Eye of the storm* [DVD]. New York: ABC News Production.

Verhaag, B. (Writer and director), & Strigel, C. (Producer). (1996). *Blue eyed* [DVD]. Munich, Germany: DENKmal Film Production.

Welty, E. (1963, July 6). Where is the voice coming from? *The New Yorker*, pp. 24–25.

Recommended Websites

American Jewish Joint Distribution Committee

http://www.jdc.org
The JDC website can be useful to access information and stories about the organization's assistance to children in need around the world.

Center for Media Literacy

http://www.medialit.org
The Center for Media Literacy's MediaLit Kit can be downloaded from the following site: http://www.medialit.org/cml-medialit-kit.

Facing History and Ourselves: Helping Classrooms and Communities Worldwide Link the Past to Moral Choices Today

http://www.facinghistory.org
We recommend Facing History's extensive resources on Holocaust history, stereotyping, bystander behavior, racism, and so on. Links for "Teaching Strategies," "Lesson Plans," "Facing Today," and so on, are easy to navigate under the site's "Educator Resources."

National Eating Disorders Association

http://www.nationaleatingdisorders.org
The National Eating Disorders Association provides resources for educators and coaches to help students with negative body images and eating disorders. The educator toolkit can be downloaded from: http://www.nationaleatingdisorders.org/information-resources/educator-toolkit.php.

No Name-Calling Week

http://nonamecalling.org
The No Name-Calling Coalition was created by GLSEN: Gay, Lesbian and Straight Education Network and Simon & Schuster's Children's Publishing, inspired by James Howe's young adult novel *The Misfits* (2001). Teachers can order a resource kit, which includes a range of resources such as an instructional video, or they can download lesson plans from the website. Middle Level Lesson Plan #2, "Using Literature as a Tool to End Name-Calling," can be downloaded from: http://www.nonamecallingweek.org/cgi-bin/iowa/all/resources/record/110.html.

Teaching for Change: Building Social Justice Starting in the Classroom

http://www.teachingforchange.org
This site includes extensive recommendations for parents and teachers.

Teaching Tolerance: A Project of the Southern Poverty Center

http://www.tolerance.org
Teachers can access essays that have been published in the magazine *Teaching Tolerance*, as well as a vast array of "classroom activities" dealing with social justice issues. Useful classroom activities on stereotyping include the following:
"We and Thee"—http://www.tolerance.org/activity/we-and-thee
"Small Steps: A Tolerance Program"—http://www.tolerance.org/activity/small-steps-tolerance-program, and "Who Are the Arab Americans?"—http://www.tolerance.org/activity/who-are-arab-americans

United States Holocaust Memorial Museum

http://www.ushmm.org/education/foreducators
This site includes useful strategies for teaching about Holocaust history, as well as specific lesson plans and recommended resources. We recommend the section "Anne Frank the Writer/An Unfinished Story," which includes an interactive and multimedia online exhibition: http://www.ushmm.org/museum/exhibit/online/af/htmlsite/.

Recommended Children's Literature

The Best Part of Me

Thinking About the Body

Asim, J. (2006). *Whose knees are these?* New York: LB Kids.

Asim, J. (2008). *Whose toes are those?* New York: LB Kids.

Blume, J. (1971). *Freckle juice.* New York: Simon & Schuster Books for Young Readers.

Blume, J. (1974). *Blubber.* New York: Yearling.

Bowman, G. (2007). *Thin.* New York: Penguin Books.

Browne, A. (1984). *Willy the wimp.* London: Julia MacRae Books.

Cisneros, S. (1984). *The house on Mango Street.* Houston, TX: Arte Publico Press.

Danziger, P. (1974). *The cat ate my gymsuit.* New York: Delacorte Press.

Ehlert, L. (2004). *Hands: Growing up to be an artist.* San Diego, CA: Harcourt Children's Books.

Ewald, W. (2002). *The best part of me.* Boston: Little, Brown Books for Young Readers.

Flake, S. (1998). *The skin I'm in.* New York: Hyperion Books for Children.

Fox, M. (1997). *Whoever you are.* San Diego, CA: Harcourt.

Hardy, M. (2008). *Nothing pink.* Honesdale, PA: Boyds Mill Press.

hooks, b. (1999). *Happy to be nappy.* New York: Hyperion Books for Children.

hooks, b. (2004). *Skin again.* New York: Hyperion Books for Children.

Korman, G. (1998). *The 6th grade nickname game.* New York: Hyperion Books for Children.

Krull, K. (1996). *Wilma unlimited.* San Diego, CA: Harcourt.

Lasky, K. (1994). *The librarian who measured the Earth.* Little, Brown Books for Young Readers.

Lord, C. (2006). *Rules.* New York: Scholastic Press.

MacLachlan, P. (1991). *Journey.* New York: A Dell Yearling Books.

Newman, L. (1994). *Fat chance.* New York: Putnam's.

Polacco, P. (1988). *The keeping quilt.* New York: Simon & Schuster Books for Young Readers.

Polacco, P. (2010). *The junkyard wonders.* New York: Penguin Group.

Reich, S. (2005). *Jose! Born to dance: The story of Jose Limon.* New York: Simon & Schuster Children's Publishing.

Rylant, C. (1985). *The relatives came.* New York: Simon & Schuster Books for Young Readers.

Seskin, S., & Shamblin, A. (2002). *Don't laugh at me.* Berkeley, CA: Tricycle Press.

Spinelli, J. (2002). *Loser.* New York: HarperCollins.

Tarpley, N. (1998). *I love my hair.* Toronto, Canada: Little, Brown Books for Young Readers.

Williams, V. (1990). *"More, more, more," said the baby.* New York: Greenwillow Books.

Wood, J. (1992). *The man who loved clowns.* New York: Putnam's.

Zeckhausen, D. (2007). *Full mouse, empty mouse: A tale of food and feelings.* Washington, DC: Magination Press.

Reading Poetry

Grimes, N. (1997). *It's raining laughter.* New York: Dial Books for Young Readers.

Grimes, N. (1999). *My man Blue.* New York: Dial Books for Young Readers.

Grimes, N. (2000). *Shoe magic.* New York: Orchard Books.

Holbrook, S. (1997). *Am I naturally this crazy?* Honesdale, PA: Boyds Mill Press.

Nye, N. S. (2000). *Come with me: Poems for a journey.* New York: Greenwillow Books.

Nye, N. S. (2005). *A maze me: Poems for girls.* New York: Greenwillow Books.

Black Self/White Self

Thinking About Ethnic and Racial Exclusion and Discrimination

Golenbock, P. (1990). *Teammates.* New York: Voyager Books, Harcourt Brace.

Hoffman, M. (1991). *Amazing Grace.* New York: Dial Books.

Hoobler, D., & Hoobler, T. (1997). *Florence Robinson, The story of a jazz age girl.* Englewood Cliffs, NJ: Silver Burdett Press.

Knight, M. (1992). *Talking walls.* Gardiner, ME: Tilbury House.

Lee, M. (2006). *Landed.* New York: Farrar Straus Giroux.

Naidoo, B. (1986). *Journey to Jo'burg.* New York: HarperCollins.

Santiago, C. (2002). *Home to Medicine Mountain.* San Francisco: Children's Book Press.

Weatherford, C. (2005). *A Negro league scrapbook.* Honesdale, PA: Boyds Mill Press.

Wolfram, W. (2000, Fall). Everyone has an accent. *Teaching Tolerance, 18,* pp. 17–23.

Stories About Civil Rights and Anti-Slavery Activism

Bridges, R. (1999). *Through my eyes: Autobiography of Ruby Bridges.* New York: Scholastic.

Coles, R., & Ford, G. (2004). *The story of Ruby Bridges.* New York: Scholastic.

Curtis, C. (1995). *The Watsons go to Birmingham.* New York: Bantam Doubleday Dell Books for Young Readers.

Fuqua, J. (2002). *Darby.* Cambridge, MA: Candlewick Press.

Giovanni, N. (2005). *Rosa.* New York: Henry Holt.

Hopkinson, D. (1993). *Sweet Clara and the freedom quilt.* New York: Knopf.

Johnson, A. (2005). *A sweet smell of roses.* New York: Simon & Schuster.

Krull, K. (2003). *Harvesting hope: The story of Cesar Chavez.* Orlando, FL: Harcourt.

Lasky, K. (2003). *A voice of her own: The story of Phillis Wheatley, Slave Poet.* Cambridge, MA: Candlewick Press.

Levine, E. (1993). *Freedom's children.* New York: Avon Books.

Miller, W. (1998). *The bus ride.* New York: Lee & Low Books.

Morrow, B. (2004). *A good night for freedom.* New York: Holiday House.

Munoz Ryan, P. (2000). *Esperanza rising.* New York: Scholastic.

Rappaport, D. (2006). *Nobody gonna turn me 'round.* Sommerville, MA: Candlewick Press.

Weatherford, C. (2002). *Remember the bridge: Poems of a people.* New York: Philomel Books.

Stories About Interracial Friendships

Altman, L. (2000). *The legend of freedom hill.* New York: Lee & Low Books.

Polacco, P. (1994). *Pink and say.* New York: Philomel Books.

Walter, M. (2005). *Alec's primer.* Middlebury: Vermont Folklife Center.

Woodson, J. (2001). *The other side.* New York: Putnam's.

Stories About Multiracial Identity

Curry, J. (2005). *The black canary.* New York: Margaret K. McElderry Books.

Igus, T. (1996). *Two Mrs. Gibsons.* San Francisco: Children's Book Press.

Kandel, B. (1997). *Trevor's story: Growing up biracial.* Minneapolis: Lerner Publications.

Meyer, C. (1997). *Jubilee journey.* Orlando, FL: Harcourt Brace.

Steptoe, J. (1997). *Creativity.* New York: Clarion Books.

Walker, R. (2001). *Black White and Jewish: Autobiography of a shifting self.* New York: Riverhead Books.

American Alphabets

Reading Alphabet Books

Chin-Lee, C. (2004). *Amelia to Zora: 26 women who changed the world.* Watertown, MA: Charlesbridge.

Demarest, C. (2005). *Alpha, bravo, Charlie: The military alphabet.* New York: Margaret K. McElderry Books.

Ehlert, L. (1989). *Eating the alphabet.* San Diego, CA: Harcourt Brace.

Elya, S. (2006). *F is for fiesta.* New York: Putnam's.

Pallotta, J. (1986). *The icky bug alphabet book.* Watertown, MA: Charlesbridge.

Pearle, I. (2008). *A child's day: An alphabet of play.* Orlando, FL: Harcourt.

Schwartz, D. (1998). *G is for googol: A math alphabet book.* Berkeley, CA: Tricycle Press.

Van Allsburg, C. (1987). *The Z was zapped: A play in twenty-six acts.* Boston: Houghton Mifflin.

Stories About Language and Cultural Diversity

Jules, J. (2008). *No English.* Ann Arbor, MI: Mitten Press.

Levine, E. (1989). *I hate English!* New York: Scholastic.

Lomas Garza, C. (1996). *In my family/En mi familia.* San Francisco: Children's Book Press.

McKissack, P. (1986). *Flossie and the fox.* New York: Dial Books for Young Children.

Mora, P. (2001). *Love to mama: A tribute to mothers.* New York: Lee & Low.

Nobisso, J. (2003). *In English, of course.* Westhampton Beach, NY: Gingerbread House.

Rylant, C. (1982). *When I was young in the mountains.* New York: Dutton Children's Books.

Smalls, I. (2003). *Don't say ain't.* Watertown, MA: Charlesbridge.

Turner, P. (1996). *The war between the vowels and the consonants.* New York: Farrar Straus Giroux.

Young, E. (1997). *Voices of the heart.* New York: Scholastic Press.

Stories About "Home"

Bunting, E. (1991). *Fly away home*. New York: Clarion Books.

Creech, S. (1994). *Walk two moons*. New York: HarperCollins.

Curtis, C. (1999). *Bud, not buddy*. New York: Yearling.

Naylor, P. (1991). *Shiloh*. New York: Simon & Schuster.

Paterson, K. (1978). *The great Gilly Hopkins*. New York: HarperCollins.

Polacco, P. (2009). *In our mothers' house*. New York: Philomel Books.

Say, A. (1993). *Grandfather's journey*. New York: Houghton Mifflin.

Taylor, M. (1976). *Roll of thunder, hear my cry*. New York: Puffin Books.

Memories from Past Centuries

Stories About General Holocaust History

Ackerman, K. (1994). *Night crossing*. New York: Random House, Bullseye Books.

Adler, D. (1994). *Hilde and Eli: Children of the Holocaust*. New York: Holiday House.

Adler, D. (1989). *We remember the Holocaust*. New York: Henry Holt.

Adler, D. (1995). *Child of the Warsaw ghetto*. New York: Holiday House.

Baylis-White, M. (1991). *Sheltering Rebecca*. New York: Puffin Books.

Dabba Smith, F. (2000). *My secret camera: Life in the Lodz ghetto*. London: Harcourt.

Hurwitz, J. (1993). *Anne Frank: Life in hiding*. New York: Beech Tree Paperbacks.

Lowry, L. (1989). *Number the stars*. New York: Dell.

Roy, H. (2006). *The yellow star*. Tarrytown, NY: Marshall Cavendish.

van De Rol, R., & Verhoeven, R. (1993). *Anne Frank: Beyond the diary: A photographic remembrance*. New York: Viking Press.

Volavkova, H. (Ed.). (1993). *I never saw another butterfly*. New York: Schocken Books.

Watts, I. (2008). *Good-bye, Marianne: A story of growing up in Nazi Germany*. Toronto: Tundra Books.

Stories About the Resistance Effort and Rescued Children

Drucker, M., & Halperin M. (1993). *Jacob's rescue*. New York: Dell Yearling Books.

Drucker, O. (1992). *Kindertransport*. New York: Henry Holt.

Foxx, A., & Abraham-Podietz, M. (1999). *Ten thousand children: True stories told by children who escaped the Holocaust on the kindertransport*. West Orange, NJ: Behrman House.

Hesse, K. (2004). *The cats in Krasinski Square*. New York: Scholastic.

Oppenheim, S. (1992). *Lily Cupboard*. New York: HarperCollins.

Stories About Cultural Difference and Tolerance

Buck, P. (1986). *The big wave*. New York: Harper & Row.

Dooley, N. (1991). *Everybody cooks rice*. Minneapolis: Carolrhoda Books.

Friedman, I. (1984). *How my parents learned to eat*. Boston: Houghton Mifflin.

Gilson, J. (1985). *Hello, my name is scrambled eggs*. New York: Pocket Books.

Intrater, R. (1995). *Two eyes, a nose and a mouth: A book of many faces, many races*. New York: Cartwheel/Scholastic.

Knight, M. (1996). *Who belongs here? An American story*. Gardiner, ME: Tilbury House.

Kuklin, S. (1992). *How my family lives in America*. New York: Simon & Schuster Books for Young Readers.

Stories About Immigration

Freedman, R. (1995). *Immigrant kids*. New York: Puffin Books.

Kidd, D. (1989). *Onion tears*. New York: Beech Tree Paperbacks.

Lawlor, V. (Ed.). (1995). *I was dreaming to come to America: Memories from the Ellis Island oral history project*. New York: Viking Books.

Levine, E. (1982). *I hate English!* New York: Scholastic.

Levine, E. (1993). *If your name was changed at Ellis Island*. New York: Scholastic.

Stanek, M. (1989). *I speak English for my mom*. Niles, IL: A. Whitman.

Stories About Bullying

Blume, J. (1974). *Blubber*. New York: Yearling.

Estes, E. (1999). *The hundred dresses*. New York: Harcourt Brace.

Flake, S. (1998). *The skin I'm in*. New York: Hyperion.

Gatto, P., & De Angelis, J. (2004). *Milton's dilemma*. Franklin, TN: Providence Publishing.

Hahn, M. (1992). *Stepping on the cracks*. New York: HarperCollins.

Howe, J. (2001). *The misfits*. Simon & Schuster Children's Publishing.

Huser, G. (2003). *Stiches*. Toronto, Canada: Groundwood Books.

Ibittson, J. (1989). *Wimp and the jock*. New York: Simon & Schuster Children's Publishing.

McCain, B. (2001). *Nobody knew what to do: A story about bullying*. Morton Grove, IL: Albert Whitman.

Meade, A. (1998). *Junebug and the reverend*. New York: Farrar Straus Giroux.

Moss, M. (1998). *Amelia takes command*. Middleton, WI: Pleasant Company Publications.

Moss, M. (2004). *Say something*. Gardener, ME: Tilbury House.

Polacco, P. (2001). *Mr. Lincoln's way*. New York: Philomel Books.

Shreve, S. (1993). *Joshua T. Bates takes charge*. New York: Knopf.

Spinelli, J. (1997). *Crash*. New York: Knopf.

Wild, M. (1995). *Beast*. New York: Scholastic.

Wilhelm, D. (2003). *The revealers*. New York: Farrar Straus Giroux.

Additional Works Cited in Memories from Past Centuries

Bunting, E. (1995). *Cheyenne again*. New York: Clarion.

Garland, S. (2000). *Voices of the Alamo*. New York: Scholastic.

Selected Photography Books

Bey, D., Terrassa, J., Smith, S., & Meister, E. (2003). *Dawoud bey: The Chicago project*. Chicago: Smart Museum of Art, University of Chicago.

DeCarava, R. (1996). *A retrospective*. New York: Museum of Modern Art.

Disfarmer, M. (1996). *Disfarmer: Herber Spring portraits*. Santa Fe, NM: Twin Palms Publishers.

Ewald, W. (1992). *Magic eyes: Scenes from an Andean childhood*. Seattle, WA: Bay Press.

Ewald, W. (1996). *I dreamed I had a girl in my pocket*. New York: W. W. Norton in association with the Center for Documentary Studies.

Ewald, W. (2000). *Secret games: Collaborative works with children 1969–1999*. New York: Scalo.

Ewald, W. (2002). *The best part of me: Children talk about their bodies in pictures and words*. Boston: Little, Brown.

Ewald, W. (2004). *In peace and harmony: Carver portraits*. Richmond, VA: Hand Workshop Art Center.

Ewald, W. (2005). *American alphabets*. New York: Scalo.

Ewald, W. (2006). *Towards a promised land*. London: Stiedl/Artangel.

Ewald, W., & Lightfoot, A. (2001). *I wanna take me a picture: Teaching photography and writing to children*. Boston: Beacon Press in association with the Center for Documentary Studies.

Hambourg, M. M., Heilbrun, F., Neagu, P., & Nadar, F. (1995). *Nadar*. New York: Harry N. Abrams.

Keita, S. (1998). *Seydou Keita*. New York: Scalo.

Lee, N. S. (2001). *Nikki S. Lee projects*. Osfildern-Ruit, Germany: Hatje Cantz Publishers.

Levitt, H. (1989). *A way of seeing*. Durham, NC: Duke University Press in association with the Center for Documentary Studies.

Namuth, H. (1989). *Los todos santeros: A family album of Mam Indians in the village of Todos Santos*. London: Dirk Nishen Publishing.

Rogovin, M. (2003). *The forgotten ones*. New York: Quantuck Lane Press.

Rogovin, M. (1994). *Triptychs: Buffalo's lower west side revisited*. New York: W. W. Norton.

Sander, A. (1973). *Men without masks: Faces of Germany, 1910–1938*. Greenwich, CT: New York Graphic Society.

Willis, D. (1998). *VanDerZee: Photographer, 1886–1983*. New York: Harry N. Abrams.

Willis, J. (2010). *Views from the reservation*. Chicago: Center for American Places.

Technical Resources

Photography Equipment Used in the Projects Featured in This Book

Film cameras: Olympus Trip (multiple models, e.g., XB400).

Digital cameras: Kodak EasyShare (multiple models, e.g., C813).

Polaroid cameras: Polaroid 600 film camera and Polaroid ProPack (Polaroid no longer makes the film for these cameras. A new, more expensive model is the Polaroid PoGo Instant Digital Camera and Instant Mobile Printer).

Digital printers: Canon Selphy (multiple models, e.g., CP770), along with Canon KP Color Ink/Paper Set (other, more expensive printer options: Canon PIXMA MP640; Epson Picture-Mate PM250).

Digital video cameras: Flip Ultra Video Camera.

Recommended Websites on Digital Photography

Digital Photography Review:
http://www.dpreview.com

Steve's Digicams:
http://www.steves-digicams.com

Digital Camera Resource Page:
http://www.dcresource.com
Imaging Resource: http://www.imaging-resource.com

Digital Camera Basics

Just like a conventional camera, a digital camera has a series of lenses that focus light to create an image of a scene, but instead of focusing this light onto a piece of film, they focus it onto a semiconductor device that records light electronically. A computer then breaks this electronic information down into digital data. All the fun and interesting features of digital cameras come as a direct result of this process. Instead of film, a digital camera has a sensor that converts light into electrical charges. For more information on how digital cameras operate, see http://electronics.howstuffworks.com/digital-camera2.htm.

Film Versus Digital Photography

Film Pros

• Having physical negatives is a storage option that is not possible with digital images. If your hard drive crashes and you have your images stored only in once place, you have lost all of your work. (However, negatives can get damaged so if you don't have them scanned or printed nicely, you are out of luck as well.)

• Film requires you to slow down and think about what you're photographing. Because we are not able to see the picture right away and we have a more limited number of images to work with, people tend to be more thoughtful and deliberate.

• Even though digital images can be printed out, the fact is that most images taken with a digital camera are never printed. We are moving away from physical photographs and moving onto looking at images on screens. Film forces us to take the time to make physical images.

- The darkroom experience has unique social and educational value that cannot be re-created using digital images. Particularly for children, being in the darkroom can be a bonding experience with teachers and classmates, and it requires a combination of skills to produce a quality result. It also involves a series of methodical tasks that must be followed, which also slows down the process of picture making, which often involves teamwork and collaboration.

Digital Pros

- The obvious benefit of digital technology is the convenience and speed. Images can be seen a split second after they were taken, allowing us to immediately see whether we captured the image we wanted to. Digital technology is by far the most common form of photography for the general public, making film more of a challenge to use. Because film is so rare these days, it is more expensive to buy and develop and more difficult to find in stores.

How to Slow Down the Digital Photography Process and Bring the Benefits of Film to Digital

Limit the number of images each person can make so he or she spends more time on each image.
- Print out contact sheets of each group of images and spend time selecting the best ones.
- Don't allow students to delete any of the images they make so they can learn from mistakes or discover unintended successes.
- Print out images and use them as physical objects in activities.
- Start by doing one film project to allow students to understand the film process before moving onto digital.

Digital Camera Features and Equipment

Focus

Digital cameras have one of four types of lenses:
- **Fixed-focus, fixed-zoom lenses**. These are the kinds of lenses on disposable and inexpensive film cameras—inexpensive and great for snapshots, but fairly limited.
- **Optical-zoom lenses with automatic focus**. Similar to the lens on a video camcorder, these have "wide" and "telephoto" options and automatic focus. The camera may or may not support manual focus. These actually change the focal length of the lens rather than just magnifying the information that hits the sensor.
- **Digital zoom**. With digital zoom, the camera takes pixels from the center of the image sensor and interpolates them to make a full-sized image. Depending on the resolution of the image and the sensor, this approach may create a grainy or fuzzy image. You can do the same thing manually with image processing software—simply snap a picture, cut out the center, and magnify it.
- **Interchangeable lens systems**. These are similar to the interchangeable lenses on a 35mm camera. Some digital cameras can use 35mm camera lenses.

Focal Length

The focal length is one important difference between the lens of a digital camera and the lens of a 35mm camera. The focal length is the distance between the lens and the surface of the sensor. Sensors from different manufacturers vary widely in size, but in general they're smaller than a piece of 35mm film. In order to project the image onto a smaller sensor, the focal length is shortened by the same proportion.

Flash

Most digital cameras have built-in flashes that have the capacity to light subjects 3–4 meters away. If the camera has a hot shoe on the top, this gives you the option to use an external flash that will allow you to control light more and increase the flash's distance if desired.

Resolution

The amount of detail that the camera can capture is called the resolution, and it is measured in pixels. The more pixels a camera has, the more detail it can capture and the larger pictures can be without becoming blurry or "grainy."

256 x 256. Found on very inexpensive cameras, this resolution is so low that the picture quality is almost always unacceptable. This is 65,000 total pixels.

640 x 480. This is the low end on most "real" cameras. This resolution is ideal for e-mailing pictures or posting pictures on a website.

1216 x 912. This is a "megapixel" image size—1,109,000 total pixels—good for printing pictures.

1600 x 1200. With almost 2 million total pixels, this is "high resolution." You can print a 4 x 5 inch print taken at this resolution with the same quality that you would get from a photo lab.

2240 x 1680. Found on four megapixel cameras—the current standard—this allows even larger printed photos, with good quality for prints up to 16 x 20 inches.

4064 x 2704. A top-of-the-line digital camera with 11.1 megapixels takes pictures at this resolution. At this setting, you can create 13.5 x 9 inch prints with no loss of picture quality.

Batteries

The type of battery you will need is determined by the type of camera you buy. Some cameras call for AA batteries and some for lithium ion. Lithium batteries are three times more powerful than AA batteries, hold up well in cold weather, and can last up to 10 years. The key thing to remember, whether you have lithium or AA batteries, is to always carry your charger and bring multiple batteries whenever possible. For AA batteries, rechargeable batteries are the most eco-friendly and inexpensive, but the quality varies; Energizer and Powerex have been proven to be the best two brands of rechargeable AA batteries.

Digital Cards

CompactFlash (CF) is one of the most common types of digital camera memory. Most high-end digital cameras, and all digital SLRs, are CompactFlash compatible. Each card type has a different size and shape, and they are not interchangeable. As a general rule it is wise to purchase cards with recognizable brand names such as ScanDisk or Transcend.

Card Readers

Many computers and portable digital printers have built-in slots for digital cards, but it is useful to have your own card reader in case you're using multiple printers, computers, and cameras. It is wise to purchase a card with multiple format types to use with different cameras if you are working with many people or if you upgrade to a new camera.

Storage

Many people rely on their computers and CDs/DVDs to store their images. This is fine for temporary storage, but should not be a long-term strategy. Computers, especially when they have lots of images stored on them, can crash or loose data. CDs and DVDs deteriorate over time.

It's always important to back up your work in multiple places. External hard drives made by Lacie or Western Digital can be used to store large volumes of images. Having DVD backups of images stored on hard drives is also a good idea. The key is multiple backups using a cross-section of media. Also, because technology is moving so quickly, it is important to update your storage devices every 2 to 3 years to make sure they are still usable and accessible.

Video Cameras

Most digital cameras have video options. It's important to know how many minutes you are able to record before downloading. Some cameras have limited abilities in low-light situations and their simplicity limits your control. The Canon Vixia (several models available) is a step up, with more features and excellent video quality.

About the Authors

Wendy Ewald has published ten books; *Literacy and Justice Through Photography* is her first work written specifically for classroom teachers. *Secret Games,* a 30-year retrospective of Ewald's work with children, was shown from 2000 to 2006 at museums across the United States. The projects and lesson plans presented here are inspired by Wendy Ewald's collaborations with children and teachers and have been developed and tested over a decade.

Katherine Hyde has a Ph.D. in sociology. She coordinated the Literacy Through Photography program for 8 years and has been the director of LTP for 4 years. She also teaches several courses at Duke University on sociology and photography.

Lisa Lord, author of *Success in Reading and Writing: Grade 3* and *Success in Reading and Writing: Grade 6*, has taught for over 35 years, and has National Board Certification and an Ed.D. in literacy.